FOOLS
RUSH IN

FOOLS
RUSH IN

Steve Case, Jerry Levin,
and the Unmaking of AOL Time Warner

Nina Munk

HarperBusiness
An Imprint of HarperCollinsPublishers

HarperCollins books may be purchased for educational, business, or sales promotional use. For information, please write to: Special Markets Department, HarperCollins Publishers Inc., 10 East 53rd Street, New York, New York 10022.

Designed by Joy O'Meara

Library of Congress Cataloging-In-Publication Data
Munk, Nina.
   Fools rush in : Steve Case, Jerry Levin, and the unmaking of
AOL Time Warner / Nina Munk.   338.7
     p. cm.   Munk
   Includes index.
   ISBN 0-06-054034-6
   1. AOL Time Warner—History.   2. Case, Stephen McConnell.
3. Levin, Gerald M.   4. Businessmen—United States—Biography.
5. Internet service providers—United States—History.   6. Online information services industry—United States—History.   7. Publishers and publishing—United States—History.   8. Motion picture industry—United States—History.
9. Consolidation and merger of corporations—United States—Case studies.
I. Title.

HE7583.U6.M66 2004
338.7'61004678—dc22   2003056900
04 05 06 DIX / RRD 10 8 7 7 6 5 4 3 2 1

for my mother and father

NOTE TO READERS

THIS BOOK IS THE RESULT OF HUNDREDS OF HOURS OF INTER-views with almost all the central figures in the AOL Time Warner debacle. Nearly every interview was recorded. Only a handful of the people I mention in this book refused to comment altogether. Others, sometimes because they were facing civil or criminal charges, spoke to me on background only. Others allowed only some of their comments to be attributed. In most cases, the people I interviewed were remarkably candid; they were also generous with their time. I am grateful for their cooperation.

Research for this book started in the fall of 2000, when I began writing an article for *Fortune* magazine about Jerry Levin and the AOL Time Warner deal. That article was shelved, so I turned to *Vanity Fair,* where two of my articles on the AOL Time Warner deal were later published (in July 2002 and January 2003). Some of the material in this book has appeared in *Vanity Fair;* for the most part, though, the book was written over twelve months, beginning in late 2002. Apart from interviews with more than one hundred people, my research included dozens of legal and financial documents, confidential e-mails and letters, internal memoranda, corporate filings, Census Bureau data, real estate deeds, high school and college yearbooks, newspaper and magazine articles, and stacks of books.

Most of the executives who were involved in the AOL Time Warner deal have left the company. Having dropped the acronym AOL, the company is now called Time Warner, but its problems are ongoing. As I write this, approximately fifty shareholder lawsuits against the company and its executives (former and current) are pending. Both the Securities and Exchange Commission and the Justice Department are pursuing their investigations. So far, having admitted that it inflated more than $190 million of revenue during a twenty-one-month period beginning in the fall of 2000, Time Warner has turned over more than one million pages of documents to prosecutors. Steve Case, Jerry Levin, and Dick Parsons have been subpoened by the SEC. More evidence is being gathered. I would like to think that *Fools Rush In* is the last, definitive word on the AOL Time Warner fiasco. We'll see.

Nina Munk
November 2003

CONTENTS

PROLOGUE

IT WASN'T A GOOD LIKENESS OF HENRY LUCE, PEOPLE SAID. Still, there it was, on the thirty-fourth floor of the Time-Life Building, propped up on an easel, in a conference room with no windows. Painted in 1972, five years after Luce's death, by the Russian-born constructivist Constantin Alajálov, the portrait of Time Inc.'s great founder was based on a photograph taken by *Life* magazine's Alfred Eisenstaedt when Luce was sixty-four years old.

Luce's portrait (a likeness of a likeness) had been in that airless room for years, consigned to the dustbin of corporate history. Then, in early 2001, after the AOL-Time Warner merger had closed, Steve Case decided to claim the portrait and with it Luce's exalted legacy. From the Time-Life Building to AOL Time Warner's headquarters it's two short blocks; before you could say "ancestor" or "heritage," Luce's portrait was hanging on the wall of Steve Case's new office.

For Case, the portrait of Henry Luce was a sign, like a coat of arms: AOL Time Warner's new chairman wasn't some crass Internet upstart who'd used inflated dot-com stock to buy his way into high corporate society. On the contrary, Steve Case was the spiritual heir of an empire builder, a visionary known for his rigorous moral standards and an unwavering commitment to the greater good. "I have long believed that Henry Luce had it right when he said that corpora-

tions must be run not just for shareholders but also in the public interest," Case declared in 2001. "And I wanted people to know that I embraced that perspective."

In retrospect, the only surprising thing about Case's laying claim
to Luce's portrait is that Jerry Levin hadn't grabbed it first. Levin had
often measured himself against the great man; one reason he'd persuaded himself to merge Time Warner with AOL in the first place
was to create a legacy comparable to Luce's. Over the years, distancing
himself from other media and entertainment moguls (the unculti-
vated and greedy ones), Levin had flaunted his high moral convictions
and his learning. With easy allusions to the Bible (Ecclesiastes), to the
French existentialist writer Albert Camus, and, in an interview with
Architectural Digest, to Heraclitus, the pre-Socratic philosopher, Levin
presented himself as a scholarly, upright man who just happened to be
the CEO of the world's largest media company. Now in his sixties,
having pulled off the AOL merger, the most ambitious deal of his
career, Levin was satisfied that he, like his predecessor Henry Luce,
would be remembered for something much bigger than a balance
sheet.

He was right, of course. This book is the story of how two men,
Jerry Levin and Steve Case, caused what may be the biggest train
wreck in the history of corporate America. Or shipwreck. Like other
willful executives and Captain Ahabs of the late 1990s, Levin and
Case ran their companies with few checks and balances. To examine
the AOL Time Warner deal closely, to scrutinize the details of its
making and unmaking, as this book sets out to do, is to recognize a sad
truth: Despite rules set by the Securities and Exchange Commission
and other regulators, the company's own stakeholders—its shareholders and employees—didn't count for much.

In broad terms, the disastrous merger of Time Warner and
AOL epitomizes the culture of corporate America and Wall Street in
the late 1990s. It speaks to the speculative mania that gripped America
at the end of the twentieth century. And it records the climate in exec-

utive suites, where as long as a company's stock price kept going up and up, a CEO was all-powerful, like a king with divine right. Unworkable mergers and acquisitions, questionable accounting practices, massive insider stock sales, giant layoffs: all were part of the game. What makes the story of AOL Time Warner stand out from other corporate scandals of the past few years, however, is the absorbing egotism of two men: Jerry Levin and Steve Case.

In 1999, during the elaborate mating rituals that led up to the AOL Time Warner deal, Levin and Case had compared ideologies. They'd talked about integrity, missions, selflessness, altruism, responsibility, and (of course) making a difference. In a moment of mutual recognition, both men discovered they embraced the principles of Time Inc.'s founder, Henry Luce: their mandate was higher than profits, more than the bottom line; their mission was to educate and serve mankind, universally. Two years later, as the merger of AOL and Time Warner unraveled, Levin and Case, deluded to the end, wouldn't admit their mistake. Instead, they wrapped themselves even more tightly in Luce's mantle of righteousness. History would be their witness.

Meanwhile, some $200 billion of shareholder value had vanished; insiders had unloaded nearly $1 billion worth of shares; a federal investigation into AOL Time Warner's accounting had begun; and shareholder lawsuits had been launched, alleging that the company and its executives had committed fraud. Before long, Jerry Levin and Steve Case would lose everything: their reputations, their power, their jobs. The way up and the way down are the same, Heraclitus wrote—or something like that.

■ ■ ■

FOR MONTHS AFTER THE COLLAPSE OF AOL TIME WARNER, Levin was "a wreck," he confessed. During our first encounters (long lunches, telephone calls, and meetings in his post-retirement office on the second floor of the Time Warner Building at 75 Rockefeller Plaza), he sounded desperate, like someone looking for a sign of re-demption and a way out. Vulnerable, he told me he was on the path of self-discovery, self-realization. He talked about maybe writing a novel. He was reading the philosopher Martin Buber, he said, whose 1923 treatise *I and Thou* focuses on the way human beings relate to the world and to others, genuinely. Freed from the corporate prison of AOL Time Warner with its inhuman demands, Levin had taken off his blinkers only to discover the fragile beauty of life itself. "I'd never cried before," he told me in a confessional mode, "I'd never cried. And now I cry all the time."

Having followed Levin for years, I'd finally concluded that the man was brilliant but fragmented; parts of him didn't cohere, didn't fit together. Part of him, the one that quoted the Bible and Heraclitus, was deeply spiritual. At the same time, as Levin himself admitted, he was ruthless. Was his spiritual quest a form of sentimentality, the in-evitable flip side of ruthlessness? Or was Jerry Levin, one of the most manipulative corporate operators of our time, suddenly experiencing a change of heart and mind, regretting what he'd done to AOL Time Warner, and crying on behalf of his shareholders and employees?

Either way, Levin's repentance was short-lived. "I've done a transforming transaction on myself," he told me, giddy, one afternoon in early 2003. He'd fallen in love; the love was "profound, almost un-real," he confided. Abruptly, during the 2002 Christmas holidays, Levin had informed his wife of thirty-two years, Barbara Riley, that he was leaving her, just like that. ("She never saw it coming," a friend of hers told me.)

"The love of my life," is how the sixty-three-year-old Jerry Levin described Laurie Perlman. A clinical psychologist, a former movie producer for Warner Bros., and a onetime talent agent, Perlman, forty-nine, was at the heart of Levin's "transforming transaction." They'd spent New Year's together on a remote island of Hawaii. Upon his return to New York, they'd spoken by phone every single day, for hours at a time. He'd given her an emerald-and-diamond ring: they were now engaged to be married. With a nod to neoplatonism, he assured me they were "soul mates" and "twins." As soon as arrangements were made, he intended to move right across the country to join Perlman in Marina del Rey, California. Late one January afternoon in New York, as he saw me to the door of his office, he announced proudly: "There's a pep in my step today because I'm off to see her in California tomorrow."

In February 2003, Levin and his fiancée appeared in *The New York Times*. Posing cheek to cheek, the couple was photographed on the beach in Marina del Rey with the evening sun setting softly behind them. "It's been wonderful to discover that I can really have a life outside Time Warner," Levin confessed to the *Times*. "Now I'm on a spiritual journey, and it's one I intend to savor every step of the way."

Reading that text, Levin's former executives and employees were outraged. "It's beyond belief," gasped one senior official. "The gall!" exclaimed another. It was unconscionable: here was Jerry Levin, carefree, on a beach, in love, savoring his spiritual journey. Meanwhile, back in New York and Dulles, his former executives and employees were mopping up the awful mess he'd left behind at AOL Time Warner. Their stock options were worthless. Their retirement plans had been decimated. And Levin, free as a seagull, soaring, and still earning $1 million a year as an "advisor" to his old company, had walked away from it all. So this was what it all came down to: a CEO could be utterly reckless, utterly ruthless, and then he could move on.

After that, Levin lost interest in me and my book. He let days go by before returning my phone calls, and when he did he had little time to talk. His eyes glazed over when I asked for details about AOL Time Warner; that was old news, yesterday's paper, I inferred. Compared to his spiritual quest, the story of AOL Time Warner was unimportant. He couldn't meet me for lunch, he explained one day, because he and his fiancée were busy writing a proposal for a self-help book. Its working title was *Soul Communion*.

PART
ONE

"Resident Genius"

From Time Inc. to
Time Warner, 1923–1998

ONE

BY ALL ACCOUNTS, HENRY ROBINSON LUCE WAS ENDOWED WITH moral certainty at birth. Born in 1898 to American missionaries in Tengchow, China, Harry, as he was known, was a precocious and serious-minded child. At the age of five, as a diversion, he delivered religious sermons to his playmates. Later, turning to journalism, which he referred to as a "calling," he wrote: "I believe that I can be of greatest service in journalistic work and can by that way come nearest to the heart of the world." His father had devoted his life to proselytizing; likewise, Harry Luce would set people on the highway to truth. Making money was not his goal, as the terms of Luce's will would later make clear: "Time Incorporated is now, and is expected to continue to be, principally a journalistic enterprise and, as such, an enterprise operated in the public interest as well as in the interest of its stockholders."

When he was fifteen Luce arrived in America to attend Hotchkiss School. From there he went on to Yale. He was an exceptionally gifted student: he wrote poetry; he became assistant managing editor of the *Yale Daily News;* he graduated summa cum laude; he was admitted to Phi Beta Kappa; and he was voted "Most Brilliant" in his class. Harry Luce was most likely to succeed.

In the early 1920s, while he was working as a reporter at the *Bal-*

timore News, Luce, together with a former classmate from Yale, Briton Hadden, decided to start a weekly magazine called *Time.* A summary of the world's most important news, it would run articles of no more than four hundred words, or seven inches of type; it would also deal "*briefly* with EVERY HAPPENING OF IMPORTANCE," as Luce and Hadden explained in their prospectus. Unlike the *Literary Digest,* an existing summary of the news, *Time* would have a clearly defined point of view: "The *Digest,* in giving both sides of a question, gives little or no hint as to which side it considers to be right. *Time* gives both sides, but clearly indicates which side it believes to have the stronger position."

In early 1923, having raised $85,675 from seventy-two investors, Luce and Hadden published their first issue of *Time.* Only twenty-eight pages long, the entire issue of volume 1, number 1, dated March 3, 1923, could be swallowed and digested in thirty minutes or less. "It was of course not for people who really wanted to be informed," sniffed W. A. Swanberg in his definitive 1972 biography of Luce. "It was for people willing to spend a half-hour to avoid being entirely uninformed."

Those who worked for *Time* were rewrite men whose job was to shrink and condense articles from *The New York Times* and *New York World,* transforming them into "Timestyle," the quirky prose for which *Time* became famous (or infamous). Together the men invented neologisms—telescoped words like "socialite," "cinemaddict," and "guesstimate," for example. They also revived arcane terms such as "tycoon" (Japanese for "great ruler") and "pundit" (Hindi for "learned man"). Deeply in love with adjectival phrases ("To Swanscott came a lank, stern Senator, grey-haired, level-browed"), Luce and Hadden claimed they'd been influenced by Homer's *Iliad* with its inverted syntax and double-barreled epithets ("white-armed Hera" and "grey-eyed Athena" and "horse-breaking Trojans").

Time was pilloried by intellectuals. Parodying Timestyle for a 1936 profile in *The New Yorker,* Wolcott Gibbs wrote: "Backwards ran sentences until reeled the mind. . . . Where it will all end, knows God!"

In 1929, just as *Time* was becoming successful, Hadden died of a streptococcus infection, and Luce took over, borrowing money to buy Hadden's share of their company. He was thirty-one years old. Before long, Hadden would be a footnote in the history of Time Inc.

With a circulation approaching three hundred thousand, *Time* was now sufficiently profitable that Luce could afford to expand. Determined to spread his "fantastic faith in the industrial and commercial future of this country," Luce launched *Fortune* in 1930. Six years later, in late 1936, he introduced his most spectacular success, *Life* magazine. Its purpose: "To see life; to see the world; to eyewitness great events; to watch the faces of the poor and the gestures of the proud."

Within hours of its arrival at newsstands, *Life* was sold out all over the country. Struggling to find enough coated paper to meet the demand, Luce couldn't publish enough copies. Even he had never imagined *Life* would be so popular. After just four weeks, *Life*'s circulation was 533,000; no magazine in American history had passed the half-million mark so quickly.

Sports Illustrated would come next. In contrast with *Life*, however, *Sports Illustrated* was not an immediate success. Launched in 1954, when spectator sports were looked down on as fodder for the working classes, *Sports Illustrated* was ahead of its time. But Luce was fully committed to his new magazine. Before long *Sports Illustrated* would broaden the appeal of spectator sports and change the way they were covered.

■ ■ ■

LONG BEFORE *SPORTS ILLUSTRATED* HAD BECOME PROFITABLE— even before it was launched—Luce had become a media baron. By the early 1940s, one in every five Americans was reading a Luce publication. Company revenues were $45 million. Emboldened by the success of his publications, Luce increasingly turned them into vehicles of political and moral propaganda. Money had never motivated Luce, but power did.

In 1941, decrying isolationism, Luce argued that it was time for America, the world's most powerful nation, to fulfill its duty to humanity. The twentieth century, he stated famously in an editorial written for *Life,* was "the American Century." Americans had to "accept wholeheartedly our duty and our opportunity as the most powerful and vital nation in the world and in consequence to exert upon the world the full impact of our influence, for such purposes as we see fit and by such means as we see fit."

Luce's magazines promoted interventionism. They also attacked the New Deal, defended Chiang Kai-shek, advocated an aggressive attack on godless communism worldwide, and encouraged Americans to vote Republican. Luce's strident voice and his partisanship enraged critics; some people said that he was single-handedly responsible for the cold war. Even his correspondents complained that their reporting was skewed to fit Luce's worldview, his agenda. Theodore White, *Time's* correspondent in China during the 1940s, protested that his dispatches were being willfully ignored. When White reported that Chiang Kai-shek had become a corrupt dictator, *Time's* rewrite men and censors in New York had him glorifying Chiang and the Kuomintang. "Any similarity between this correspondent's dispatches and what appears in *Time* is purely coincidental," read a sign posted on White's office door. T. S. Matthews, an editor at *Time* from 1929 to 1953 (and managing editor from 1949 to 1953), left after falling out with Luce. Luce, he wrote, "began to entertain the delusion common among press lords: that he could control and direct the enormous influence his magazines exerted on public taste."

Utterly convinced of the "righteousness" (a word he used often) of his causes, Luce dismissed his critics. "I am a Protestant, a Republican and a free enterpriser," he declared. "I am biased in favor of God, Eisenhower and the stockholders of Time Inc.—and if anybody who objects doesn't know this by now, why the hell are they still spending 35 cents for the magazine?"

By the 1960s, Time Inc. had reached its glorious peak. *Time* had become a staple of the (not entirely uninformed) American middle class. Tall, slender, blue-eyed, gray-haired, thick-browed, Luce (a heavy smoker) influenced every aspect of American life. As his obituary in *The New York Times* would later confirm, Luce "helped shape the reading habits, political attitudes, and cultural tastes of millions." At the beginning of the decade, the company moved into the new Time-Life Building at Rockefeller Center, an awesome $83 million, forty-eight-story steel-and-glass skyscraper that reflected the empire Luce had built. The building's lobby featured shimmering brushed-steel wall panels, an undulating gray-and-white terrazzo floor modeled after Copacabana paving in Rio de Janeiro, and two immense abstract murals, one by Josef Albers, the other by Fritz Glarner. The ground-floor restaurant was designed by Alexander Girard. The eighth-floor auditorium was designed by Gio Ponti. As for the executive floor, where Henry Luce's office was located, it "proclaims the presence of powers," a critic remarked at the time: "Sleek, sharp and obviously expensive, these offices achieve the impossible: overstyled understatement."

Of every advertising dollar spent on consumer magazines in the 1960s, thirty-three cents went to Time Inc. publications. *Life,* which by that time had a circulation of seven million, accounted for seventeen of those thirty-three cents. In all the American corridors of power, *Time* was required reading: every Sunday night in the early 1960s, at the personal request of President John F. Kennedy, an early copy of the magazine was delivered by special messenger directly from the printing plant to the White House.

Radiating the confidence of an enterprise that knows its place at the heart of the world, Time Inc.'s culture was based on entitlement and old school ties. Back then, virtually all Time Inc.'ers were male Ivy League graduates; most of them were WASPs. On closing nights at *Time* magazine, bow-tied waiters served beef Wellington (filet of beef covered with foie gras and wrapped in puff pastry) and chicken divan (sliced chicken breast and spears of broccoli covered with sauce Mornay and baked until golden brown). A well-stocked drinks cart was pushed through the offices, with highballs (whiskey and soda) and French wine for *Time*'s gentlemen writers and editors, until reeled the mind. On the street, chauffeurs in Carey Cadillacs were waiting to take them home.

Outsiders rarely gained access to Time Inc.'s exclusive club. John Gregory Dunne, who worked at *Time* from 1959 to 1964, explained how the system worked: "I was twenty-seven when I was hired, and an ignoramus, vintage Princeton '54," he wrote in overstyled understatement:

> I got my job because a woman I was seeing on the sly, Vassar '57, was also seeing George J. W. Goodman, Harvard '52, a writer in *Time*'s business section. . . . Goodman, I was informed by Vassar '57, was leaving *Time* for *Fortune,* which meant that if I moved fast there was probably a job open. I applied to *Time*'s personnel man, a friend, Yale '49, and was in due course interviewed by Otto Fuerbringer, Harvard '32, and *Time*'s managing editor. The cut of my orange and black jib seemed to satisfy him, and the $7,700 a year I was offered more than satisfied me, and so a few weeks later I went to work as a writer in the business section, although I was not altogether certain of the difference between a stock and a bond, and had no idea what "over the counter" meant.

Here and there on the editorial staff you'd find the odd Jew or African American. (Not on the business side, though.) One black writer felt so vulnerable at Time Inc. that he carried a knife to work. The most senior Jew at *Time* was Henry Anatole Grunwald, an extraordinarily talented editor who'd escaped from Austria in 1938 when it was annexed by the Nazis. Asked whether Grunwald would ever be promoted to the top job, a colleague remarked: "He's short; let's face it, he's fat; and he's Jewish. Can you see him as a boss of all those WASPs at *Time?*"

There was really only one boss, one editor, at Time Inc., and it was Luce. Refusing to take the title of "chairman," "president," or "publisher," Luce referred to himself as "editor in chief" of Time Inc. (The editors of the individual magazines were known as "managing editors.") Luce's first responsibility was not to his shareholders; his title made that clear. His company's mandate was to educate and serve the public—the millions of readers who were being shown life and the world and great events through Luce's eyes.

To make ends meet, someone had to sell advertising, of course; but moneymaking was undignified. In the words of one executive, the people working on the business side of Time Inc. were "galley slaves." Control was in the immaculate hands of editors, who were all-powerful and infallible. In Lucean terms, they represented "the Church," to which "the State" (the publishing or business side) deferred. "The managing editor of a Time Inc. magazine," Luce once remarked, "comes as close as anything in America to being a czar."

When Harry Luce died on February 28, 1967, just short of his sixty-ninth birthday, Time Inc.'s revenues were $600 million. At his death, he beneficially owned 1,012,575 shares of Time Inc. Representing 15 percent of the shares outstanding, Luce's stake was worth $109 million and paid an annual dividend of $2.4 million.

Luce's funeral was held on March 3 at the Madison Avenue Presbyterian Church, where he had worshipped since 1924. Among the eight-hundred people present that day were former vice president Richard Nixon, New York governor Nelson Rockefeller, and Barry Goldwater, the former senator and presidential candidate. The church was filled with 140 floral arrangements; a cross of white flowers was sent by General and Mrs. Dwight D. Eisenhower. In a public statement, President Lyndon B. Johnson declared: "Henry Luce was a pioneer of American journalism." To commemorate his death, Luce's photograph appeared on the covers of both *Time* and *Newsweek*.

■ ■ ■

FOR A FEW YEARS AFTER HIS DEATH, THE COMPANY HENRY LUCE had built remained unmistakably his. It was high-minded, self-righteous, and Protestant; it was also insular.

Imitating the gestures of the proud, Time Inc.'s editors still took it upon themselves to dictate the course of national affairs. Here's a telling anecdote. During the 1972 presidential campaign, editorials in *Time* and *Life* suggested that Richard Nixon's vice president, Spiro Agnew, was not fit to be president. In response, Agnew invited Hedley Donovan, Time Inc.'s editor in chief, and Henry Grunwald (who after Luce's death had, after all, been named managing editor of *Time*) to the Executive Office Building for lunch. The editorials had been unfair, Agnew objected. Why, *Life* had said he was not intellectually qualified to be president! "My I.Q. happens to be 130," Agnew asserted. "And in any case, is it for *Time* to decide who is qualified to be President?"

Donovan, looking Agnew in the eye, replied matter-of-factly: "First of all, Mr. Vice President, you work for us. You're a public servant. The reason we say these things about you is that we believe they are true. You are not qualified to be President, and we have a responsibility to tell our readers."

Time Inc.'s editors had always been arrogant, but now they were increasingly out of touch. By the early 1970s, fewer and fewer people cared what *Time* had to say about anything. The magazine had grown stale. Comparing *Time* to its biggest competitor, an advertising executive told *The Wall Street Journal* in 1969, "Newsweek has a fresher feel to it; Time seems rather tired." *Fortune,* meanwhile, was losing readers to *Business Week,* to *Forbes,* and to *The Wall Street Journal.* As for *Life* magazine, it was shut down in 1972, having accumulated $47 million of losses in the previous two years alone. To the horror of Time Inc.'s Brahmins, their once noble company was increasingly being defined by supermarket magazines. Insiders referred to *Sports Illustrated,* with its annual swimsuit issue, as *Muscles* or *Jock,* just as they referred to the company's new *Money* magazine as *Greed. People* magazine was launched in early 1974—"A cross between *Women's Wear Daily* and *Silver Screen,"* observed one insider. Someone else added: "It violates everything Luce stood for. It has no redeeming social or educational qualities whatsoever."

■ ■ ■

JERRY LEVIN MADE HIS WAY INTO TIME INC.'S PATRICIAN ENclave almost by accident. *Time* might have reported it this way: To Time Inc. in the early 1970s a clever, ambitious, slight, slopeshouldered, mustached, son of a butter-and-eggs man from South Philadelphia, a Jew, came. "You'll never make it there," his father, David Levin, predicted. "Everyone knows they're anti-Semitic." But his son Jerry had arrived at just the right moment: Time Inc. had been in decline since 1967, the year of Harry Luce's death.

Television, not print, had become the great mass medium. An entire generation was being raised on *The Brady Bunch, Hawaii Five-O,* and Swanson TV dinners with their little compartments. As fate would have it, Jerry Levin wound up in a small, overlooked corner of the Time Inc. empire devoted to television.

In the 1970s, Time Inc. was saved by a minor, almost casual in-

vestment in a New York City cable television company—Sterling
Communications, founded by Charles ("Chuck") Dolan. At a time
when cable TV was almost unheard of, Dolan had come up with the
crazy idea of wiring Manhattan for cable. Because its densely packed
skyscrapers interfered with television signals, Manhattan had some
of the worst TV reception in the country. It was the perfect market
for cable, but still, wiring the city for cable was a huge job. In remote
parts of America, cable operators could deliver television to customers
by stringing wires on telephone poles. But there *were* no telephone
poles in Manhattan, with the result that Dolan's Sterling Communications had to dig up streets, snake wires through narrow underground ducts, drag them up and through apartment buildings, and,
finally, connect the cable to individual apartments. In the Midwest,
cable could be laid for about $10,000 a mile; in Manhattan, Sterling
was spending $300,000 a mile. By 1965, having laid just seventeen
miles of cable, Dolan ran out of money. That's when Time Inc.
stepped in.

For Time Inc., investing in Sterling was one way to make up for
lost time. It was too late to buy or start one of the big networks (the
company had missed out on that one), but by getting into the cable
business, Time Inc. might make headway in the fast-growing
medium of television. Thus in 1965 the company paid $1,250,000 for
20 percent of Dolan's cable company. At first, the investment looked
like a disaster. By 1967, Sterling was out of money again, having
blown $2 million wiring no more than thirty-four city blocks. What's
more, few Manhattan residents were willing to pay a premium for
clear TV reception; by mid-1967, Sterling had only four hundred customers. Time Inc. had a choice: invest more of the company's money
or lose the whole investment. Guaranteeing a $10 million bank loan
for Sterling, Time decided to press on. But even $10 million wasn't
enough. No matter how much money Time Inc. invested, Sterling
swallowed it all and then some.

In 1971, just as Time Inc. was ready to throw in the towel, Chuck Dolan had a stroke of genius. Cable television wasn't just about better picture quality, he recognized; it should be about carrying high-quality programming. Dolan proposed they create a cable network with programming available *only* to Sterling subscribers who paid an additional monthly fee; in other words, he'd come up with the core idea for Home Box Office, or HBO. In May 1972, once his investors at Time Inc. had given him the go-ahead on HBO, Dolan hired a smart young lawyer named Jerry Levin to help roll out his new pay TV channel. That's where it started.

Levin had just turned thirty-three. He didn't know anything about television or about the entertainment business in general. By training he was a lawyer, whose career had started in 1963 at the high-class Wall Street firm of Simpson Thacher & Bartlett. But as Levin quickly discovered, practicing law was not for him "because you were giving advice to people who were really doing something." Determined to really do something and commit himself to society, Levin thought about joining the Peace Corps or going into politics. Instead, in 1967 he joined an international development company run by David Lilienthal, the charismatic New Dealer best known as the founding director of the Tennessee Valley Authority and, later, as chairman of the Atomic Energy Commission. From Lilienthal, Levin claimed he'd learned "management as a humanist art." As Lilienthal stated in 1967, management "is based on the capacity for understanding individuals and their motivations, their fears, their hopes, what they love and what they hate, the ugly and the good side of human nature."

Working for Lilienthal, Levin helped Colombia's Indians start a business exporting flowers (carnations) to the United States. He also spent a year in Tehran, working on a massive, quixotic project to transform part of Iran's desert into farmland. As time passed, Levin became more and more convinced that business could be noble, and more, that noble business was his true calling. He could have it all: "I realized that maybe business itself is the highest art form," he explained a few years later.

On his return from Iran in the early 1970s, Levin started looking for a job in cable television. "I became fascinated with it because the concepts had many of the same principles as the work I'd been doing on massive flood control and electrification," he said, forcing an analogy between his work in the Iranian desert and the early days of HBO. "There's very little difference between water, electricity and television."

With Levin as vice president in charge of programming, HBO was inaugurated on November 8, 1972. That same evening, the eyes and ears of 365 subscribers in Wilkes-Barre, Pennsylvania (the only place to have signed on for HBO) were focused on Jerry Levin as he welcomed them to the new network. Then they were shown a hockey game between the New York Rangers and the Vancouver Canucks at Madison Square Garden (5–2 for the Rangers); that was followed by a screening of *Sometimes a Great Notion,* starring Paul Newman and Henry Fonda. HBO signed off around midnight. Determined to replicate his viewers' experience, Levin watched the entire show in a suburban living room set up at HBO's studio in New York.

Now, having invested more money in Sterling Communications and HBO than it cared to admit, Time Inc. reluctantly converted its loans into equity to become HBO's sole owner. Chuck Dolan, never having made a penny for Time Inc., left the company. In late 1973, with Dolan gone, Jerry Levin was promoted to president of HBO for one good reason: According to Time Inc.'s then CEO, Andrew Heiskell, "he was the only one who understood it." That wasn't an understatement. In the geography of Time Inc., cable TV was a third world nation; it was a business run by upstarts who knew nothing about Lucean ideals or chicken divan and who depended on huge subsidies from its parent company. In the view of just about everyone at Time Inc. except maybe Levin himself, HBO was a hopeless proposition.

Just to break even, HBO needed at least 225,000 subscribers, but by the end of 1974 barely more than 50,000 had signed on. Worse, the cost of reaching new subscribers was growing exponentially. HBO's signal was transmitted by primitive microwave relay towers; depending on the terrain, the towers could be spaced no more than twenty to thirty miles apart. The only way to reach additional subscribers was to build one microwave tower after another—slowly, inefficiently, and at great expense. Apparently, no one at Time Inc. had thought through the absurd business of multiple towers. "When it was first brought to me, we talked about microwave towers as the transmission process, but we never thought about how we were going to get to the Midwest, much less to California, in order to become a national business," Heiskell admitted. "If we had thought about how impossible it would be, we would never have started it. If I had finished Harvard Business School, I might have known enough never to start HBO at all."

We have reached Jerry Levin's moment of greatness. To save HBO, Levin argued in 1975, Time Inc. would have to distribute its programs by satellite. In itself, the idea wasn't new. Satellites could be used to bounce around TV signals; people in the industry knew that, just as they knew that their future would one day depend on satellites. Some 22,300 miles above earth, Western Union's Westar, the nation's first domestic communications satellite, was already in orbit. RCA's Satcom satellite was about to be launched. But so far no one had been daring or foolish enough to send TV signals via satellite; the cost would be prohibitive. Communications satellites, with their limited capacity, had been designed for simple voice and data transmission, not video. With its death notice all but written, HBO seemed an unlikely candidate to make the first move into satellite TV.

Somehow (no one remembers the details exactly) Levin convinced Time Inc. to spend the then immense sum of $7.5 million to be a pioneer in the TV distribution business. On September 30, 1975, HBO became the first TV network to broadcast its signal by satellite, relaying all the way from Manila the most anticipated sporting event of the year: Muhammad Ali's heavyweight title defense against Joe Frazier. It was, Levin would later remember, "an electrifying kind of experience." Whereas the big three broadcast networks would have to wait a day or two until tapes of "The Thrilla in Manila" could be flown in from the Philippines, HBO subscribers had watched the fight as it happened, live, all fourteen dramatic rounds of it, as though they were part of the frenetic crowd at the Philippine Coliseum.

In response to HBO's fantastic achievement, Time Inc.'s stock price shot up. News of the amazing satellite broadcast made the front page of *The Wall Street Journal.* Single-handedly, it seemed, HBO had revitalized Time Inc., which, with the exception of *People* and *Sports Illustrated,* seemed all but moribund. "It was sort of a turning point for me and maybe Time Inc.," recalled Richard "Dick" Munro, who as head of Time Inc.'s video group at the time was Levin's boss. At a meeting with analysts at the Harvard Club that year, almost every question was directed to Munro: "Suddenly the whole meeting began to be HBO-oriented. Magazines were ignored. Everybody was looking down the table at me. I didn't know a hell of a lot, but I was the only one who had any idea of what they were talking about—satellites, dishes."

Who could have predicted it? To Time Inc. came the thirty-five-year-old Jerry Levin. Satellites, dishes, cable TV, wires, and connections—they were the future of Time Inc., and Levin was in charge of it. From then on, he would be known as Time Inc.'s "resident genius." Andrew Heiskell, who at one time had called Levin "a snake-oil salesman," switched to hyperbole: "Levin is our resident genius—there is only one at Time Inc., and it is he," he pronounced. Around the office, speaking to no one in particular, Heiskell was heard muttering: "There is *no one* like Jerry Levin."

Levin believed it. He was the genius of the place, the tutelary spirit of Time Inc., inspired to put HBO on satellite. It was a moment of greatness Levin would never recapture.

■ ■ ■

IN 1907, JERRY LEVIN'S PATERNAL GRANDPARENTS, SAMUEL AND Anna (née Fraler) Levin, arrived in the United States from czarist Russia, part of a huge wave of Jews fleeing the pogroms. Back in Russia, Samuel had been a broom maker, according to information he provided for the 1910 U.S. Census. Soon after arriving in America, he opened a dairy shop at 2344 South 7th Street in South Philadelphia; in honor of his wife, Anna, the shop was called A. Levin Butter & Eggs. Yiddish was the couple's native language, the census taker noted. Samuel could read and write, whereas Anna could not.

Eleven years after coming to America, Samuel Levin died in the flu epidemic of 1918. He left his wife, Anna, age thirty-two (who couldn't speak English); three children between the ages of five and nine; one infant; and, according to his estate filing, "goods, chattels, rights and credits" worth $1,000, plus real estate valued at $100 after "encumbrances." Living with her four young children on the second floor of A. Levin Butter & Eggs, the newly widowed Anna took charge of the store. Her eldest son, David, then nine years old, became the part-time delivery boy, carrying packets of eggs and butter to customers after school. Every day for the next fifty-two years, until he retired in 1970 at the age of sixty-one, David Levin, Jerry Levin's father, would report for work at A. Levin Butter & Eggs in Philadelphia.

When he was in his late teens, David Levin met his future wife, Pauline Shantzer. He may have been paying a bill that day, or he may have been buying eggs for the store. In any case, he found himself at the New York Creamery Co., a Philadelphia dairy wholesaler on South 8th Street owned by Joseph Shantzer. That's when David met Pauline, Shantzer's niece and bookkeeper. Born in Romania in 1909,

Pauline had arrived in America that year with her parents, Simon Shantzer and his wife, Rebecca.

After a brief courtship, David and Pauline were married in July 1928. They were nineteen years old. Having finished high school, David was working full-time as a butter-and-eggs man. Pauline, whose formal education ended after junior high school, earned some money teaching piano. In 1929, she gave birth to their daughter, Marilyn. In 1932, in the depths of the Great Depression, the couple took out a $3,000 mortgage, payable in monthly installments of $7.50, on a row house at 720 Copley Road, Upper Darby, a working-class suburb of Philadelphia, where some of Pauline's relatives had settled. It was there that Gerald Manuel Levin was born on May 6, 1939, four years after the birth of his brother, Samuel. By then, their sister, Marilyn, was in an institution; she was retarded, it was said, though details of her condition remain vague. The subject of Marilyn was off-limits in the Levin household. Jerry Levin remembers seeing his sister only once, institutionalized, "in grotesque circumstances." She died in 1945.

The family residence at 720 Copley Road was unremarkable, a modest two-story row house with a porch and a small (eighteen-by-twenty-foot) front yard. Nonetheless, it was a step up from the teeming tenement buildings of South Philly. For the most part, immigrants didn't settle in Upper Darby. Nor, for that matter, did Jews. In a town of twenty-three churches (eighteen Protestant, five Catholic) and not a single synagogue, the Levins were one of a handful of Jewish families in Upper Darby. "Jew boy" is how Samuel Levin, Jerry's older brother, recalls being taunted by his Upper Darby neighbors.

The Levins were not especially religious. David Levin had been raised in an Orthodox home, and early in his marriage he and the children worshipped at an Orthodox synagogue in South Philly, not far from A. Levin Butter & Eggs. His wife was less observant. David was strictly kosher, separating meat from dairy and avoiding pork and shellfish (and other foods prohibited in the Bible), whereas Pauline would sneak the boys out for bacon-lettuce-and-tomato sandwiches. By the mid-1940s, David stopped going to Orthodox services altogether; instead, the family attended high holiday services in Upper Darby, where, shortly after World War II, a Conservative "synagogue in formation" was founded. Held variously in homes, above stores, in restaurants, and in churches, services were conducted by visiting rabbis.

The Levin household was structured. There were music lessons (cello for Samuel, clarinet for Jerry) and day-to-day chores. Every hour and every dollar were carefully accounted for. Clothes were passed down to Samuel from his cousins, from Samuel to Jerry, and from Jerry to other cousins. "My father was European," explained Samuel, which is to say he was strict and old-fashioned. "He ruled the roost. My mother followed his orders."

Evenings, Pauline would play classical music on a small upright piano in the living room. On weekends, the family often got together with relatives. Between them, Pauline and David Levin had ten brothers and sisters, all of whom had children of their own. The boys played games with their cousins. With Pauline at the piano, the women sang songs. Later, after dinner was served and the women washed up, the men would play cards or shoot craps.

Occasionally, as a special treat, David Levin would take his young family to the local Hot Shoppe, a drive-in fast-food chain where "running boys" delivered ice-cream sundaes and milkshakes on trays that clipped onto the windows of the family's 1941 Chrysler. David loved newfangled gadgets. He was one of the first on his block to get a 45 rpm record player. After the war, when television was still a novelty and programming limited to a few hours a day, he splurged on an RCA Victor television receiver, a $226 tabletop model with a seven-inch screen enlarged by an attached magnifying glass. Once a week, Samuel and Jerry Levin watched *The Howdy Doody Show*.

The boys' fondest childhood memories were of Camp Kweebec

in Schwenksville, Pennsylvania, a coed summer camp they attended
for more than a decade in the 1940s and 1950s. Less than forty miles
northwest of Philadelphia, Camp Kweebec might have been in another country; that's how different it was from their home. At Kweebec, Jerry Levin discovered his love of acting: he played Billy Bigelow
in *Carousel* and Curly in *Oklahoma!* He learned to ride horses and
build campfires. And he met a girl named Carol Needleman, who
would later become his wife.

In 1951, when Jerry was twelve, the Levins sold their row house
in Upper Darby for $8,000 and moved to Overbrook Hills, a solidly
middle-class neighborhood in Lower Marion on Philadelphia's Main
Line. They paid $26,500 for a two-story brick house at 150 Trent
Road. It had a nice wide yard and a finished basement. As Samuel
Levin put it, it was "a big step up," so big that David Levin had resisted the move. For one thing, he was nervous about financial pressures;
for another, by personality, he resisted change. But his wife and children were eager to move to a bigger house in a better neighborhood,
and finally they wore him down.

To cover the mortgage on the new house, David Levin worked
punishing hours, spending twelve to fourteen hours a day, often seven
days a week, at A. Levin Butter & Eggs. His mother, Anna Levin, had
retired. And though his youngest brother, Benjamin ("Benny"), and a
delivery boy named Abe now worked for him, David rarely left the
store. On weeknights he'd come home long after his boys had eaten
dinner, sometimes after they'd fallen sleep.

Jerry admired his father. But it was his grandmother Anna
whose influence he felt strongly. Anna Levin doted on Jerry; she was
confident that the future would be his, that the world lay before him.
"I was close to my parents, but my grandmother was the matriarch,"
Jerry Levin recalled. "She had great aspirations for me. She was very
loving and thought to an extent that went beyond reality that I was
bright and good-looking, and she wanted me to be the president of the
United States or something like that."

Anna's instincts were sound. Even as a young boy, Jerry Levin showed self-discipline and self-control. He was a prodigy. When Levin was ten or eleven, he told me (and almost everyone else who has ever interviewed him), the rabbi in Upper Darby failed to show up one day; whereupon the gifted young boy took the rabbi's place, leading the service in Hebrew. And all who heard him were astonished at his understanding. "Jerry was very studious," recalled his brother, Samuel. "He was a very serious-minded individual and an extremely good student. He got straight As in everything. I, on the other hand, was a B student." At every school Jerry Levin attended, he graduated at or near the top of his class. "In terms of personality, I was more outgoing and a bit of a troublemaker," Samuel added. "Jerry was not that way at all. He always did what he was supposed to do; he was really a very, very good child." Jerry concurred: "My brother was wild, and I was very quiet and never got into trouble."

At Lower Merion High School, where he graduated second in his class, Jerry Levin was named to the Honor Society. He was one of the year's "Outstanding Students," according to the school's 1956 yearbook, where his activities are cataloged: member of the Spanish Club and the Photography Club, president of the Thespian Society, "literary associate" of the yearbook, baseball player, and more. As well, there's a photograph of Levin playing District Attorney Charles Montgomery Flint, the lead role in Ayn Rand's drama of 1933, *Night of January 16th*; good and evil merge in her plot, and it's hard to tell truth from fiction.

Like many graduates of Lower Merion High School, Jerry Levin's older brother, Samuel, attended Temple University in Philadelphia. Jerry was exceptional, though, and everyone knew that. "When I met Jerry, he was sixteen going on forty-seven," recalled his first wife, Carol Needleman. "He had this maturity and sense of self." Levin attended Haverford College in Haverford, Pennsylvania, a small (480-student) all-male liberal arts school founded by the Quakers. "At the time, Haverford was one of the most difficult schools to get into," Samuel explained. "You had to be A-plus number one to get in. In suburban Philly, where we lived, it was *the* place to go. It was a *big* deal. It was very, very prestigious."

Haverford was unlike anything Jerry Levin had ever known. For the first time, he was intellectually challenged. He studied philosophy, modern literature, and religion. Intoxicated by the world of ideas, he absorbed them all. Majoring in biblical studies, he first considered becoming an academic. "He was disciplined beyond any normal standard," recalled George Parker, a classmate of Levin's at Haverford who was dazzled by him. Forty years later, Parker would say: "I think the world of him—I just think the absolute world of him. I'm awestruck by him and honored to have had him as a friend."

Encouraged to think in new ways, and surrounded by creative young men with nimble minds, Levin began to regard his background as embarrassingly parochial. How restricted his life had been! Slowly Levin was rejecting the world of Judaism and embracing something called universalism: everyone would be saved. The more he read, the more he was drawn to Haverford's Quaker ethic—its emphasis on humility, industriousness, and moral purity, for example. "The symbol of Jesus—the notion of humility, ego submersion, the meek will inherit the earth—became so powerful to me that, although I was first in my class, I refused the award that went with it," he later said. "To this day I'm not sure why, but I also burned every paper I wrote in college, including my honors paper, on the theory that no one needed to applaud it or read it." Quakerism, Levin noted, "endowed me with a moral certainty about certain things that I carry to this day."

One book, Albert Camus's bleak existentialist novel of 1942, *The Stranger,* made an indelible impression on Levin. He'd read it first in his sophomore year at Haverford; then he kept reading it. The plot of the novel is straightforward: An ordinary young Algerian named Meursault kills a man for no apparent reason and is condemned to death. The absurdity of the trial is central to Camus's novel. Meursault is detached, memorable for his lack of guilt and his inability to express human emotion. When his girlfriend asks him if he loves her, he writes clinically, "I answered the same way I had last time, that it didn't mean anything and that I probably didn't." *The Stranger* was the catalyst for Levin's first great epiphany—in his words, "that humankind's fate is to rally against injustice but that the universe is indifferent."

Identifying with Camus's protagonist in *The Stranger,* Levin saw himself as a detached observer, misunderstood, helpless in the face of an absurd universe. "It just resonated," Levin said from the depths of his human predicament. "That we impute meaning and purpose to things that are totally adventitious or accidental; that there is no God; that there just is; that there's no life after death. It was a pretty bleak philosophy, but it became my philosophy."

When Levin came home from Haverford during holidays, his parents were shocked by his transformation. His mother resented his new philosophy, perhaps because it implied contempt for her beliefs. She had hoped that her son would become a rabbi. But now, recognizing that religion was nothing more than an excuse for evading one's own liberty, Jerry Levin turned his back on Judaism. "She thought that my mind had gotten poisoned by all this stuff, and she never quite understood it," said Levin.

When he graduated from Haverford in 1960, Levin was named class valedictorian and elected to Phi Beta Kappa. Newly married to Carol Needleman, the girl he'd met back at Camp Kweebec, and with his first child on the way, Levin decided to pursue a practical and lucrative career. In 1963, he graduated first in his class at the University of Pennsylvania Law School.

By the time he entered his new situation at Time Inc. ten years later, Levin had cut most of his ties to the past. He was detached, literally, having left his wife and three young children in 1970. Two months after his divorce, he married a woman from Kansas named Barbara Riley, who had worked as a secretary for David Lilienthal's international development company. Jerry Levin was starting over.

TWO

BY 1980, THE MOST POWERFUL MEN IN THE TIME-LIFE BUILDING were accountants, lawyers, and MBAs. That year, for the first time, Time Inc.'s video group, comprising HBO and various cable systems, made more money than all the company's magazines put together. Two years later, in 1982, the video group was responsible for an astonishing two-thirds of Time Inc.'s total profits. It was hard to believe, but there it was: Time Inc.'s most important assets no longer depended on Henry Luce and his legacy. *Time, Fortune, Sports Illustrated,* and *People* were good, steady businesses, but compared to cable television and its enormous potential for growth, Time Inc.'s magazines seemed doomed.

In 1980, Dick Munro, who had been running the video group since the early 1970s, was elected Time Inc.'s new president and CEO. Now, with Jerry Levin succeeding Munro as its head, the video group was all-powerful. Cultures clashed at Time Inc., with people on the magazine side accusing people in the video group of being "market oriented." In other words, they intended to make money. "Compared to Time Inc., we're overly aggressive and overly arrogant," a video group executive admitted. "Publishing is more gentlemanly."

In the days of Henry Luce, editors were gentlemen, and Time Inc. was high-minded. By the 1980s, however, America was moving into a new age. Wall Street now controlled corporate America, and Wall Street demanded efficiency (which may have been inseparable from aggression and arrogance). The traditional employment contract—loyalty in exchange for lifetime employment and a gold watch—no longer made any sense. Hundreds of thousands of workers were fired. From now on employees would be self-sufficient, responsible for their own future. Ruthlessly, costs were cut. Companies that didn't or couldn't adapt became targets for corporate raiders. The economy was on speed. It was the age of corporate raiders, yuppies, insider trading, leveraged buyouts, junk bonds, limousines, cocaine, *Bright Lights, Big City,* Michael Milken, and Ivan Boesky.

Luce's handpicked successor, Andrew Heiskell, retired in 1980, just in time. In many ways he was the last gentleman of Luce's Time Inc. Heiskell was tall (six feet five and a half inches); he was cultured (a member of the board of the New York Public Library); and he was international (born to American parent in Naples, raised in Italy, Switzerland, Germany, Austria, and France, and fluent in three languages). "When I became chairman, I didn't know what a balance sheet was," he once said, suggesting that the world of finance was slightly beneath him. Heiskell's first wife was the glamorous movie actress Madeleine Carroll. His second wife was Marian Sulzberger, daughter of Arthur Hays Sulzberger, publisher of *The New York Times.* Andrew Heiskell was universally regarded as "urbane."

By contrast, Dick Munro was a meat-and-potatoes man. A former U.S. Marine and a combat veteran of the Korean War, he'd spent a year in hospital recovering from shrapnel wounds. Having attended Colgate University on the GI Bill, he'd arrived at Time Inc. in 1957, a decade before the death of Henry Luce. Munro wasn't sure he'd ever met the great man ("I can't recall ever shaking his hand," he said). He disliked traveling abroad. When forced to cross the Atlantic, he'd bring along jars of peanut butter. "He is a man who has absolutely no interest in food or drink, who confuses Château Margaux with

Château Gallo, or for that matter with cream soda," said Heiskell, who was charmed by Munro's lack of pretensions.

Munro was thoroughly likable, someone who boasted of never having eaten fish, as though fish eaters were soft or un-American. He was a populist, working in shirtsleeves and more at ease with Time Inc.'s elevator security guards than with its senior executives. He was modest and self-effacing. From the perspective of Time Inc.'s directors, his greatest contribution was his success with the video group: Munro had built the company's most profitable division.

But despite his admirable qualities, or because of them, Dick Munro was not suited to run a major public company in the 1980s. For one thing, he wasn't good at big strategic thinking. And complex financial models made him nervous; he couldn't always grasp them. After all, when he'd arrived at Time Inc. in the gentle 1950s, the emphasis was not on numbers and charts. "In those days," he recalled, "all you had to do was add and subtract. Almost no one ever heard of a balance sheet. Business then was all profit and loss."

To compensate for his lack of financial sophistication, Munro was forced to rely heavily on his two former lieutenants in the video group—Levin, and Nick Nicholas, a Harvard MBA and a mathematical wizard. Born in September 1939 and descended from Greek immigrants, Nicholas had arrived at Time Inc. in 1964, fresh out of business school. Quickly he proved to be a sharp and focused turnaround artist, dedicated to the bottom line. He was unsentimental, tough-minded, and very ambitious. He was not self-effacing. Before long, Nicholas and Levin were widely regarded as Time Inc.'s most promising young executives. "They were my protégés," explained Munro.

Levin was the big thinker, the so-called resident genius who'd put HBO on satellite, and Munro was impressed by him. But despite his considerable intellect, the truth is that Levin couldn't make money. Carried away by the big idea, he had never mastered the art of turning a profit. Time and again in the late 1970s and early 1980s, Nick Nicholas was dispatched to clean up after Levin, who made one expensive mistake after another. For example, under Levin, the video group lost $35 million on something called Teletext, a service that delivered text news and information to TV sets via cable wires. The video group also lost $87.4 million, an immense sum of money at the time, in one of the costliest failures in Time Inc.'s history—an experiment with subscription television. Then there was TriStar Pictures, a film studio started in 1982 by HBO with CBS and Columbia Pictures. In a startling (but not uncharacteristic) act of shortsightedness, Levin had failed to limit the amount of money HBO would invest in movies made by the studio. No matter how much TriStar decided to spend on its films, Time Inc. found itself on the hook for a third of that sum. By the time the terms of the initial agreement were changed, in the late 1980s, Time Inc. had wasted somewhere in the range of $500 million.

In 1983, Levin and Nicholas were named to Time Inc.'s board of directors. A year later, in 1984, they were made executive vice presidents, reporting directly to Dick Munro, who openly (and naively) announced that he intended to retire by 1990. Suddenly the two forty-four-year-old golden boys, Nicholas and Levin, became rivals, enemy twins, as it were, in the race to become Munro's successor. Nicholas won and in 1986 was named president and chief operating officer of Time Inc. Levin, by sad contrast, was given the titular position of "chief strategist." It wasn't Levin's only humiliation. Three months after Nicholas's promotion, Levin was removed from Time Inc.'s board of directors. "I didn't think Gerald had the balls for the job and I thought Nick did," explained Munro, adding, "I was proven wrong."

Levin was devastated. Moping around the place, he appeared to be inconsolable, a broken man in an indifferent universe. At the age of forty-seven, Levin had suffered his first public setback. Nevertheless, if Nicholas thought for a moment that his opponent would pack up and leave, he had misread Levin badly. "The conventional view was, as a colleague put it, that Levin had his eyes on the mountaintops while Nicholas was good at fighting through the swamps," recalled Henry Grunwald, Time Inc.'s editor in chief at the time. "The reality was more complex. Nicholas was not as tough as he looked, and Levin a lot tougher."

Patiently, biding his time, Levin stayed the calculated course. His day would come; he knew that. Meanwhile he would position himself as Nicholas's closest, most trusted adviser. "The reason I didn't quit was not just because of blind love for the company," Levin later explained. "There was some unfinished business. It was finding the destiny of the company. I was going to do it."

■ ■ ■

FOR THE REST OF HIS LIFE, FROM 1980 UNTIL HIS DEATH IN THE summer of 2003, Andrew Heiskell would regret having appointed Dick Munro as CEO of Time Inc. In Heiskell's view, Munro, or rather his proxy, Nicholas, had destroyed Luce's great company. "Within a relatively short period of time Munro was not making any decisions of his own but was being propelled by Nicholas," wrote Heiskell in his memoirs, published in 1998. "After a while I began to wonder, who the hell is Dick Munro? What have I done? A failure. My big failure."

Indeed, once Nicholas had been made president of Time Inc. in 1986, Munro seemed to be little more than a figurehead. Meanwhile, Levin had allied himself tightly with Nicholas, who regarded his new partner as "his right arm." Together, under Munro, the two men devised a tough new program for Time Inc. The company would be driven by financial targets, the sorts of targets that in the past had been thought to stifle creativity. "Capital redeployment," "strategic benchmarks," and "return on equity": those and related catchwords now defined the goals of Time Inc. If Wall Street demanded accountability and efficiency, then the company had to be operated in the interest of shareholders, period. Luce's mission to run Time Inc. in the "public interest" was outdated.

In the view of Wall Street, Time Inc. was in trouble. "The company is perceived on both Wall Street and internally as uncreative, overly cautious, investor-driven, and risk-adverse," concluded an internal report of 1988. By the late 1980s, the breakup value of Time Inc. exceeded its market capitalization; corporate raiders were circling the company like so many buzzards.

Under Nicholas, Time Inc.'s overriding goal was a return on equity (ROE) of 20 percent, well above the 13.7 percent ROE that Time Inc. had averaged in the 1970s. To meet that goal, underperforming divisions were shut down or, in the case of Temple Eastex and Inland Container, the company's forest-products divisions, spun off. Hundreds of employees were fired, expense accounts were curtailed, and the company's airplanes were sold. Even the editors would now be paid according to their magazine's financial performance.

Inside the company, Nicholas became known as "Nick the Knife" and "Neutron Nick." Neither epithet bothered him particularly; in his view, Time Inc. needed to be shaken up. "There was no choice," he recalled. "I just kept saying, 'Hey, everybody, wake up! This should have been done five years ago, but it wasn't. So now it's our job. We've got to bite our upper lip and do it.' And I had the will to do it."

In the all-out drive to cut Time Inc.'s costs and improve ROE, even Andrew Heiskell was given an ultimatum: Either he'd vacate his modest postretirement office in the Time-Life Building or he'd have to start paying $50,000 a year in rent (he chose to pay the $50,000). What's more, in an act of iconoclasm that marked a break with Time Inc.'s history, Nicholas removed the official portraits of Heiskell and of Hedley Donovan, who had succeeded Luce as Time Inc.'s editor in chief. "This is not a company that worships deities," Nicholas stated. "Who is Andrew Heiskell? Andrew was the latest guy to come along.

Hedley Donovan was the number two editor in chief. We're now into number four. Big deal. Give me a break."

■ ■ ■

By 1987, Nicholas and Levin agreed on a strategy: Time Inc.'s salvation depended on what Levin called a "transforming transaction." (In the 1980s, just about every company in America equated salvation with making a big deal.) From the perspective of Levin and Nicholas, Time Inc. was too insular, too resistant to change, to transform itself; it needed a catalyst. To quote Levin: "I remember going to one of our strategy sessions . . . and looking around at the top 75 or 80 people in the company; nearly all of them had been here since they got out of school." Hiring outsiders wasn't the solution, he explained: "Time has what we call an immunologic system, and it rejects them."

In May 1987, Nicholas met what seemed to be his future salvation in the person of Steve Ross, the head of Warner Communications. Warner was one of Time Inc.'s biggest competitors in the cable business, and the companies' offices were less than two blocks from each other. Still, Ross and Nicholas had never met. Michael Fuchs, who had worked closely with Nicholas and Levin at HBO since 1976 and was now head of HBO, suggested the meeting. "I went to Nick and I said, 'Look, we've never spoken to Ross.' You know, Warner was considered a little dirty in those days—I mean, they were really swingers, those guys. So I said, 'You know, Steve Ross is a block and a half away, Nick, and we've never gone to talk to him.' So we went to talk to him." Fuchs added, "I don't claim it was my idea for the merger; it was my idea for them to sit down."

Years later, Nicholas would describe Steve Ross as "the Henry Luce of Warner." But the only thing Ross and Luce had in common was an addiction to power and cigarettes. The son of an oil burner salesman, Steve Ross, born Steven Jay Rechnitz in the Flatbush section of Brooklyn on September 19, 1927, was a canny operator, a shrewd promoter who'd transformed his father-in-law's funeral parlor and parking lot business into the world's largest entertainment company. A deal junkie drawn to serial acquisitions, Ross was blessed with charm and a brilliant mathematical mind ("I hate calculators," he once said, "they're the equalizer"). Between 1966, the year Ross took Warner public, and 1988, one year before he announced the merger with Time Inc., his company's market value had grown from $12.5 million to $5.6 billion.

In its early days, Ross's company, then known as Kinney Service Corporation, was an unexciting conglomerate made up of more than 150 companies. From his father-in-law's funeral parlors, Ross had expanded into almost every imaginable service business: parking lots, rental cars, security guards, commercial cleaning, printing, data processing, painting, plumbing, and more. "Service Is Our Middle Name!" was one of Kinney's early slogans.

In 1967, Ross added a touch of glamour to his collection of companies: he bought a large Hollywood talent agency whose founder, Ted Ashley, soon suggested that Ross buy a run-down movie and music company called Warner–Seven Arts. That's where it all began for Ross.

The Warner Bros. studio had been started in 1923 by four brothers, Harry, Albert, Sam, and Jack Warner. The Warner boys had entered the movie business in 1903. Together with their father, a Jewish immigrant from Poland, they bought a nickelodeon in New Castle, Pennsylvania. From owning theaters, they moved into producing and distributing movies before opening a studio in Burbank, California. Their big break came in 1927, the year Warner Bros. released the first major "talking picture," *The Jazz Singer,* starring Al Jolson.

By the late 1930s, Warner Bros. had become one of the most powerful studios in Hollywood. Jack Warner, who became the company's leader, was respected for his daring and his imagination; he was also widely feared. His stars, whom he controlled absolutely, included

Errol Flynn, Humphrey Bogart, James Cagney, Olivia de Havilland, Bette Davis, and Rin Tin Tin. Among the studio's hits were *Casablanca, 42nd Street,* and *My Fair Lady.* "As much as it is possible for one man to dominate a publicly owned company, Mr. Warner dominated Warner Brothers," Vincent Canby of *The New York Times* would later note.

In 1956, Jack Warner bought out his brothers' interest in Warner Bros. Two years later, he got into the music business by starting Warner Bros. Records. By the late 1960s, however, Warner Bros. was in decline. The movie business was under assault from television and regulators. As for Jack Warner, he was losing his touch. In 1967, at the age of seventy-four, he sold his one-third interest in Warner Bros. to Seven Arts for $32 million. The age of all-powerful studio heads had come to an end. Even Jack Warner knew that. "Yeah, today I'm Jack L. Warner," he is said to have remarked at the time, "but wait until tomorrow: I'll be just another rich Jew."

Only a year after Jack Warner sold his company, it was picked up by the charismatic Steve Ross. Before long, with Ted Ashley running the business day to day, the studio was restored. By the early 1970s, Warner Bros. was once again making hit films, among them, *A Clockwork Orange, The Exorcist,* and *Dirty Harry.* The music division, too, which now included the Warner Bros. label as well as Atlantic Records, Elektra Records, and Asylum Records, was producing one hit album after another, by Aretha Franklin, the Rolling Stones, the Doors, Carly Simon, and others. By this point in the story, Ross had transformed himself into a Hollywood mogul. Abandoning Kinney Service Corporation, Ross sold all his assets except his movie and music company, which he renamed Warner Communications Inc.

■ ■ ■

PEOPLE WILL TELL YOU THAT STEVE ROSS WAS "LARGER THAN life." Sometimes he'd embellish his true-life stories for color and effect. He said he'd played professional football for the Cleveland Browns. He said that in World War II, as a member of the U.S. Navy, he'd seen heavy combat action in the Pacific. In fact, as Richard Clurman reports in his book of 1992, *To the End of Time,* the war in the Pacific was over by the time Ross joined the USS *Hopping* in 1945; and he never did play professional football. Tall (six feet three), handsome, magnanimous, and extraordinarily generous, Ross seduced everyone he met. "I learned about people in the funeral business," he told Connie Bruck, whose 1994 book, *Master of the Game,* recounts Ross's ascent from Flatbush to the top of the entertainment world. "It's a service business. You service people in an emotional time—you learn about their needs, their feelings."

In retrospect, it should be no surprise that in May 1987, after his meeting with Nicholas, Ross suggested their two companies might come together, perhaps by way of their cable systems. Time Inc. was having a hard time, an emotional time, and Ross understood that. He knew what they needed. Anyway, how could he resist proposing to Time Inc.? For the boy from Flatbush, Henry Luce's Time Inc. was the princess with the golden hair he'd always dreamed of. As Ross himself put it, "Time has such pizzazz."

Before long, prompted by Ross's idea of a joint venture, Nicholas decided that a merger between Time Inc. and Warner Communications could be the solution to Time Inc.'s problems. In the view of Time Inc.'s top executives, if something wasn't done soon their company would be left behind or be bought out. To compete in the global marketplace, it was believed, Time Inc. had to get big fast—and what better way to accomplish that goal than by merging with Warner? A combined Time and Warner would dwarf every company in the industry. Building on Nicholas's logic, Levin drafted a confidential memo to Dick Munro in August 1987, making a strong case for the deal. Together with Warner, "the new Time Inc.," Levin wrote, "would be an entertainment-oriented communications company."

Later, Jerry Levin would claim that the idea for the merger with Warner Communications had been all his. ("Nick maintains he gave me the idea, but that is not true," he said.) Nicholas brushed off Levin's version of events as fantasy, assuring me that the idea of the merger had been his. Meanwhile, Dick Munro insisted that the idea came out of Time Inc.'s strategy group. One way or another, Levin and Nicholas worked closely together that summer. While Levin, the lawyer, looked after the technical and legal details, Nicholas, the numbers man, focused on the financial strategy. Of course, they knew that the idea of merging with Warner, a company run by Hollywood types, would be unpopular with Time Inc.'s senior executives and board of directors. Thus every day, for months, Levin and Nicholas met to prepare their arguments and map out a rhetorical strategy. Ross was pushing to get things moving, but Nicholas and Levin needed time to build support at Time Inc.

Dick Munro shared their point of view, but it wasn't easy to win over Time Inc.'s board. In the first place, many directors worried about Ross's "character." Henry "Hank" Luce III, for example, Harry Luce's son and a Time Inc. director, was utterly opposed to the deal. He evoked the terms of his father's will: Time Inc. must "continue to be, principally, a journalistic enterprise, and, as such, operated in the public interest." He objected to Ross's outrageously lavish employment contract. He was disgusted by "the ethics and foul tongues of Hollywood types." Finally, Hank Luce zeroed in on rumors about Mafia connections over at Warner.

For years, Steve Ross had been plagued by those rumors: he and his company had links to the Mob and organized crime, it was said. There had been criminal charges (price fixing), and people talked about a mysterious briefcase kept in Ross's office and stuffed with cash (gambling winnings, Ross insisted). Munro assured the board that most of those stories about Ross were unproven; besides, any problems he may have had when he was in the parking lot business were past history. "Steve is such a warm, embracing human being," Levin attested. "He has this huge emotional reservoir, which is, I think, what makes him unique."

It was hard to ignore the contrasts between Warner Communications and Time Inc. Steve Ross had his hair styled and blow-dried every day. He was an intimate friend of such Hollywood stars as Barbra Streisand and Steven Spielberg. He was glamorous. At the company's expense, Ross kept a fleet of Gulfstream jets, as well as a helicopter that shuttled between Manhattan and his estate in East Hampton. To accommodate Ross's favorite executives and celebrities, Warner Communications bought up chunks of real estate: five apartments in Manhattan's Trump Tower, two fully staffed chalets in Aspen, and a hacienda overlooking Mexico's Acapulco Bay. Villa Eden, as Ross called the Mexican hacienda, was a prop, designed to service people in a narcissistic time and feed their sense of entitlement. It included indoor and outdoor tennis courts, two swimming pools, fourteen bedrooms, five massage rooms, a screening room, and a "pro shop," where once, in a single year, $25,999 was spent on providing company guests with complimentary tennis balls and running shoes. "Steve is like a kid in a candy store," his good friend Spielberg once remarked. "It just happens that he runs the candy store."

That kind of excess (or vulgarity) was too much for Time Inc.'s directors, who were convinced that Warner's executives were not (to put it politely) their kind of people. The board would agree to a deal with Warner, but only on one condition: Time Inc.'s "culture" had to remain intact. In a word, the combined company would have to get rid of Steve Ross and his excesses as soon as possible.

Month after month, like a pendulum, Time Inc.'s chief negotiator, Jerry Levin, went back and forth between the Time-Life Building and Warner's headquarters at 75 Rockefeller Plaza. His legal background, his devotion to getting the deal done, and his unflappable personality made him the obvious man for the job. He considered and discussed every nuance of the deal. Munro planned to retire in May

1990; until then he and Ross would be co-chairmen and co-CEOs of the new combined company. After that, with Ross as chairman, Ross and Nicholas would serve as co-CEOs. Eventually, when Ross retired (he was already in his sixties), Nicholas would take charge. Meanwhile, Jerry Levin would be the number three man, officially a vice chairman. As for Ross's lavish ten-year employment contract, it couldn't be altered.

Typically, Levin focused so intensely on his idealized vision of the merger that he managed to overlook the uncomfortable and unresolved details. "Well, sure, the cultures were different," Levin explained. "But the real question is, Does it make sense to make Time Inc. a full-media company? That's really the question." To Levin, the answer was obvious, and the end always justified the means. "At some point it will work its way through because it's the right thing to do," he said, echoing an argument he would make again and again to justify his decisions. "At some point, if it makes sense, it'll work its way through."

On March 4, 1989, two years after negotiations began, Time Inc. and Warner Communications announced their impending deal, a simple all-stock, tax- and debt-free merger. Three months later, and just two weeks before shareholders were scheduled to vote on the proposed deal, a hostile bid came out of left field: Gulf & Western (soon renamed Paramount Communications) offered to pay an incredible $200 a share—in cash—for Time Inc., then trading at $125 a share. All hell broke loose. Time Inc. was not going to be swallowed up by just anyone, and *especially* not by Paramount's CEO, Martin Davis— an unprincipled parvenu, in the view of Time Inc. Why, compared to Davis, Steve Ross was saintly! As Munro put it, "Ross is a gentleman. Davis is a son of a bitch."

Week after week, desperate to save their company, their jobs, and their reputations, Time Inc.'s flustered senior executives and outside advisers huddled in "the War Room," a conference room on the thirty-fourth floor of the Time-Life Building. How should they respond to Davis's hostile bid? It was chaos. It was pandemonium. Who could have anticipated this turn of events? Nicholas, overwhelmed by the pressure, flipped and flopped. Munro, the war veteran, was shocked; he'd read about wily corporate raiders, of course, but he'd never imagined that Time Inc. would be sabotaged like this. What's more, Munro kept repeating, Davis had pretended to be his friend! Only a few months earlier, according to Munro, Davis had promised not to bid for Time Inc.! "Maybe I was naive," said Munro, still riled by it all 15 years later, "but in the world I was raised in, you fought fair." On day two of the turmoil, when Davis put in a telephone call to Munro, Munro refused to take it. "Tell him to go fuck himself," he shouted to his secretary.

In the midst of the hysteria at Time Inc., Jerry Levin, cool and knowing, stepped in to fill the power vacuum. "It's like mobilizing a military force: somebody had to be in charge. It wasn't Nick. It wasn't Dick," Levin said, recalling the precise moment he'd understood that his destiny was to run Time Warner. "Maybe it was because I negotiated the deal or I have a legal background or I managed all the bankers, that I took charge. I slept at the office for two months. We met every morning and I ran the meetings." In the disarray, Levin discovered his great strength: he was a superb tactician who knew just how to spot and exploit weakness in others.

"It was a pivotal experience for me," Levin noted. "How many times in business do you go through a situation where your survival is at stake?" he continued rhetorically. "Where you have to engage in this warfare that's all about tactics?"

Levin may not have had Nicholas's financial genius. He didn't have Munro's personal touch, and he lacked Steve Ross's charm. Levin's power lay in something less obvious: his emotional detachment. Calmly, rationally, he would do whatever it took to make sure the deal with Ross went through.

To save themselves from Davis, Levin and his troops at Time Inc. came up with a desperate counterproposal: The company would buy Warner outright, with cash it didn't have. According to the terms of the original plan, a merger of Time and Warner would have required a vote by shareholders; and which Time shareholder in his or her right mind would have turned down Paramount's $200 offer for stock then trading at $125? On the other hand, an all-cash acquisition of Warner required no approval at all from Time Inc.'s shareholders. The scheme was foolproof.

In response, Paramount sued, contending that as a public company, Time Inc. had a fiduciary responsibility to its shareholders to accept Davis's offer of $200 a share. Evoking the terms of Henry Luce's will, Time Inc.'s executives testified that the company wasn't like other public companies. It was a breed apart. Their most prized assets included editorial integrity, a commitment to serve the public, and a belief that business was about more than dollars and cents. According to Luce's will, Time Inc. was "an enterprise operated in the public interest as well as in the interest of its stockholders." By contrast, Time Inc.'s executives argued, Davis had nothing but money to offer.

Remarkably, the judge agreed with Time Inc. In his seventy-nine-page decision, William Allen, chancellor of the Delaware Court of Chancery, wrote: "The mission of the firm is not seen by those involved with it as wholly economic." It was a huge precedent for corporate America, that decision. Time Inc.'s duty to serve the public was more important than the fiduciary rights of company shareholders.

Shareholder activists were aghast. In his textbook *Corporate Governance,* Robert Monks, known as the dean of shareholder activists, states: "Just about everything the courts said about the duty of directors to shareholders in the early takeover cases was reversed in the case involving the Time Warner merger. That case represents probably the greatest incursion in United States business history into the rights of shareholders."

Chancellor Allen's decision confirmed the right of Time Inc.'s directors and executives to manage their company largely as they saw fit. It allowed them to justify their corporate decisions by evoking integrity and principles and public service and a "mission" that was not "wholly economic." Forget about the short-term interests of shareholders, executives, and employees. "What a beautiful thing," Levin said wistfully on the subject of Chancellor Allen's decision in *Paramount v. Time*. What a beautiful thing.

■ ■ ■

ON JANUARY 10, 1990, TIME INC. ACQUIRED WARNER COMMUNI-cations for $14.9 billion. With revenues of more than $10 billion, the new Time Warner Inc. was now the world's biggest media and entertainment company. As a direct result of Paramount's hostile bid, however, what had initially been planned as a simple all-stock merger of Time and Warner had turned into a massive leveraged buyout. Time Warner wound up so bloated with debt, it could scarcely move. It was like a beached whale on life support. Interest payments alone on the $11.5 billion of debt would cost Time Warner $3 million a day. Even in the greatest bull market the world had ever know—and may ever know—it would take seven and a half years for Time Warner shares to climb to the equivalent of Paramount's $200-per-share offer.

For the employees and shareholders of Warner, and especially for Ross himself, the deal was a windfall. Time Inc. paid cash, up front, for their company's shares. In total, Warner's employees and executives made $677 million by selling their company to Time Inc. Ross alone earned $78.2 million in 1990, of which $74.9 million represented payment for his shares in Warner. Further, in accordance with the fantastic employment contract he'd negotiated, Ross would receive another $121 million over the next seven years. Meanwhile, once the merger closed, Warner's executives were granted most of the newly issued stock options. Over at Time Inc., by sorry contrast, almost everyone lost his or her shirt. "Because of that son of a bitch at Paramount, we had to acquire Warner in cash," Hank Luce told me, still angry more than ten years after the fact. "That made all of the Warner people rich and all the Time people resentful."

Officially, Time Inc. had bought Warner Communications; still, there was no doubt who was in charge of the new combined company. "We bought them. They got rich. Then they treated us like they owned us," raged Michael Fuchs, who was then head of Time Inc.'s HBO division. Steve Ross was chairman and CEO of Time Warner Inc., and he made all the crucial decisions. Nick Nicholas was co-CEO, but his title didn't mean much; confronted by Ross and the high-flying culture of Warner, Nicholas was out of his league. He couldn't cope. "Time Inc., at the time, was a very rarefied environment—we didn't mix with just anyone else. We mixed with *our* kind of people. We weren't ready for the real world, and Warner was the real world *plus*," recalled Fuchs. "After that merger, Nick got, like— what's it called when you get sick from heights? Agoraphobia? No. You know, fears of heights." Acrophobia? "Ya, that's it. Acrophobia. So Nick really let us down—they all let us down—the Warner guys were pissing all over us."

Ross took charge, and Nicholas rebelled, disagreeing openly on how Time Warner should go about paring its huge debt. He criticized Ross's imperious style of management. He contradicted Ross's views in public. For his part, Ross found Nicholas's amateur meddlings insufferable, and before long the two men were barely communicating. Once again, Jerry Levin stepped in to fill the vacuum.

Ross was sixty-four, and in Nicholas's mind it was only a matter of time before he, Nick Nicholas, would be in charge of Time Warner. For many years, Ross had smoked at least two packs of cigarettes a day. He ate steak and eggs for breakfast. He'd had a heart attack in the early 1980s. A few years later, in 1985, he'd been diagnosed with prostate cancer, which, after radiation and surgery, had gone into remission. By 1991, his cancer had recurred. In a brief two-sentence press release, Ross claimed that his doctors were optimistic about his recovery; he also claimed his work was not affected by his minor illness. But Nicholas and Levin knew he was dying. "Ross was propped up in a deathbed and had lawyers and doctors with him who basically lied, you know, telling us he was fine," Nicholas recalled. "But I knew he was a dead man even before the merger."

It's like a scene out of Shakespeare. Focusing on Ross's crown, Nicholas, the heir apparent, assumed that Levin was his ally. But Levin was ambitious. To Ross, whose cancer was spreading rapidly, Levin hinted at dark and dire things to come: once Nicholas was in charge at Time Warner, everything would fall apart. Levin approached Ross's wife, Courtney, reassuring her that he, Levin, would make sure that Time Warner remained true to Ross's memory and noble legacy. During the Christmas holidays of 1991, alone in the woods behind his house in Vermont, Levin made up his mind to stage a coup. By February 1992, Levin had Ross's approval: Nick Nicholas would be fired as co-CEO, and Levin would take his place.

Before the final stroke could be delivered to Nicholas, a final matter had to be settled: Levin needed the approval of Dick Munro. Of the twenty-three directors on the Time Warner board, twelve were loyal to Steve Ross; in the vote to fire Nicholas, they would side with Levin. However, to ensure the support of the remaining directors (those from the Time Inc. side of the company), Levin needed Munro's backing. In mid-February 1992, with Nicholas and his family safely on vacation in Vail, Levin visited Munro at his home in Connecticut. "It was like Jacob going to his father, Isaac, to get his blessing," Levin explained to me. (If we're on the same page of scripture, Jacob deceives his blind father, Isaac, in order to get his blessing, thereby supplanting his older brother, Esau.) "I'm not characterizing myself as a messiah," Levin added quickly, "but I knew what this company should be, and I had to see it through."

Years later, Munro would recall that meeting with anger and regret. "About half way through his dissertation, it dawned on me that Levin wasn't there to seek my approval. I remember being stunned. It was done. It was over. He wasn't looking for my approval; it was just a courtesy call," Munro remembered. "I've often reflected on what I should have done or could have done. There are times in your life where you wished you had behaved differently and that was one of those times: I have always felt deep down in my soul I should have done something to save Nick. But it was too late; it was over."

On Wednesday, February 19, blithely skiing in Vail, Nicholas received a phone call from a director, informing him that his twenty-eight-year career at Time Warner was over. Not for a minute had Nicholas seen it coming. Ten years later, he was still astounded by how smoothly, how effortlessly, Levin had manipulated him. He recalled: "A week before it happened, Levin came into my office and said, 'You know, Nick, I'm completely comfortable with this relationship.' He just came into my office and said that! It was apropos of nothing."

Levin did not dispute Nicholas's account of things, nor did he defend his actions. "It is absolutely true that I plotted the departure of Nick Nicholas after working with him for twenty years," conceded Levin. "And I don't have justifications for it other than I'm a strange person." He did imply, however, that like Meursault in Camus's *The Stranger* or Frederic Henry in Hemingway's *A Farewell to Arms,* he was driven by something larger than bourgeois codes of human behavior. "When your existence is up for grabs, you don't know how you are going to react," he mused. "It's like a Hemingway thing—you know, you're an individual survivor."

Gaining control of Time Warner's board was the next item on Levin's agenda. While Steve Ross lay dying of prostate cancer, Levin forced the resignation of nine board members, many of whom were Ross loyalists. Plans to pare down the unwieldy Time Warner board had been in the works for some time—even Ross apparently agreed that the board was too large. But when the press release announcing the makeup of the new board was issued on December 20, 1992, the very day Ross died, many people were shocked by the coincidence, and some of those people accused Levin of bad faith. Ross's widow, Courtney, had to be pressured to invite Levin to her husband's funeral. "It was the timing of when [Levin] made his move and how he did it," explained someone who was close to Ross. "Levin woos you and then he kills you—he's like a black widow spider."

THREE

Munro had retired. Nicholas had been pushed out. Ross was dead. And Jerry Levin, age fifty-three, had maneuvered himself into the exalted role of chairman, CEO, and president of the world's biggest media and entertainment company. Now in control of Time Warner's destiny, the individual survivor wandered the corridors of the vast twenty-ninth floor of 75 Rockefeller Plaza. Most of the offices were deserted. "With Steve Ross's passing, I have lost a friend, a colleague, and a co-worker," Levin said plaintively in one of his first public statements after Ross's death. "I want Time Warner's success to be part of Steve Ross's legacy."

Who was this new CEO? Levin rarely spoke to the press. His executives and directors were kept at a distance. He had few friends. He didn't confide in his family. According to Levin's eldest child, Laura, the daughter of his first wife: "Maybe it's shyness, or a reticence to expose himself to people, but he's private in his public persona and to his children, too. If something's bugging my mom, you know it. But with my dad—you don't know what he's thinking."

One thing is certain: Levin was no Steve Ross. Invariably, articles written about the merger of Time and Warner described Ross as "charismatic," "dynamic," and "entrepreneurial." Ross was a Colossus bestriding the narrow world. Levin, on the other hand, was "colorless," "laconic," and "stooped and graying." Without an ounce of compassion, *Vanity Fair* focused on Levin's weak chin. For a 1995 cover story, *Forbes* commissioned a caricature of a diminutive Levin who, awkwardly and impossibly, is trying to follow a track of giant footsteps—presumably left by Steve Ross.

It didn't help that Time Warner was in free fall. The sprawling, incoherent empire was losing more money than it made. Its stock price was going nowhere. Rumors of takeover attempts began to circulate; in 1993, it was revealed that the president of Seagram Co., Edgar Bronfman Jr., was amassing a large position in Time Warner. As for the company's overwhelming debt, under Levin it kept growing until, by the mid-1990s, it had reached an obscene $15 billion. According to one estimate, the interest alone on that debt was costing the company $90,000 an hour.

Meanwhile, Time Warner's division heads were squabbling, tearing the company into bits. Steve Ross had known instinctively how to control the giant egos of his men; under Levin, however, much of their time was spent in petty power struggles. In the course of planning for the merger, it had seem obvious that Time Inc.'s HBO division and Warner's movie studio would work together. But now each side refused to give up any control to the other. At Time Inc., HBO's Michael Fuchs had been the company's undisputed star. Under Fuchs, HBO had become known for producing some of the highest-quality programming on television. It was also fantastically profitable. Fuchs, confident, even arrogant, saw the merger with Warner as his opportunity to move into feature films. But the men who ran Warner's studios, Robert Daly and Terry Semel, wouldn't give him an inch. Day in, day out, while Levin tried to stabilize Time Warner, Fuchs battled with Daly and Semel. One observer likened the situation to medieval England, "where the barons really have all the power, the king is almost titular, and the subjects—i.e., the shareholders—don't even come into the equation."

Before long, enraged shareholders were demanding that Levin

be replaced by someone competent and sensible. Levin's position at Time Warner was so precarious that the *New York Post* started to print a daily "Jerry-o-Meter" that gauged his good chances of being fired.

Frustrated at the lack of respect accorded him, Levin, the prophet without honor, embarked on an act of historical revisionism. To distance himself from the "charismatic" and "dynamic" and "entrepreneurial" Steve Ross, Levin had Ross's name dropped from official accounts of the company's history. He removed Ross's portrait from Time Warner's executive suites. Now, according to Levin, "the founders of Time Warner," and thus Levin's forebears, were Henry Luce and Jack Warner. In 1995, openly contemptuous of Ross, his benefactor, Levin told a reporter: "Steve was smart enough to put some of the best assets together, but he wasn't a creator like Luce."

Levin presented himself as a creator, a visionary, an original thinker. The media could say what it liked: "I thought that it was all perception, and most of that wasn't me anyhow," he explained. "I was able to hold on to my inner self. I could withstand a lot." On his office wall, he hung a framed quotation from George Orwell's novel of 1949, *Nineteen Eighty-four:* "The voice came from an oblong metal plaque like a dulled mirror which formed part of the surface of the right-hand wall. . . . The instrument (the telescreen, it was called) could be dimmed, but there was no way of shutting it off completely."

Ignoring his critics, Levin, under siege and desperately seeking his next triumph, divined a new strategy for Time Warner. The company would no longer simply produce content; it would also take the lead in distributing that content. Just as he had foreseen the importance of satellite, he now understood the potential of cable wires to transform his company. By squeezing data and information and compressing them digitally, cable wires could carry more than just a few movies and sitcoms at a time; they could carry loads and loads of content all at once. What's more, with a little tweaking, cable wires could both send and receive data. Levin wasn't thinking of the Internet (it was too early for that); instead, in 1994, looking far into the future, he believed that Time Warner customers would one day use their television sets to order pizzas, play interactive games, buy groceries, pay bills, and request movies on demand. If all went well, they would even use their Time Warner cable connection to make telephone calls.

"Someday, 15 percent of New Yorkers will be paying their phone bills to Time Warner," Levin predicted. "And on their cable bills could be charges for movies, electronic games, and news on demand, just to name a few of the services Time Warner plans to offer." Everything was coming together; televisions, telephones, and computers were converging; it was the dawn of the information highway, and Levin intended to build and own the roadways and tollbooths.

Interactivity, convergence, the information highway—they weren't invented by Levin, of course. If anyone could be said to have popularized the concept of using cable to deliver a digital interactive future, it was John Malone, whose Tele-Communications Inc. was the nation's biggest and most powerful cable operator. At a cable conference in December 1992, Malone had announced that before too long, American television viewers would have at their disposal five hundred channels. He'd pulled the number out of a hat, pretty much, by figuring that digital compression would allow a cable wire to carry ten times the fifty or so channels that existed at the time. Malone's hazy concept of an interactive five-hundred-channel digital future was so marvelous that it electrified the nation.

■ ■ ■

ON WEDNESDAY, DECEMBER 14, 1994, FROM THE STAGE OF A hotel ballroom in Orlando, Florida, Levin introduced what was meant to be his greatest accomplishment since putting HBO on satellite. It was called the Full Service Network (FSN), and he had promised to spend between $3 billion and $5 billion of Time Warner's money getting it up and running. "I've staked my career on it," he told *The Wall Street Journal.*

Before an audience of nearly five hundred, holding a remote control in his right hand, Levin demonstrated the wonders of his Full Service Network. He pressed the ON button and moved through a series of commands until his requested movie, *The Specialist,* starring Sylvester Stallone and Sharon Stone, appeared on the giant screen. Fast-forwarding, he paused at his favorite scene: Sharon Stone placing flowers on the grave of her murdered parents. With Sharon and her flowers on hold, Levin called up a second movie, John Grisham's *The Client,* and pressed the pause button again. Then came the denouement. Still navigating the remote control, Levin clicked over to FSN's expansive "shopping mall"; there, on a TV screen in a ballroom in Orlando, Florida, he bought postage stamps and a $10 Bugs Bunny baseball cap.

The magic show wasn't over. Levin's final dramatic act took place in the interactive gaming area, where he played a round of virtual gin rummy with Karl and Susan Willard and their children, Jaclyn and Brad, an Orlando family who lived just down the street. As the game ended and Sharon Stone and her flowers came back on the screen, the whole room burst into applause. Levin smiled broadly, satisfied. "The debut of the Full Service Network is a turning point for the communications industry," he proclaimed. Before long, the audience was told, fourteen million Americans would be connected to FSN.

Three years later, in 1997, Time Warner quietly abandoned the Full Service Network. It was not a triumph after all. From the beginning it had been an unwieldy, ill-conceived project with almost no customer demand. The cost alone of each cable TV set-top box needed to bring the Full Service Network into a home was somewhere in the range of $5,000 and $15,000, depending on your source. The technology behind the project was mind-boggling. "FSN required more lines of computer code than was needed to put men on the moon," said Joseph Collins, head of Time Warner's cable division. Despite all that code, the system couldn't handle more than 20,000 users at once. As for the Willard family and their game of gin rummy with Jerry Levin, Karl Willard had only this to say: "I was one card away from beating him."

■ ■ ■

IN BUSINESS, AS IN MOST THINGS, TIMING IS THE KEY. AND WITH the exception of putting HBO on satellite in 1975, Jerry Levin never really managed to get his timing right, not once. Eventually, after his career at Time Warner was over, cable would become central to the digital interactive future. In the meantime, though, with his eyes fixed on the mountaintop, Levin failed to grasp the importance of this thing called the Internet.

In January 1993, nearly two years before Levin launched the Full Service Network, Marc Andreessen, a twenty-one-year-old student at the University of Illinois at Urbana-Champaign, introduced a computer program called Mosaic. Soon to be renamed Netscape, Mosaic would come to be known as a Web browser. It would change the world.

Until Marc Andreessen arrived on the scene, the Internet was a mysterious little underworld, frequented first by academics and military researchers, then by fringe groups and even radicals. As *Time* magazine ominously explained in 1993 in one of its very first articles on the subject, the Internet is "an anarchistic electronic freeway that has spread uncontrollably and now circles the globe." It attracted hackers and cyberpunks, the sorts of people who, as *Time* noted, took ecstasy and went to raves; it was a place with electronic bulletin boards labeled alt.sex.masturbation and alt.sex.fetish.feet. It was edgy and dangerous. It was weird.

Whatever the Internet represented in the early 1990s, it was still a cultural phenomenon, not a business. There were commercial computer networks, of course—companies like America Online (AOL), Prodigy, CompuServe, and GEnie that had started in the mid-1980s.

But those companies weren't really the Internet; they were more like gated communities, whose members used computers and a device called a modem to connect to one another. Besides, companies like AOL were modest businesses, and they appealed to a tiny subset of Americans.

Out of hand, Jerry Levin dismissed computer networks such as Prodigy and America Online with their primitive chat rooms. Compared to a big media and entertainment company like Time Warner, they really had nothing much to offer. For example, they couldn't offer movies on demand or phone service, as Time Warner hoped to. "It's a little like holding the Indy 500 on a two-lane plank road," Levin remarked when asked about computer networks. His vision of interactivity was far grander. Whereas the Internet transmitted simple data along twisted-pair copper phone lines, Time Warner's Full Service Network used powerful fiber-optic cable wires capable of transmitting movies and music at superhigh speeds. Imagine the difference between a garden hose and a fire hose. Besides, while practically every home in America had cable, the Internet's potential was limited. Everyone knew it was impossibly difficult to navigate. Intrepid souls who did venture onto the Internet not only needed a computer and a modem; they also had to understand and operate something called Unix and be able to use a set of communication protocols known as TCP/IP.

Not that Time Warner was ignoring the Internet entirely. As early as 1993, *Time* magazine had agreed to allow some of its articles to be carried by America Online. And in late 1994, about the same time Levin launched the Full Service Network, Time Warner started a Web site called Pathfinder that compiled articles from the company's various magazines. But the Internet was clumsy and it was slow; Levin wasn't impressed. Cable was the future; he was absolutely convinced of that. It was the key to his vision of an interactive future. Year after year in the early and mid-1990s, he spent billions of dollars amassing cable networks across America. By 1995, Time Warner had

11.5 million cable subscribers, almost as many as John Malone's Tele-Communications Inc.

Despite those numbers, most of Wall Street despised cable. In the view of investors and analysts, Time Warner's "software" assets (film, music, and publishing) were far more valuable than cable. Cable was a lumbering, capital-intensive business with dimming prospects and meddlesome government regulators who kept imposing lower rates on companies. Even if you did believe in the future of some sort of interactive digital five-hundred-channel universe, Time Warner was in no position to keep throwing away money. Already the company had $15 billion of debt divided among a dizzying array of financial instruments. There were nineteen different tranches, or classes, of Time Warner debt, including zero coupons, convertibles, and floaters. There were ten series of preferred shares. So complex was its debt structure that Time Warner's 10k, the annual financial statement required by the SEC, was a daunting nine hundred pages long.

By 1995, everyone was begging Levin to stop pushing cable. Wall Street was frustrated by Levin's single-mindedness, as were his senior executives and board of directors. His division heads, especially those who'd come from the Warner side of the business, men like Daly and Semel, viewed Levin as stubborn and inept and unrealistic. Time Warner's new president, Richard "Dick" Parsons, pleaded with Levin to give up on cable. But Levin, digging in his heels, refused to back down. "I don't suffer fools wisely," he said, recalling how he'd dismissed his critics in the mid-1990s. "I said, 'Dick, we're going ahead, because they're wrong. If I get pushed out, that's okay. I know I'm right on this.' "

Meanwhile, Marc Andreessen's Netscape browser was transforming the Internet. It added color and graphics to what had formerly been a bleak, all-text universe; it made the Internet easy to navigate; it made it luddite-proof. At the same time, adding to the Internet's advantage, the price of computers dropped by half, and high-speed modems were being given away. The Internet may have been a two-lane plank road, but it was accessible to almost anyone, and everything it had to offer was free.

Overnight, depending on your point of view, Levin's cutting-edge cable and his Full Service Network were old-fashioned; or they were so futuristic, so ahead of their time, that they were wildly impractical. Even if everything worked out as planned, how could Time Warner possibly charge enough to recover its massive investment? Compared to the Internet, cable was a losing proposition. Compared to companies like America Online and Yahoo!, Time Warner was a single-lane plank road.

That the Internet was the key to the future became clear on August 9, 1995, the day of Netscape Communications's initial public offering (IPO). Netscape had no profit, it had been in business for only sixteen months, and for the most part, it gave away its browser gratis. For all that, on its first day as a public company, Netscape's stock, priced at $28, soared as high as $74.75. So frenzied was the demand for Netscape stock that on that one day alone, each of the five million shares traded hands almost three times. In total, fourteen million Netscape shares were bought and sold on August 9. By the end of the day, with the stock having settled down at $58.25, Netscape was valued at $2.2 billion, about as much as General Dynamics Corp., the giant defense contractor founded in 1952. No one had ever seen anything like Netscape's IPO. It was transformative.

That same day, Time Warner's uninspired stock closed at $43. In the past two years, it had dropped 8 percent. In the five years since the merger of Time Inc. and Warner Communications, Time Warner's stock had grown by a compounded average rate of 7.8 percent a year, whereas Standard & Poor's S&P 500 index had grown at an annual rate of 12.2 percent. Jerry Levin's performance as CEO of the world's largest media and entertainment company had been nothing short of dismal.

■ ■ ■

TIME WARNER WAS GOING NOWHERE. IN FACT, HAVING FALLEN
behind its competitors, it was no longer the world's biggest media and
entertainment company. That distinction now belonged to the Walt
Disney Corp., which in August 1995 offered $19 billion to buy Capital
Cities/ABC. There was no avoiding the problem; Levin had to clean
up Time Warner's balance sheet. For months now he'd been trying to
sell Time Warner's 21.9 percent stake in Turner Broadcasting System.
It wasn't glamorous work, selling off assets and paying down debt,
but what other choice did Levin have?

Then suddenly, unexpectedly, Levin had an ingenious idea: Instead of selling his stake in Turner, he'd *buy* Turner. The idea for this
latest "transforming transaction" came to Levin out of nowhere. He
hadn't conferred with any of his executives or discussed the idea with
investment bankers. "Jerry went off to the mountaintop, so to speak,
and came back with this thought on his own," is how Dick Parsons
explained it.

On September 22, one month after the Disney–Cap Cities/ABC
deal was announced, Jerry Levin made an announcement: He intended to pay $7.5 billion in newly issued Time Warner stock for the
78.1 percent of Turner his company didn't already own. The deal
with Turner was an obvious way to buy growth and assert Time
Warner's position as the most powerful media and entertainment
company in the world. In the days of Henry Luce, Time Inc., like
most other companies, had grown "organically" by plowing its profits
into new ventures. That kind of strategy requires time and long-
range planning; it's much easier simply to pay for size and scale. Time
Inc. had saved itself from near irrelevance by spending $14.9 billion
on Warner Communications; now Jerry Levin would save himself by
buying Turner Broadcasting System.

Like all big deals, this one would distract his critics, for a few
moments. Besides, once he'd pulled off a deal of this magnitude,

everyone would know that Levin was in charge at Time Warner. It would become his company. No one would associate it with Steve Ross or Nick Nicholas or even Henry Luce. "I finally want to make as clear a break as possible into the future," Levin explained, planning to start a new life without baggage and nostalgia. "It will never be the old Warner Communications or the old Time Inc. again. It is going to be something totally different, as it must be."

Ted Turner was no fan of Levin's. His deal with Time Warner represented a marriage of convenience and resignation. Turner had always dreamed of owning one of the big three televisions networks, but by the time Levin suggested they merge their companies, it had become clear to Turner that owning those networks was out of the question. First Disney had bought Cap Cities/ABC. Then Westinghouse had announced it would buy CBS. Confronted by these huge media consolidations, Turner worried that his company was too small to compete. Moreover, like Levin, he was trapped by a mountain of debt and an immovable stock price. "I'm tired of being little all the time," Turner said at the press conference announcing his deal with Time Warner. "I'm nearing the end of my career and I want to see what it's like to be big for a while."

Turner was fifty-seven. Not for a minute did anyone believe that he was nearing the end of his career. He was starting over. For one thing, Turner would be Time Warner's largest individual shareholder, with about 10 percent of the shares outstanding. For another, Turner seemed to think that in Levin he'd found a partner he could dominate. "I'm used to being in charge," Turner told a reporter. "I've been in charge for 33 years. Jerry's only been in charge for three or four."

■ ■ ■

ROBERT EDWARD TURNER III HAD PRESENCE. NEXT TO HIM, Levin appeared smaller and more colorless than usual. Turner, who at the time was married to Jane Fonda, really *was* a visionary and empire builder. Born in Cincinnati on November 19, 1938, and raised in Savannah, Georgia, Turner had inherited his father's outdoor advertising business at the age of twenty-four; he proceeded to turn it into a media empire. His Turner Broadcasting System owned Cable News Network (CNN); the New Line Cinema and Castle Rock Entertainment movie studios; the MGM film library; Hanna-Barbera Cartoons; and cable channels like TNT (Turner Network Television), Turner Classic Movies, and the Cartoon Network. Turner also owned various sports teams, including the Atlanta Braves and the Atlanta Hawks.

Turner wasn't just a successful businessman; he was an original, a maverick with an outsize personality. Tales of his excesses were legendary. In 1977, after winning the America's Cup as skipper of his boat *Courageous,* Turner was so drunk that he could barely stand up to collect his trophy. "Show me your tits!" he shouted to a group of women standing nearby. On another occasion, in 1983, during an interview, Turner smashed the reporter's tape recorder; he then grabbed his bag, threw it to the floor, stomped on it, and finally, swearing and shouting, hurled it at the reporter's head. "Captain Outrageous" was one of Turner's nicknames. He'd also been called a crackpot.

Turner liked to think of himself as an underdog. Even after he'd become a billionaire many times over, he'd continue to rail against the big established networks and their "unfair" advantages. He was a romantic who idolized Rhett Butler; having seen *Gone With the Wind* dozens of times, Turner named one of his sons Rhett, wore a pencil-thin mustache styled after Clark Gable's, and hung a life-size portrait of Scarlett O'Hara in his living room. "I like the romance of the Confederacy, you know, going down against overwhelming odds," he told *Playboy* magazine in 1978. "I liked Rhett Butler in *Gone With the Wind,* because he was trying to help a lost cause. . . . I was reading about war all the time as a kid. Fighting and soldiers and all that stuff. What I wanted to be was Horatio, Admiral Nelson, Napoleon, Alexander the Great and Pericles; they were the greatest warriors."

For all of Turner's contradictions, he was an America hero. Long before the nation worshipped CEOs, he was a celebrity. In part, this was because Turner spoke the confessional language of self-help paperbacks. Openly, he discussed his battle with depression, his reliance on lithium, and his complex relationship with his father. In 1963, when Ted was twenty-four, his father, Ed Turner, put a .38-caliber pistol in his mouth and shot himself through the head. Ed had been a tyrant, a heavy drinker, a manic-depressive, and a control freak, who believed that all successful people are ambitious and insecure. When Ted was a child, his father beat him with wire coat hangers. When he decided to major in classics at Brown University, his father, who wanted his son to study something practical, wrote: "I am appalled, even horrified, that you have adopted Classics as a Major. As a matter of fact, I almost puked on the way home today. . . . I think you are rapidly becoming a jackass, and the sooner you get out of that filthy atmosphere, the better it will suit me." As it happened, Ted Turner was kicked out of Brown in his junior year for sneaking a girl into his dorm room.

In 1964, after his father died, Ted took over his billboard advertising company. A few years later, he decided to move the company in a new direction: first he bought a radio station in Chattanooga; then, quickly, he added two more, in Jacksonville and in Charleston. In 1970, Turner got into television, using the profits from billboard advertisements to buy a struggling TV channel in Atlanta.

Before long, Turner dreamed about owning a big national network. Since he couldn't possibly afford to buy CBS, NBC, or ABC, he looked for some way his little Channel 17 could compete with the major networks. It was then, in 1975, that Turner first crossed paths with Jerry Levin, Time Inc.'s resident genius, who had just launched HBO on satellite. By airing "The Thrilla in Manila" on HBO, Levin had made the big three networks seem outdated. Recognizing his opportunity, Turner flew to New York to be briefed by Levin on satellite transmissions; in 1976, Atlanta's Channel 17 became the second cable channel to be carried across the nation by satellite.

With no money to spend on original programming, Turner did what he could to fill airtime. He showed old movies, cartoons, and reruns discarded by the networks. He secured the rights to such unglamorous sporting events as professional wrestling; and instead of competing with news organizations, he hired someone to read Associated Press wire copy on air. To fill even more airtime, he bought local sports teams along with the rights to air their games. By the early 1980s, the newly named TBS Superstation (TBS for Turner Broadcasting System) was reaching twenty million homes.

Turner's greatest success was the Cable News Network. CNN, the world's first all-news network, was launched on June 1, 1980. It was a laughable exercise at first, widely derided as the "Chicken Noodle Network" and with no ratings to speak of. In its early years, CNN lost tens of millions of dollars. What was Turner thinking? Everyone knew there was no money to be made from news. The big three networks were rolling back their news operations, closing overseas bureaus, and devoting ever less time to "hard" news.

If Turner had conducted focus groups before launching CNN, he would have known not to start an all-news channel. But he did not conduct focus groups, nor did he care what people thought; he depended on gut instinct. And the unexpected happened: the more news CNN gave Americans, the more they wanted. With all those hours of airtime to fill, CNN could cover every angle of a news story. Politicians, even minor ones, quickly discovered that they could have their say on CNN. Then came the Gulf War of 1991. When the Bush administration urged reporters to leave Baghdad, the broadcast networks complied; CNN, however, stayed put. "I will take on myself the responsibility for anybody who is killed," Turner said defiantly, in his best Rhett Butler mode.

For ten days, as bombs fell on Iraq, CNN's Peter Arnett had Baghdad to himself. Using a suitcase-size satellite phone, broadcasting with the screams of air-raid sirens behind him, Arnett provided continuous live coverage of Operation Desert Storm. Like *Time* magazine in the 1950s and 1960s, CNN was now one of the most important news outlets in the nation. George Herbert Walker Bush, Mikhail Gorbachev, and Saddam Hussein depended on CNN for their information. "I learn more from CNN than I do from the CIA," the first President Bush confided.

Ted Turner was named *Time*'s Man of the Year for 1991. That was the year he married Jane Fonda; the couple held hands on *Larry King Live*. With Fonda at his side, Turner settled down, becoming less erratic and less compulsive. Like it or not, he was by that time part of the establishment. Only one thing was missing: a broadcast network. In the mid-1980s, Turner had made a failed hostile bid for CBS. In the early 1990s, he looked at buying ABC and entered negotiations for NBC. But each time he wanted to buy a network, he was foiled by the consortium of cable companies that effectively controlled his company.

Back in 1985, using junk bonds for financing, Turner had borrowed $1.4 billion to buy the MGM film studio from Kirk Kerkorian. Financially, the purchase was a disaster for Turner: soon overwhelmed by the debt he'd taken on, he was forced to sell most of MGM's assets back to Kerkorian for less than he paid. Though Turner kept MGM's film library and used it to start Turner Classic Movies, the deal had nonetheless trapped him. He needed a bailout, and to his rescue came a group of cable operators, most prominently Time Warner. In return for $560 million, Turner's new partners were granted 37 percent of his company, seven of his fifteen board seats, and veto power over any expenditure above $2 million.

It wasn't long before Time Warner became Turner's greatest stumbling block. Almost every purchase Turner wanted to make was vetoed by Jerry Levin. In September 1994, during a rambling speech to the National Press Club, Turner turned abruptly to the subject of clitoridectomies. "Between 50 and 80 percent of Egyptian girls have their clits cut off. I mean, how about that? You talk about a barbaric mutilation—well, I'm in an angry mood, I'm angry at that too. *I'm*

being clitorized by Time Warner." As the audience laughed in disbelief, Turner continued, "That's exactly right—and I don't like it any
more than they do."

One year later, however, Turner had softened on Time Warner.
Thinking practically, he recognized that owning 10 percent of Time
Warner was, after all, better than owning 30 percent of a company he
no longer really controlled. Given Jerry Levin's abysmal performance
as CEO, there was little doubt in Turner's mind that he, Turner,
would wind up at the helm.

Like others before him, Turner had underestimated Levin; he
hadn't recognized his ruthlessness and cunning—his Janus face.
Years later, after he was betrayed by Levin, Turner would say simply:
"The biggest mistake I made was trusting Jerry too much."

■ ■ ■

JERRY LEVIN WAS TOUGH AND WILY. PERHAPS THE MOST REMARK-
able feat of his long career at Time Warner was his ability to beat the
odds of being fired. People kept betting that he'd be ousted, and year
after year he proved them wrong. Michael Fuchs, who worked closely
with Levin for eighteen years at Time Inc., then at Time Warner,
compared Levin's genius for self-preservation to that of a boxer:
"There were fighters—there used to be more in the old days—who
fought you in a way that you could never hit them. They had such
body movement that if you did get a glove on them, it would glance
off. They were either keeping you off balance or able to slip everything that you threw at them."

By the late-1990s, deflecting criticism or tuning out, Levin grew
increasingly isolated. He lost what had once been a quick sense of
humor. Never gregarious, he became almost a recluse. Levin's passion, his only passion, was his job. He was known for mastering every
aspect of the company in what can only be described as obsessive detail. He read all the trade magazines and industry newsletters, care-

fully circling articles of note. He analyzed the latest box office returns, tracked each new analyst's report, and drafted one memo after another. His weekends were devoted to reading the company's magazines cover to cover, watching advance release versions of Warner Bros. movies, and listening to Warner's latest musical releases. "He's compulsive about absorbing, learning, sucking in new information," a Time Warner executive explained, awed. His single-minded devotion and dedication to the company was remarkable. "Jerry is one of the hardest-working people you've ever encountered," Dick Parsons, who became president of Time Warner in 1996, would later tell me. "I don't know how he does it, I really don't. He consumes all of the product in this company . . . He's *always* working this account. He doesn't sleep much—you know, the guy sleeps four hours a night—so he's on the case twenty hours a day."

All this mastering of detail seemed to be a crucial part of Levin's management strategy. "On the way up [the corporate ladder], he said, all the time, that the man who controls the information controls the company," recalled Fuchs. "When he got to the top he still hoarded the information. I said to him, 'Jerry, you have the power already and you own all the information.' All of this reading and note taking and sending notes and seeing everything . . ." Fuchs's voice trailed off.

Having learned the ropes from personal experience, Levin recognized, perhaps unconsciously, that there were two ways to maintain power: to control the information and to surround himself with impotent executives—executives who didn't covet his crown. If there was no one to replace him, how could he ever be replaced? One by one, often with stealth, he managed to eliminate people who posed a threat to his control, replacing them with yes-men and puppets. Or he'd give his executives so few responsibilities, they were never able to prove themselves.

In late 1995, it was Fuchs's turn. All of a sudden, the man who was widely viewed as Levin's heir apparent was fired. By then Fuchs was running both HBO and Warner Music Group. He was perhaps the most powerful executive at Time Warner, and more and more, he let it be known that he, Michael Fuchs, would make a better CEO than Jerry Levin. If Fuchs was right, it might explain why Levin was so keen to get rid of him. But there was this, too: Fuch's battles with Semel and Daly, his rivals at the Warner Bros. studio, threatened to destroy Time Warner and, with it, Levin himself. Nonetheless, for Levin to dump his closest associate, someone he'd worked with since 1976, was brutal.

"After all these years, I'm objective. You know, Jerry had the right to fire me—all is fair in love and war—he was CEO," Fuchs said. "It's the way he did it I can't forgive. Jerry deceives you and then turns on you. . . . You feel dirty when you get through with him because you've really been fucked over. And you feel stupid. But he's able to do it over and over. It's a talent."

Executives who'd been pushed out or toppled or displaced by Levin over the years described him as "cunning," "disingenuous," and "Machiavellian." Still, it wasn't easy to reconcile those views of Levin with his apparent modesty, his piety, and his pure dedication to the company. Levin wasn't like other moguls you read about. Articulate and obviously intelligent, Levin spoke in complete paragraphs. He quoted the Bible, grappled with deep philosophical questions, and seemed to be carrying the burden of humanity on his narrow shoulders. He wasn't motivated by money and things. He bought his suits off the rack, wore cheap shoes, and clipped coupons from the Sunday papers. Knowing that his wife tended to be extravagant, he didn't trust her to do the shopping; instead, every weekend, coupons in hand, he went to the supermarket to buy the family's groceries.

Nor did power appear to motivate Levin. When he was enraptured by an idea, any idea, his convictions were so absolute that more than once he gambled his job on the direction the company would take. Questioned by his executives or directors, he claimed to be guided by moral convictions and by destiny. "Jerry can be extraordinarily daring and willful: he's brave and fearless to the point of recklessness," explained Peter Haje, Time Warner's general counsel between 1990 and 1999. "He cares about how he's perceived—but more how he perceives *himself.* He cares about being morally correct and about being a strong decisive leader."

There was something else, something poignant about Levin that made him different from other moguls and Fortune 500 CEOs. In June 1997, Levin's son Jonathan was murdered. Shortly after midnight on June 3, the police arrived at Levin's Manhattan apartment: Jon had been found in his one-bedroom walk-up on the Upper West Side, face up in a pool of dried blood. By then, his body was decomposing. His feet bound with duct tape, his chest riddled with knife wounds, Jon Levin had been killed by a gunshot through the head.

The youngest of Levin's three children from his first marriage, Jon was thirty-one at the time, a teacher at a public high school in an impoverished part of the Bronx. In many ways, he was what his father had once aspired to be, or what his grandmother had hoped his father would be. "Jon is my mother's son," said his older sister, Laura. "He was a remarkably caring, compassionate, funny, and kind human being. That's what my mom is."

For years, Jerry Levin had not been close to Jon or to any of the three children from his first marriage. Then, encouraged by his second wife, Barbara, he'd established a relationship with Jon in the early 1990s. They'd attended prizefights together in Las Vegas and discussed politics. Occasionally, Jon would drop in to visit his father at the office. "He was very close to Jon," Laura attested. "My brother would say things to my dad that no else would, like 'Wake up! Life is short! Work isn't everything!' "

Jonathan's funeral was held at the Park Avenue Synagogue on June 4. Levin was a wreck. Supported by a bodyguard on one side and by his wife, Barbara, on the other, he was led into the synagogue sobbing. His son's death, he said, was "a watershed." In shock, Levin stayed home for three full weeks. For a man who never left the office, someone who needed to control all the information, those three weeks were "a lifetime," in the words of one associate. Briefly, Levin considered quitting his job. But what else could he possibly do? "I lay low," Levin said, recalling the weeks following his son's death, "and then went back to the narcotic."

That narcotic, his job at Time Warner, allowed Levin to focus on the point of a pin and pretend it was the universe; it kept his ego more or less intact. Under the narcotic's influence, Levin was, in his own words, "imperturbable, impenetrable, unemotional." Critics could say what they pleased; in all events, they had a hard time saying anything. After Jonathan's death, Levin became almost untouchable. When a man has lost his son that way, how can someone accuse him of bad will? Of deception? Of treachery? Of duplicity? Some years later, following a talk Levin gave at the Onondaga County Convention Center in upstate New York, a member of the audience would stand up, go to the microphone, and extol Levin as "a combination of Jesus, Buddha, and Gandhi."

■ ■ ■

BY LATE 1997, ONLY SIX MONTHS OR SO AFTER THE TURNER DEAL had closed, Levin had once again managed to redeem himself. The Turner deal was acclaimed as a brilliant strategic acquisition. With Ted Turner himself promising to forge cooperation among the company's operating units, to cut costs, and to shake the place up, Time Warner seemed reborn. For the first time since Levin had been named CEO, Time Warner's cash flow was actually improving.

Levin got lucky: all of a sudden cable was back in favor. In the summer of 1997, Bill Gates, the co-founder and CEO of Microsoft, had invested $1 billion in Comcast Corp., the nation's fourth-largest cable operator. As a headline in *The Economist* put it: CABLE TELEVISION: ENTER GOD, WITH $1 BILLION. Overnight, trying to imitate the great Bill Gates, the sheep on Wall Street flocked to cable. Cable stocks surged.

No one talked about interactive television or a five-hundred-channel universe anymore. Levin's wondrous Full Service Network had been disbanded; it had not, after all, been "a turning point for the communications industry." Never mind. According to Gates, what now defined cable was the Internet; what now defined the Internet was cable. Compared to cable, using phone lines to hook up to the Internet was like communicating with a string and two tin cans. While the fastest computer modems transmitted data along twisted-pair copper phone lines at speeds of 56,000 bits per second, new cable modems could move data, video, and music thirty times more quickly. Cable modems were not yet widespread—of the nation's sixty-four million cable TV subscribers, only an estimated twenty-five thousand had cable modems in 1997. But in the view of Gates and others in Silicon Valley, the future of the Internet depended on cable. And everywhere, everyone was focusing on the Internet.

The enthusiasm that had begun with Netscape's IPO in 1995 was now mania. People were talking about the New Economy: the Internet was transforming the world. Silicon Valley was suddenly the most important place on the planet. Yahoo!, started by two graduate students at Stanford University, had its spectacular initial public offering in 1996: issued at $13, its stock soared as high as $43 before settling at $33 on its first day as a publicly traded company. That first-day gain was bigger even than Netscape's had been. One year later, in May 1997, Amazon.com went public. Despite revealing that it spent $25 on each book sold for $20, Amazon.com soared. It was taken for granted that online retailing, or e-commerce, would be one of the biggest industries of the new century. In the face of Amazon.com, no traditional bricks-and-mortar bookstore would survive. As for Steve Case's America Online, which Levin and others like him had dismissed only a year earlier, its revenues now exceeded $2 billion. In the past twelve months alone, between the fall of 1996 and 1997, its stock price had climbed by nearly 300 percent!

Mary Meeker, one of Wall Street's most influential Internet

stock analysts, explained in a report of September 1997: "The world
has never experienced as rapid/violent a commercial evolution of a
fundamental business change as that being caused by the accep-
tance/usage of the Internet as a communications and commerce tool."
Despite her convoluted prose, the message was clear: A revolution
had begun.

But Time Warner had no Internet strategy. Levin thought we'd
be ordering pizzas and paying bills using the remote control on a TV
set. What Time Warner did have was cable. By 1998, shares of Time
Warner were trading at an all-time high. Levin had taken a huge
gamble—he'd risked his company on cable and on a deal with Turner.
"The same market insiders who once considered him aloof, ineffec-
tive, and unmotivated now routinely describe him as strong, decisive,
and farsighted," marveled *Fortune*. It was almost as good as getting
HBO on satellite.

PART TWO

Enter the
Internet Cowboys

AOL, 1985–1999

FOUR

NO ONE EVER USED WORDS LIKE "COOL" AND "CUTTING EDGE" TO describe America Online and Steve Case, its CEO. From the high perch of Silicon Valley, AOL was commercial and unsophisticated; it was technology for dummies. *Wired* magazine described AOL as the "Carnival Cruise line of interactivity." Others called it the Internet's "training wheels," as though Case and his fellow AOL'ers were pedaling around a kiddie Infobahn. Big deal. By the late 1990s, America Online was the most powerful brand in cyberspace because it had demystified the Internet, making it so innocuous that no one was intimidated by words like "baud" and "megabyte." "The geeks don't like us," Case once remarked. "They want as much technology as possible, while AOL's entire objective is to simplify. . . . We want to be the Coca-Cola of the online world. . . . We don't really care about the technology."

America Online was based in Dulles, Virginia, a tired stretch of land in the middle of nearly nowhere, whose one excuse for being was its proximity to Washington's Dulles International Airport. Located at 22000 AOL Way, AOL's headquarters comprised a series of nondescript office blocks overlooking a version of pastoral: fields, an aging silo, and a Wal-Mart. The focal point of AOL's utilitarian lobby was Steve Case's mission statement, inscribed on a metal plaque: "To build a global medium as essential to people's lives as the telephone or the television . . . and even more valuable."

In contrast with other founders and CEOs of Internet companies, Case was hopelessly square. Tall, with a round face and short brown hair, Case looked like someone who ordered his clothes from an L. L. Bean catalog—the sort of man you'd meet on a Carnival Cruise playing shuffleboard. The media described him as "bland." Even his colleagues and employees found it hard to glamorize their boss. "He spends a lot of time with his kids. He's very devoted to his family," confided a senior AOL executive who'd known Case for many years. "He goes to his daughter's soccer games." Another long-time colleague who considered himself a friend of Case's repeated the soccer motif: "He does make sure he's at his kids' soccer games. He's an extraordinarily strong family person—a devoted family person." A third senior AOL executive, someone who'd worked closely with Case for more than five years, cataloged Case's personal interests, when pressed: "He travels with his wife in the summer. He likes good wine, I know that." There had to be something else. He paused; then, overwhelmed by the almost impossible burden of humanizing Steve Case, he answered: "I don't know. I don't know if he reads, I don't know if he goes to the movies, I don't know if he plays ball, I don't know if he's a sportsman. I don't have any idea. None. None."

Case was aloof. Everyone knew that about him. He didn't make small talk. He was uncomfortable at parties, bewildered, as if he didn't get the point of being there. In photo after photo, he stares out with the same forced and frozen smile. "He doesn't create a warm and fuzzy," to quote yet another AOL executive, who added: "One of the longest six hours of my life was sitting next to him on a plane going across the country."

Despite his lack of warmth, Case was revered by his employees in Dulles; they didn't presume that such an extraordinary man would make small talk and ask about their child's first day at school. One after another, people who worked with Case said he was "really smart." They were awed by the way he handled information: by his uncanny ability to absorb, process, and sort huge, complex amounts of data and, finally, to translate it into a stripped-down concept anyone could grasp. Brainpower alone didn't explain the respect paid to Case at 22000 AOL Way. His tenacity and resolve were just as impressive. Over the years, time and again, his vision of the Infobahn had seemed incredible to outsiders: it was folly; it was the stuff that dreams are made on.

Throughout much of the 1990s, according to the media and Wall Street, AOL was nearly dead. If various Internet service providers didn't finish off AOL, the thinking went, Microsoft would. Nonetheless, Case's belief in the future of AOL was unshakable. "Since the early 1990s, Steve has had this burn in his belly that what he was creating with AOL was not just something you did with your computer—like word processing—it was something huge and something that would one day be as big and pervasive as the telephone or the television," explained Barry Schuler, an AOL executive who worked with Case for more than a decade. "That belief of his burns inside of him like radioactive uranium; it's ever-present, it's the drive that propels him."

Case's goal wasn't to make money; he'd have been happy to run AOL as a nonprofit, people close to him said. It was his version of messianism. "To the people at AOL, AOL is not just a company, it's a religion," Schuler continued. "If AOL is your religion, Steve is your spiritual leader." Case was a visionary, a prophet. "There were a half dozen seminal moments in the history of the company, and Steve always made the right decision," said Jack Davies, who ran AOL's international division for six years. Jack Daggitt, a former executive on AOL's technology team, concurred: "Steve kept making the right decisions: one time, two times—you chalk that up to luck—but when you keep doing it, it moves to the realm of skill."

For Steve Case, AOL was part of something as profound, as meaningful, as the Industrial Revolution.

■ ■ ■

A FIFTH-GENERATION HAWAIIAN WHOSE ANCESTORS HAD AR-
rived from England, Germany, and the mainland United States in the
nineteenth century, Stephen McConnell Case was born in Honolulu
on August 21, 1958. Even though he grew up in the turbulent sixties
and seventies, his childhood reflects the cozy, comforting clichés of the
Ladies' Home Journal as it once was. "Aloha from The Cases" is the
message printed on a Christmas card of 1971, featuring all four Case
children, smiling brightly, along with their two Corgis, Tuffy and
Tabe.

Steve Case's mother, Carol, was an elementary school teacher
who stayed home to raise the children. His father, Daniel Jr., a successful corporate lawyer, represented the island's powerful sugar and
pineapple companies. At the Cases' house, located on a cul-de-sac in
suburban Honolulu, favorite family pastimes included paddle tennis,
croquet, and cribbage. On Sundays, the family attended the Congre-
gationalist Central Union Church, where Steve Case was an usher.
From kindergarten through the twelfth grade, all four Case children,
Carin, Dan III, Steve, and Jeff, attended the private Punahou School.
As though they were living out an American novel, the Case children
had paper routes and limeade stands. While they were still teenagers,
Steve and his older brother, Dan founded a company called Case Enterprises, selling Christmas cards, flower seeds, and wristwatches
door-to-door, depending on the season.

"I believe in love, availability and direction": that's how Carol
Case, Steve's mother, once described her approach to parenting. "We
gave our children chores and jobs, even on vacations. After dinner we
would play cribbage. The loser did the dishes. That's the structure,
but I would try to make myself available when they needed me. I'd be
around the house and have a glass of iced tea with them."

Despite the limeade stands and paper routes and cribbage games
and iced tea, Steve Case was not a typical upper-middle-class subur-

ban boy. He was not a conformist, for one thing. "I was always more conventional," his brother Dan told *GQ* in 1997. "Steve always did things his own way. He defined his own turf rather than play on someone else's." Dan was the prototypical firstborn son: a straight-A student, a Junior Achiever, a Princeton grad, a Phi Beta Kappa, a Rhodes Scholar. At the age of thirty-three, he was named CEO of Hambrecht & Quist, the San Francisco–based venture capital and investment banking firm. Their older sister, Carin, followed her mother's example, becoming a kindergarten teacher. Their youngest brother, Jeff, went into the insurance business, becoming a senior executive at Aon.

As for Steve Case himself, early on he found himself at a start-up company that had a harebrained idea: Make it simple for people to connect to one another through their personal computers. His success was not unexpected. Scott Lankford, who lived with Case for three years at Williams College, put it this way: "He knew he was going to be a businessman from the moment he walked into Williams. He didn't care particularly about grades. He would shoot for Cs, and he knew why he was shooting for Cs. . . . He knew that the game was not, 'Get an A'; the game was, 'Take over the world.' "

If Case was not a dedicated student—and according to three of his roommates and at least one of his professors, he was not ("I would not want to reveal his grades," James MacGregor Burns, professor of political science at Williams and a Pulitzer Prize–winning scholar, said elegantly. "But he was among my median students")—it was because his full-time campus occupation was to start and then promote one business venture after another. "He was a yuppie before the word *yuppie* existed," said Lankford.

We're in the late 1970s. Using his dorm room as an office, and signing up various roommates as business partners, Case launched Williams Fruitbaskets, offering parents a way to send their children healthy, nourishing snacks during exams. He also started a record label, Purple Cow Records, whose only known LP, a Simon &

Garfunkel–inspired compilation entitled *The Best of Williams— Volume I, 1978,* sold for $4 (a special "discount price," Case told the campus newspaper). Case took control of Magic Bus, a student-run shuttle that transported students from Williams to Albany Airport at the end of each semester. From a haphazard operation, Magic Bus turned into an efficient and (barely) profitable one.

Then there were Steve Case's famous themed parties at Williams: for a 1978 *Saturday Night Fever* party, billed as a "multi-media extravaganza," Case and his partner, roommate Bill Beckett, spent $1,125 on rented lights, a disco ball, special effects, champagne punch, and dark and light beer. All of this was too coarse, too commercial, for Williams's undergraduates. For one thing, they complained loudly about the $2 cover charge. Calling the party "plastic," an article in the *Williams Record* accused Case of "laissez-faire capitalism." More, as if to prove that Case was in it for money, not for fellowship and love and community and all that, the article noted that he didn't dance, not a step.

As it happened, Case never did make much money at Williams. He lost $350 on the *Saturday Night Fever* party, for instance. And as co-chairman of the All-College Entertainment Committee, he spent so much of the school's money hiring big-name acts like Don McLean ("American Pie"), Livingston Taylor, and Southside Johnny and the Asbury Jukes that he was accused of "deliberate mismanagement" of funds by the school paper. After one sparsely attended concert, a writer for the *Williams Record* reported: "Sprawled out on a foam cushion between sets, a distraught Steve Case . . . estimated that total losses would probably approach five thousand dollars or more, necessitating the cancellation of Homecoming concert plans." For Case it was only a temporary setback on the thruway to greatness.

After graduating from Williams in 1980 with a degree in political science, Case joined Procter & Gamble as an assistant brand manager. There he helped develop a practical but short-lived product called Abound, a disposable conditioner-soaked towelette for the hair.

It had a memorable slogan: "Towelette? You bet!" He also worked to revive something called Lilt, a home perm kit. Then, restless after two years at P&G, Case joined Pizza Hut as a manager for new development.

It was during his time at Pizza Hut, living by himself in a rental apartment in Wichita, Kansas, that Case was granted his epiphany, his moment of revelation that led to AOL; all of a sudden everything became transparent. Described time and again—in almost every in-depth interview Case ever gave, on his personal Web site, and in his speeches—the story was polished into a myth. It goes like this: Case had bought himself a Kaypro II personal computer and a primitive modem; he then paid $100 to subscribe to the Source, the first computer network service for consumers (as opposed to businesses). It was 1982, a lifetime ago in the history of computing. Case's Kaypro II weighed twenty-six pounds (despite being described as a "portable computer"); it came with a 2.5 MHz processor, 64K of RAM, and a nine-inch green phosphor screen. "When I finally logged in and found myself linked to people all over the country from this sorry little apartment in Wichita, it was just exhilarating," professed Case.

One year after his Emersonian exhilaration, at a 1983 Consumer Electronics Show in Las Vegas, Case's brother Dan introduced him to the man who created the Source, William Von Meister. A consummate inventor and entrepreneur, Von Meister was running Control Video Corporation, whose sole product was something called Game-Line. Using a 1,200-baud modem and an ordinary telephone line, GameLine allowed subscribers to download video games onto their Atari 2600 home game machines. At the time, Atari was huge, it really was. And insiders suspected that Control Video would be huge as well: at the 1983 electronics show, Von Meister and his chief technologist, Marc Seriff, took orders for tens of thousands of Game-Line units. On the spot they also hired Steve Case, age twenty-five, as a marketing consultant. "He had no credentials; he was a pizza-marketing guy," recalled Seriff. But Case was enthusiastic and bright and optimistic—more, his brother Dan, or rather, Dan's firm, Hambrecht & Quist, had invested in Control Video.

Only a few months later, however, the home video game industry collapsed, and Atari seesawed on the edge of bankruptcy. Of the fifty thousand or so GameLine modules made, almost all ended up in a Dumpster behind Control Video's offices in Tysons Corner, Virginia. Determined to salvage their investment in Control Video, the company's backers pushed out Von Meister and installed Jim Kimsey as CEO, despite the fact that Kimsey knew nothing at all about computing. He was a decorated veteran of the Vietnam War whose only business experience was running a string of successful bars in Washington, D.C. But he was an old and trusted and reliable friend of venture capitalist Frank Caulfield, one of Control Video's largest investors; the two men had been at West Point together. With Seriff in charge of technology and Steve Case responsible for marketing, Kimsey started over, using the core idea behind the GameLine modules to launch Quantum Computer Services, which offered an online service for Commodore 64 computers. Called Q-Link, the service, introduced in 1985, was the beginning of what would become America Online.

Case had heard the prophetic call. "More and more, it became sort of religious," said Kimsey, describing those first, early years. "I was driven more by everybody telling me, 'It can't be done.' I've always been motivated by that. But my motivation was a short-term, you know, 'I can save it, I can do it, and the more you tell me I can't, the more I'm convinced that I can.' Steve was driven by a much longer-term vision." Marc Seriff concurred: "This is going to sound so corny, but Steve is one of those destiny kind of guys. He knew what was going to happen. He didn't grandstand, he just went and made it happen."

Most famously, what Case made happen was a deal with Apple Computer, a deal so unfathomable that, in the words of an AOL'er who witnessed it live, it was "like grabbing a gumball from a crocodile's mouth." Rather than compete directly for consumers with the industry's big computer network services (the Source, then owned by Reader's Digest; H&R Block's CompuServe; and General Electric's GEnie), Quantum started out by building proprietary online services for computer manufacturers. Still, common sense dictated that if Apple wanted a proprietary online service, and it did, Apple would do a deal with one of the big players. Quantum was not just unknown; it was a tiny, poorly financed company with a shaky history and, in Commodore, only one customer. Unintimidated by the odds, and establishing a pattern that would become typical for him, Case was going to do a deal with Apple, and nothing would deter him, nothing.

So in late 1986, he packed a suitcase, got on a plane, and moved into a rental apartment just down the road from Apple's headquarters in Cupertino, California. Every day for three months, obsessively, patiently, biding his time, he focused on one thing: wearing down Apple's resistance. After the deal was signed, after the miracle, Case returned to Quantum as a hero. Then, one after another, Case pulled off a string of equally miraculous deals; whereupon his people convinced themselves that Case was superhuman: he could walk on water and change it into wine. "The deals he did—there was no logical reason for them to be done," Seriff noted. "Apple, Tandy, IBM. None of them should have happened. We were a nobody."

Officially, Kimsey was still the company's CEO. But inside the company, it was clear that Case had become the leader. When CompuServe offered $50 million for America Online (as it was now called) in 1991, Kimsey came close to selling out. AOL, with revenues at the time of about $20 million, was still the smallest online service by far. How much further could it go on its own? reasoned Kimsey. But Case insisted they had to remain independent: he wasn't looking just to make a quick buck. "Hell, I was looking for an endgame all the time," recalled Kimsey. "I mean, I was going to sell to CompuServe—

Steve reminds me of this all the time—and for ten more million dollars, I probably would have."

Around that time, Case was named CEO of AOL. He was thirty-three years old. One year later, in 1992, he was forced to give back the CEO title to Kimsey on practical grounds: America Online was getting ready to go public, and in the views of its board of directors, Case was way too young to give the company the credibility it needed for an initial public offering. Kimsey recalled: "So I took him to lunch at Clyde's in Tysons Corner. I remember the Elmer Fudd look on his face. We sat there for two hours and I really had to go through it. I will tell you, I admire him tremendously for how he took it and how he conducted himself. . . . You know, he could have said, 'Screw you, I'm outta here.' He could have been petulant, he could have tried to undermine me. He was a good dude. He took it. I know it killed him. It had to." Wasn't Kimsey worried that Case might quit? "I knew he was too psychically invested to do that," Kimsey confided. Not long after AOL's IPO in March 1992, Case was re-named CEO.

■ ■ ■

In building America Online, Case was inspired by Alvin Toffler's futurist book, *The Third Wave* (1980). In his five-hundred-page polemic, Toffler divided history into three waves, three revolutions: agricultural, in which nomadic hunter-gatherers settled down to create agrarian communities; industrial, the era of mass production when people moved from farms to cities and toiled in factories; and, finally, technological. During the third wave, Toffler predicted, once people were freed from factory life and from the tyranny of Orwellian uniformity, they would be truly liberated. "[The computer] makes possible a flood of new theories, ideas, ideologies, artistic insights, technical advances, economic and political innovations that were, in the most literal sense, unthinkable and unimaginable before now,"

Toffler wrote. "What is happening is not just a technological revolution but the coming of a whole new civilization in the fullest sense of that term."

Convinced by Toffler's vision of the technological future—fueled by the belief that he was building something at AOL that would change the world—Case worked fifteen-hour days, inspiring his employees to do the same. They weren't working simply to pay the rent; they were idealists on a profound and universal mission. "To build a global medium as central to people's lives as the telephone or the television . . . and even more valuable."

Late at night, Case could usually be found online, hanging out in AOL's chat rooms, posting messages on its bulletin boards, and composing sincere, companionable letters to members that he signed "Steve." In a cross-country road trip called "Getting America Online," Case set out to meet his members in person, face-to-face, at AOL rallies held at the local Hard Rock Café and in high school gyms. AOL wasn't an impersonal second wave business, was Case's message; AOL was a brotherhood of passionate, inspired men and women who were discovering their soul mates in cyberspace.

"It was intoxicating," said Randy Dean, a former bartender who joined AOL in 1988. "You had a bunch of people similar in age, similar in life circumstances, and everybody's just rolling up their sleeves, and that was exciting. How many people can say that they go to work and do something that nobody's ever done before? We were saying that every day."

AOL's employees didn't just work together; they ate together, they hung out together, they got drunk together, they even slept together. America Online was their life. For the most part, they were fresh out of college. Any jobs they may have held before joining AOL were mostly unrelated to technology or business. Julia Wilkinson, hired at AOL in 1988, described her previous work experience: "I had worked cleaning houses, cleaning toilets, and cleaning dishes; slinging grub at a bakery, deli, and Tastee-Freez; hawk[ing] wares at a jewelry store, five-and-dime, and two clothing stores; hostessing at two restaurants; delivering papers; filing magnetic tapes for a phone company; and finally, playing glorified comma jockey as a proof-reader."

AOL'ers were a family, and Case was their indulgent father. No cribbage or croquet or limeade stands this time around. Instead, he joined them in paintball games, bought kegs for their Friday after-noon beer bashes, judged their annual Halloween contest, and, with goodwill, endured being laughed at in the *Quantum Quirk,* the company's "underground" satirical newsletter. In a parody of AOL's adolescent culture, the *Quantum Quirk* published this job posting: "Responsibilities include: Wandering around aimlessly, getting drunk on Friday afternoons, juggling fruit in the halls, spraying caus-tic chemicals at co-workers. . . . If you are an unmotivated, team-oriented rabble-rouser, fill out the following application and arrange an immediate interview."

"It was gorgeous": that's how Mark Walsh, who left his job as president of GEnie to join AOL in 1995, recalled those early, inno-cent, fun-filled days. "There are very few times in your business life that you truly believe with a capital B. When it happens, it's like your first love—you never forget it. You never forget the time you really, really frickin' believed."

■ ■ ■

JIM KIMSEY TELLS A STORY ABOUT CASE'S VISIT TO PARIS. THERE for a business meeting with Minitel, an early online service owned by the French government, Case refused to stop in at the Louvre. It was beside the point. "That just tells you everything you need to know about Steve," said Kimsey. "He was so focused on going to the Minitel thing, he didn't even want to stop for two minutes and look at the Louvre."

Yes, Steve Case did have what's called a personal life. In 1985 he married Joanne Barker at a church in her hometown of Rumson, New Jersey. They'd met at Williams, where Barker, then a student at Smith College in Northampton, Massachusetts, had spent a year as an exchange student. She was outgoing, she was attractive, and according to Case's classmates, they made a very fine couple indeed. She became a schoolteacher. They had three children. In retrospect, it is not surprising that Case's marriage to Joanne Barker unraveled somehow, or that his second wife, Jean Villanueva, would be a senior executive at AOL. Day and night, night and day, for Case there was only AOL; it was all-consuming, that company. As Randy Dean, who concedes that he had more than one love affair with a fellow AOL'er, put it: "We didn't have any other social life."

As scandals go, Case's romance with an executive at AOL was minor. Still, the news rattled AOL'ers; it proved to them that their spiritual leader was human after all. Case and Villanueva (who ran AOL's corporate communications) took their love affair public in the spring of 1996. First they told AOL's board of directors and executives; then, trying to control the news and subsequent damage, they leaked the story to *The Washington Post*. In the event that someone misunderstood and got the timing wrong, Case and Villanueva swore that their romance had started *after* their respective marriages had come apart. For a time, Villanueva continued on at AOL as if nothing had changed; by the end of 1996, however, under pressure from AOL'ers and from outside investors, she quit her job, stating publicly that she had to "address pressing family matters." Two years later, in a private ceremony, Billy Graham pronounced Case and Villanueva man and wife.

The furor caused by Case's office romance exposed his fragile ego, his need for approval, and a deep-seated puritanism. As news of the love affair made its way through the media, even appearing in *People* magazine, it became clear that Case cared about his public image. When he heard that *Business Week* intended to mention his relationship with Villaneuva in a cover story about AOL, he exploded;

in retaliation, tit for tat, he withdrew permission for the use of his personal photos. That wasn't an isolated incident: a few years later, just as a major profile of Case written by Mark Leibovich for *The Washington Post* was going to press, Case started to quibble over details. He was rankled, for example, by the suggestion that as boys, playing basketball with the neighbors, he and his brother Dan were known to change the rules of the game if they were losing. Case, alleging that Leibovich hadn't done enough reporting, raised his voice; then he left Leibovich a long defensive voice mail challenging this unflattering detail and that one.

But we're getting ahead of ourselves. It's 1996, and Case is on the cover of *Business Week*. He's been photographed in his khakis by Richard Avedon for a Gap ad ("Do your best. Work in khakis. What's best is always a benchmark"). He's also become fodder for local gossip columnists. Which is only to say that AOL was now on America's radar screen. Since going public in 1992, the company had grown from $38 million in revenues to more than $1 billion. Case had buried the old competition—GEnie, the Source, CompuServe, Prodigy—by promoting AOL as a simple online service for the masses. Clever marketing didn't hurt: every household in the country, it seemed, had received by mail at least one copy of AOL's free software, along with the promise of a free month of service. Wherever you looked, AOL's software disks were there, too: bundled with copies of *Reform Judaism*, hidden in cereal boxes, served with meals on United Airlines, and packaged with mail-order filet mignons from Omaha Steaks. On those easy terms, it was hard to resist the digital future.

Then, suddenly, madly, sometime in the middle of 1996, AOL was spinning out of control. More and more, the cost of providing those millions and millions of free software disks was outpacing the revenue they brought in. At the same time, a frightening number of AOL users were abandoning AOL and its high hourly rates for other, brand-new Internet service providers that offered cheap flat rates and unlimited access. Legal troubles started. In June 1996, New York's attorney general announced that it was investigating AOL's automatic billing practices. Within weeks, fourteen other states and the Federal Trade Commission said they too were examining the company's billing policies. Then came an accounting scandal: AOL was forced to restate its books and in the process wiped out every profit the company had ever shown. As if all this weren't enough, in August 1996, AOL's overwhelmed, overloaded, exhausted, stressed-out networks went down for nineteen hours straight. All over the Internet, like mushrooms in damp, rich soil, homemade Web pages were springing up. Three tell the story: AmericaOnlineSucks.com; AmericaOutta line.com; and WhyAOLsucks.com. Between February and October 1996, AOL's stock price dropped nearly 70 percent.

"The company was in tremendous turmoil. The press was saying we were going to die," recalled Barry Schuler. "People [at AOL] were hurting. They wanted someone to stand up and comfort them." That comforter would not be Steve Case. He may have been a visionary, he may have been a genius, he may have had faith in the power of technology to change the world and create utopia. At the same time, Case was deeply unsentimental. In his single-minded pursuit of the big dream, obstacles were swept aside or bulldozed. "In his mind, it was noise," continued Schuler, describing Case's take on the pain and suffering and despair and trauma at AOL. "He thought that was baby stuff, you know, like, 'Grow up!' "

Ignoring the static by tuning out, Case isolated himself, focusing narrowly on the overwhelming question: Should AOL move to flat-rate pricing? Day in, day out, logically, rationally, systematically, as if he had all the time in the world, Case ran the numbers, compared the options, weighed each possible pricing plan, and took votes on them from his various managers. Meanwhile, as the decision-making process dragged on and on, AOL's ship kept taking on water. Finally Barry Schuler spoke up. Raging, he sent an e-mail to Case that read, "This company needs a CEO! Stop acting like a brand manager. You're not at P&G anymore."

Despite the pressure, Case kept himself cloistered in his office, communicating largely by e-mail and instant messages. Inevitably, it seemed, AOL would have to introduce flat-fee pricing: Internet users were no longer prepared to pay by the hour. Yet no matter how Case tweaked the numbers, it became clear to him that a flat fee would wipe out AOL's profits. How would the company make money? Setting aside that question, and trusting his intuition, Case reached a decision. In October 1996, AOL announced a flat $19.95 monthly fee. The response to the flat fee was overwhelming, literally. People stampeded to sign up; whereupon AOL's computer servers, its central nerve system, collapsed. Subscribers dialing into AOL were hit with busy signals and frustration. The media, having renamed the company "America on Hold," accused Case of conning his customers by promising what he couldn't deliver. The New York attorney general threatened to sue AOL for fraud and for "repeatedly and persistently engaging in deceptive acts and practices." One competitor, CompuServe, took advantage of the fiasco by launching a toll-free number for potential customers: 1-888-NOTBUSY.

■ ■ ■

AOL WAS NO LONGER A START-UP. AND STEVE CASE, THOUGH slow to recognize it, soon understood that he wasn't cut out to manage a sprawling, increasingly chaotic organization. Someone needed to take charge. Someone had to act like a professional CEO—which is how Robert Warren Pittman comes into the story. An ambitious executive who'd turned around the last two companies he'd run, and a member of America Online's board of directors since 1995, Pittman joined AOL in October 1996, in the middle of its worst crisis ever.

Pittman was unlike anything AOL'ers had ever met. Impatient with Case's long-term, dreamy, futurist thinking, and determined to make AOL profitable, Pittman demanded short-term, tangible results. AOL, he insisted, had to start functioning like a sober public company. He introduced rigorous controls; managers had to meet aggressive financial goals; decisions had to be made quickly. Ruthlessly, he slashed costs. Very soon after Pittman's arrival, AOL announced its first large-scale layoffs. The "November '96 Massacre," as the layoffs came to be known internally, was painful: hundreds of so-called content providers, the sincere and dedicated "freaks" who'd built AOL one chat room at a time, lost their jobs. As a sign of the times (practical, rational, no-nonsense times), AOL reassured investors that the layoffs were on no account a retrenchment; they marked a change in priorities: those hundreds of creative "freaks" would be replaced by more than a thousand new employees, who would be working in such practical, revenue-generating areas as sales and customer support.

It was like oil and water, the combination of Pittman and AOL. First of all, Pittman decorated his office at 22000 AOL Way in Dulles, Virginia, overlooking a silo and a Wal-Mart, as if he were moving into a Manhattan skyscraper: with lime green chairs, a white shag carpet, and Japanese shoji screens. Then he brought to Dulles a retinue of polished advisers, notably Kenneth Lerer, a partner with the powerful public relations firm Robinson, Lerer & Montgomery. Lerer, who'd started his career running political campaigns, was best known for having represented junk bond king Michael Milken in the late 1980s, generating sympathetic press for his clever client even while he was being accused by the SEC of stock manipulation, insider trading, fraud, and other violations of federal securities laws. So effortlessly did Lerer shape the media's coverage of Milken that, according to James Stewart's 1991 book, *Den of Thieves,* he once referred to his PR task as "breast-feeding" journalists.

Some people at AOL blamed the company's troubles on Jean Villanueva, AOL's head of public relations (and Case's significant other). Unprepared for the public's violent response to AOL's problems, clumsy in her handling of the media, and sidetracked by her affair with the company's CEO, Villanueva, they said, had let things get out of control. To Pittman and Lerer, the short-term solution was clear: The press needed to be reined in, fast. Approaching AOL's access crisis as if it were a political scandal, Lerer shrewdly created TV advertisements starring Case in the role of AOL's sincere and apologetic founder; then he hired a polling firm to monitor AOL's public image and developed uniform "talking points" (convincing rhetoric) for AOL's executives. Asked about their company's rotten service, AOL's executives now explained to reporters that the initial stampede to get online, while regrettable, only confirmed AOL's power. After all, AOL really was as central to people's lives as the telephone or the television.

Lerer and Pittman made a great team. While Lerer was busy courting the media, Pittman was seducing Wall Street, where he came to be known as "Bob Pitchman" and AOL's savior. AOL wasn't just another Internet provider, Pittman insisted; for heaven's sake, it was a branded consumer product, a Coca-Cola or a Gillette or a GM. It also resembled a cable television network, not unlike MTV, where Pittman had been CEO in the early 1980s. With a smile and a wave of his hand, Pittman dismissed AOL's troubles: they were temporary, like hiccups. AOL's skeptics were like the shortsighted souls who had once questioned the future of cable television. "I've seen this movie before," he assured reporters shortly after his arrival at AOL, comparing his task at AOL to his former job of selling MTV to a world of doubters. "I've been here before."

AOL's free and easy culture seized up under Pittman's new regime. Many AOL'ers had never been told to meet a budget; on the contrary, over the years they'd been encouraged to spend freely, to experiment with new things, to make mistakes, even expensive ones, and to learn from them. They hadn't paid all that much attention to Wall Street. Until Pittman's arrival, their goal had been to attract more and more subscribers. Period. Now, all of a sudden, they were being ordered to make money.

Deeply suspicious of Pittman, Steve Case saw him as little more than a carny barker, a smooth operator with no respect for AOL's history. Threatened by Pittman's success with the media, overshadowed inside and outside AOL by Pittman's sociability and learned charm, Case was under siege; if he wasn't careful, Pittman would grab control of AOL. It was obvious: Case couldn't help but compare himself to the visionary Steve Jobs, who'd founded Apple Computer in 1976 at the age of twenty-one. In the mid-1980s, Jobs had been marginalized, then ousted by John Scully, the executive hired by Jobs to run Apple. Case had the script down cold.

For his part, Pittman chafed at Case's meddling. He'd agreed to come to AOL only under the condition that Case would leave him alone; though he officially reported to Case, he refused to work for Case. Whereas Case was an idealist, committed to the idea that AOL could change the world, Pittman was motivated by simpler goals: he was a mercenary. "Bob always wanted to be rich and famous," his brother, Thomas, said. "That was clear. He wanted to be rich and famous. . . . He said so."

FIVE

BOB PITTMAN WAS BORN IN JACKSON, MISSISSIPPI, ON DECEMBER 28, 1953, the second of two boys. His father, Warren Pittman, was a Methodist preacher. His mother, Lanita Pittman, worked as a substitute schoolteacher and helped out in her husband's office. By the time Bob Pittman was in the seventh grade, the family had moved four times, from parish to parish. After Warren Pittman was named district superintendent for the region's Methodist churches, the family settled in Brookhaven, a quiet town of ten thousand people in southwest Mississippi, one hour south of Jackson on Interstate 55.

The Brookhaven of Bob Pittman's childhood was peaceful and unremarkable, a town with eighty-four churches, antebellum homes, and a main street that centered on the town's train station, a stop on Amtrak's Chicago–New Orleans line. As Bob's brother, Tom, described it: "Brookhaven had wide streets and trees that overarched the streets and touched above and everybody knew everybody." The Pittmans lived in the church parsonage, and each boy had his own room; almost every morning before school, the family sat down to a breakfast of eggs and toast prepared by Lanita. Family vacations usually involved piling into the car and driving south to beach towns on the Gulf of Mexico; on occasion, the Pittmans would drive north to Washington, D.C.; once they drove all the way to California. Early on,

Bob Pittman announced to anyone who cared that he planned to escape from rural Mississippi.

The Pittman boys were popular at Brookhaven High School. They attended football games and school dances and took dates to the local drive-in. Both of them were good students and good boys; but while Tom was diligent and worked very hard for his grades, winning a scholarship to Ole Miss (the University of Mississippi), Bob needed a prod: he did well at school once his father started paying him fifty cents for every A he pulled off. There was no doubting Bob Pittman's brainpower. "He was smart as a whip. Just brilliant. A fine young man," recalled W. L. Roach, who served as principal of Brookhaven High School for thirty-three years. "He would get an A in half the time it took other students."

Bob Pittman's childhood is marked by something that happened when he was six years old. On a visit to his grandparents' farm in Holly Springs, Mississippi, he was thrown from a horse and kicked in the face by the horse's hoof. That's when he lost his right eye. In interviews given over the years, Pittman suggested that the loss of his eye made him work harder to be accepted. "As a kid, the last thing you want is to be different," Pittman said. "If you have an artificial eye, you're different. The dream of every kid is to fit in and be like all the other kids." Over the years, as if to prove that being monocular was no impediment, Pittman was drawn to hobbies that depended on a keen sense of sight. He devoted himself to fly-fishing, shooting, and photography, for example. In high school, after a family friend gave him a ride in a two-seater plane, he took up flying. "It changed my life," he told *The New Yorker,* referring to that first plane ride. "I couldn't imagine anything greater."

In fact, what changed Pittman's life was not the plane ride itself, but the job he took to pay for flying lessons. Turned down by the local Piggly Wiggly Supermarket and by Jack's Shop, a men's clothing store, Pittman, age fifteen, was hired as a part-time announcer at WCHJ-AM, the less popular of Brookhaven's two radio stations. It was 1968, he was earning $1.60 an hour, and every cent was being plowed into flying lessons. By 1970, his senior year of high school, Pittman had earned his commercial pilot's license, having been granted a waiver from the Federal Aviation Administration that allowed him to fly despite his glass eye.

Meanwhile, working at WCHJ-AM, he'd created a new identity. Listening to him on the radio, no one would have guessed that Pittman was a skinny, one-eyed kid from Brookhaven, the son of a preacher man. "You'd hear him on the radio and then meet him in person—completely different," marveled David Phillips, a high school friend of Pittman's. "It was like he could just turn on his radio voice. Even though he was seventeen years old, you couldn't tell him from an adult. If you didn't know who he was, you wouldn't know that they were the same people." Bill Jacobs, who was two years Pittman's junior at Brookhaven High, remembered Pittman's radio personality as "more flashy than we were used to in a small town, more of a big-city disc jockey then we were used to. I guess if he turned out to be ahead of the curve in life, then he was probably ahead of the curve at that point."

Working for the Brookhaven station after school, Pittman also got a weekend gig as a disc jockey at the "cutting-edge" WJDX-FM in Jackson, rising at four-thirty A.M. every Sunday to start his six A.M. shift. His motivation was clear: Even more than flying, radio had become Pittman's escape route from rural Mississippi. After graduating from high school, where he was named "Most Likely to Succeed," he enrolled at Millsaps College, a private liberal arts school in Jackson founded by Methodists. By then, he was working at WJDX-FM full-time. At the end of his freshman year, when he was offered a job at a radio station in Milwaukee, Pittman packed up his Dodge Dart and left Mississippi for good.

From Milwaukee, Pittman moved on to a radio station in Detroit, then to Pittsburgh, and finally, in 1973, to Chicago, where he was named program director of WMAQ-AM, an unsuccessful radio station owned by NBC. Determined to turn it around, Pittman devised a massive marketing campaign: three million WMAQ bumper stickers were stuck onto on cars, buses, and trucks; $50,000 was given away in instant cash prizes. Over and over and over on local TV, a commercial promoting the radio station featured a never-ending shower of dollar bills; while dollars were raining from heaven, a fat lady kept screaming, "WMAQ's gonna make me rich! WMAQ's gonna make me rich!"

Within months of Pittman's arrival in Chicago, WMAQ-AM had jumped from twenty-second place to the third-most-listened-to radio station in its market. Even today, some thirty years on, that singular feat is mentioned by the Museum of Broadcast Communications as one of the greatest success stories in the history of radio turnarounds. Delighted with himself and the power of advertising, Pittman sent his friends back home copies of articles from the local press, including one that was titled "He's the Country Boy Who Made WMAQ Rich."

Now twenty-three years old, the country boy from Brookhaven, Mississippi, was on his way to New York City as program director of WNBC-AM. Inspired maybe by the young Kris Kristofferson, Pittman grew a beard, blow-dried his wavy, shoulder-length hair just so, hung gold chains around his neck, and wore faded blue jeans to work at NBC's uptight offices. "The Hippie from Mississippi," they called him. After Pittman had made WNBC-AM into the nation's number one radio station, they called him "Boy Wonder." "He was the best program director in the history of radio," effused Charles ("Charlie") Warner, who recruited Pittman to WNBC. "He was the smartest kid I ever saw. He was smooth and articulate. He was brilliant." Relying on market research and listener surveys, Pittman adapted his programming to suit his audience, putting a small number of hit songs into heavy rotation and then dumping them as soon as his listeners tired of them. He had a feel for the moment. Way before they became broadcasting clichés, he was using terms such as "narrowcasting" and "psychographics." As Pittman would later explain to a reporter for the *Mississippi Business Journal,* he knew just how to cater to his public because "I was the small, skinny kid growing up, so to avoid getting picked on I figured out how to read people and get along."

In 1979, four years after Jerry Levin transformed the cable TV business by launching HBO on satellite, Bob Pittman joined Warner Amex Satellite Entertainment, a joint venture of Steve Ross's Warner Communications and American Express. His job was to devise programming for the company's nascent cable TV channels. At the same time, Pittman's boss, John Lack, came up with an idea for an all-music channel. Struck by the possibilities of that idea, Pittman envisioned a cable channel modeled after radio, where record companies provided the content for free and programming targeted a niche audience. In this case, to quote Pittman, the cable channel would target "television babies who grew up on TV and rock and roll." The result was MTV, launched at midnight on August 1, 1981, with the line "Ladies and gentlemen, rock 'n' roll."

MTV took off big-time, and Bob Pittman was famous. The press referred to him as "wiz kid" and "wunderkind." He was profiled in *Time, Esquire,* and *GQ* ("The Cool, Dark Telegenius of Robert Pittman," was *GQ*'s breathless title). Urged on by his new wife, the beautiful and ambitious Sandy Hill, Pittman turned into a quintessential 1980's yuppie. He had it all: a sun-filled apartment on Central Park West, perfect for entertaining; a fifteen-thousand-square-foot converted barn tucked away in Connecticut with sunsets; a private plane (a Cessna 340); and a seat on the board of the New York Shakespeare Festival. He preferred pin-striped suits, Hermès ties, Gucci loafers, and a gold-and-steel Rolex watch.

By the late 1980s, Pittman and his wife were conspicuous on New York's social scene, a striking couple making their way up the social ladder a rung or two at a time. Sandy was tall (five feet eleven), with wavy brown hair and the kind of luminous skin you see in cold cream ads. Raised in Northern California, where her father was in the business of renting out portable toilets, she began her career in New York as a buyer for Bonwit Teller; from there she moved over to women's magazines, first as a merchandising editor at *Mademoiselle,* then as *Allure*'s beauty editor.

Sandy Hill and Bob Pittman met on a flight from New York to Los Angeles. Attracted by his confidence and rakish good looks, and determined to make exactly the right first impression, Sandy pulled out from her bag a copy of *The New Yorker* (" 'cause that says a lot about a person," she once explained). It was love at first sight, the couple later said. When fate diverted their flight from Los Angeles to San Francisco, Sandy proposed they spend the night at her parents' house. (Her parents were out of town.) As reported by *Vanity Fair,* Sandy and Bob made "passionate" love on the living room floor. Six months later, in July 1979, they were married. Sandy was twenty-four, Bob was twenty-five.

Sandy's magazine career took second place to her social ambitions. "Many coattails were wrinkled by Sandy Pittman latching on to them," a former colleague of hers once remarked. Sandy then latched on to the sport of mountain climbing (an apposite metaphor), setting out to become the first woman to climb the Seven Summits (McKinley, Aconcagua, Vinson Massif, Kilimanjaro, Elbrus, Carstensz Pyramid, and Everest). Nothing deterred Sandy Hill Pittman, who posed in fashionable climbing gear for *Vogue* and agreed to be profiled by *The Wall Street Journal* (SOCIALITE SCALES HIGHEST PEAKS was the headline). NBC was granted the rights to transmit her electronic diary direct from Mount Everest. Listing the essential items she'd packed for her arduous trek, Sandy wrote: "I wouldn't dream of leaving town without an ample supply of Dean & DeLuca's Near East blend and my espresso maker."

Soon the tenacious Sandy Pittman became known as "the Martha Stewart of the outdoors" and "the socialite everyone loves to hate." In July 1990, a cover story on the Pittmans appeared in *New*

York magazine. Dubbed THE COUPLE OF THE MINUTE, they were characterized as social climbers ("ambitious, attractive, directed, and well-spoken to the point of glibness"), and their opulent parties were described in detail. Their charitable contributions, the story alleged, were desperate attempts to be accepted by New York's establishment; moreover, it was said, Bob Pittman, in an act of self-promotion, had referred to himself as MTV's "creator," ignoring the music network's other founders. Summing up the widely held view of the Pittmans as arrivistes and parvenus, a source told *New York,* "I'm awed and appalled by the intensity of their desire to climb."

By this time, Bob Pittman had left MTV to start his own entertainment company, Quantum Media. Backed by Steve Ross, his old boss at MTV, and by MCA, which invested $15 million in Pittman's new company, Quantum produced TV shows, home videos, and record albums. But in 1989, as Quantum's losses were outnumbering its wins, Pittman abandoned his goal of being an entrepreneur. Instead, he became Steve Ross's adviser. Ross admired Pittman; he admired his scrappy ambition and considered him a protégé. And Pittman revered Ross. "Steve Ross had probably one of the greatest impacts on my life," said Pittman. "He was a father figure in the business and really took me under his wing." The two men were so close that in some quarters Pittman was regarded as Ross's heir apparent.

In 1990, after Warner merged with Time Inc., Pittman was named CEO of Time Warner Enterprises, a new division charged with developing novel ventures for Time Warner. He persuaded Ross to buy Six Flags, a run-down national chain of theme parks that Pittman proceeded to make fresh and relevant. They featured extravagant themed restaurants. The new rides were based on Warner Bros. characters like Batman. In short, Pittman promoted Six Flags parks by latching on to Disney's coattails. One early series of ads, with its slogan "Bigger Than Disney and Closer to Home," so angered Disney CEO, Michael Eisner, that he pulled all his company's advertising from Time Inc. publications. Another series of ads for Six Flags featured a folksy Pittman himself, saying: "We're America's No. 2 theme park company, which means we have to work harder."

In 1995, under pressure to pare debt, Time Warner decided to unload Six Flags, and Pittman arranged to sell 51 percent of the company to Boston Venture Partners in a deal that valued Six Flags at $1.2 billion, nearly double what Time Warner had originally paid for the theme parks. As part of the agreement, Pittman would continue to run Six Flags. But then he got grabby: on top of his multimillion-dollar salary, he demanded a large equity stake in Six Flags worth as much as $100 million. Boston Ventures was outraged by Pittman's demands, as was Time Warner's CEO, Jerry Levin. When Pittman refused to back down, Levin had him fired.

Driven by ego and by greed, Pittman had miscalculated, badly. With the death of Steve Ross in 1992, Pittman no longer had allies and conspirators in high places at Time Warner; in fact, his allegiance to Ross may well have tainted him in Levin's eyes. What's more, Pittman's relentless self-promotion had stirred up resentment among some of the company's division heads, in particular Bob Daly and Terry Semel, the powerful duo who ran the Warner Bros. studio. Slyly, Daly and Semel lobbied Levin: Time Warner really didn't need Pittman to oversee its remaining interest in Six Flags, they argued; instead, *they* should be directing Six Flags. In the end, Daly and Semel did take control of Six Flags; and Dick Parsons, Time Warner's new president, was dispatched by Levin to fire Pittman. Things got ugly. Parsons and Pittman fought hard over severance terms; losing control of himself, Pittman picked up a chair and threw it to the ground.

Now Pittman was forty-two years old and out of work. Dismissed from Time Warner, he'd also aggravated his former colleagues at MTV by taking sole credit for the company's success. And the one company he did start, Quantum Media, never got off the ground. The former "wiz kid" and "wunderkind" and "telegenius" was old news. At the same time, his marriage to Sandy Hill Pittman had come apart; and in October 1995, Bob Pittman moved out of their Central Park West apartment with its stunning views from the twenty-sixth floor. He was tired of playing second fiddle to his wife's mountain climbing, it was rumored. "I don't know what's gotten into him," a shocked Sandy Hill reportedly told friends.

So it was that Pittman wound up running Century 21 Real Estate Corp., a washed-up, down-at-the-heels outfit best known for the signature mustard-colored blazers (real polyester) worn by its brokers. Putting his best spin on the downward move, Pittman claimed he'd joined Century 21 because he was keen to learn about something other than entertainment and media. As a matter of fact, according to some of his friends, the real estate business bored him. In October 1996, less than a year after joining Century 21, Pittman joined America Online, a company as hobbled as the man himself. That's when he furnished his sad office in Dulles, Virginia, with lime green chairs and a white shag rug. His office, you'll recall, overlooked a silo and Wal-Mart.

■ ■ ■

UNTIL PITTMAN ARRIVED IN DULLES, AMERICA ONLINE HAD been earning money almost exclusively from subscriber fees. With the move to a flat monthly rate, however, it became clear that the original business model could no longer be sustained. Now that they weren't paying by the hour, AOL's customers were spending more and more of their day online: over the course of just six months, they went from using AOL for a combined forty-six million hours a month to a remarkable 125 million hours a month. Such devotion sounds like a good thing. But, of course, the more time its users spent online, the more money AOL had to spend improving and upgrading and expanding its service, and the more money it lost, month after month, in a vicious circle. A monthly fee of $19.95 just wasn't enough to cover costs, yet the market for Internet service was so competitive, AOL couldn't increase its rates. Any way you looked at it, selling Internet access was a losing proposition.

The obvious solution for AOL was to sell ads, lots of them. But ads were anathema to AOL, a company that in the early 1990s had promoted itself as ad-free. As envisioned by Steve Case in those heady times, AOL was a company devoted to the "user experience"; it was all about bringing people together and enriching their lives; it was not about hawking consumer products. Besides, Case thought, if AOL came to depend on advertising, it might resemble television, a once promising medium that in his view had been cheapened and corrupted by advertising.

Still, Case was a realist; he recognized that AOL needed new streams of revenue. In the mid-1990s, shortly before Pittman's arrival at AOL, Case had hired a smart salesman by the name of Myer Berlow to drum up advertising for them. Berlow had been in the ad business for twenty-five years; he was a fast-talking wheeler-dealer, a chain smoker who wore Armani suits and Ray-Ban sunglasses and combed back his hair with Aveda Self Control. A charmer and a bully, Berlow was a tight ball of nervous energy, with nails bitten to the quick and no mind for detail. Because of his acute attention deficit disorder, and in order to focus, Berlow was on Ritalin.

Raised in an upper-middle-class and assimilated Jewish household (his father was a pediatrician), and educated in religion and politics at Kenyon College, Berlow nevertheless seemed to be someone out of *The Godfather.* Selling was Berlow's vocation, his passion; everything and everyone had a price tag. If seduction didn't work, he'd start yelling, but one way or another, by hook or crook, he'd close the sale. "He was unabashedly commerce related," is how Mark Walsh, then a senior vice president at AOL, described Berlow. By way of example, Walsh tells a great story. "Myer had been in the ad business in Miami. So one day we were having lunch together and I said, 'Boy,

Miami is a tough market for advertising; you got to be really sharp to get it down as an agency guy in Miami. Tell me, Myer, what was it like?' And he said, 'Mark, let me tell you what it was like. One of my partners asked me once, Would you sleep with a client for a $5 million account? And I said back to him, A man or a woman? Man: $50 million, yes. Woman: $5 million, yes.' And that's when I realized that Myer had a rate card for everything. He'd actually thought it through: man or woman, everyone had a price."

Berlow made almost no headway during those early years at AOL. Yes, Case had hired him to sell ads, but AOL wasn't really commerce related, not yet. One of the first deals Berlow signed in 1995 was with a small advertiser who agreed to pay $10,000 a month for a spot on AOL. To close the deal, Berlow needed AOL's technology department to design a "button" leading straight to the advertiser's Web site. AOL's technologists ignored Berlow's request. Advertising was not a priority in their view; their job was to improve the so-called user experience, thus increasing AOL's market share. Berlow confronted the manager responsible for designing his "button," demanding to know why it wasn't ready to go. Earnestly, the manager explained that having thought over Berlow's request, he'd concluded that advertising was a bad idea, generally. Berlow exploded: "It's done—it's fucking sold! I want these fucking ads up now." Shocked by Berlow's coarseness and aggression, but unwilling to concede easily, the manager agreed to have the ad ready in six weeks. "Six weeks!" Berlow said. "In six weeks, we're going to lose $15,000!" Berlow was put on hold.

"Six weeks to the day go by, and it still wasn't done," recalled Berlow. "So I pick up the phone and I call the guy who was coordinating it. Of course, I get his voice mail, because none of these guys would ever pick up their phone. I leave a message that says, 'Who do I have to fuck to get you people to do your job?' "

By the late 1990s, Berlow would be AOL's top salesman, helping to draw in some $2 billion worth of advertising a year. But on that day back in 1995, swearing and yelling and acting out, he was almost fired.

AOL was, after all, a cultivated, refined organization, and part of its mission was to protect its online community from materialism. Case was open to the idea of selling ads—he would tolerate them; on the other hand, he certainly didn't want to encourage them. Once, when Berlow bagged a then giant $5 million–a-year advertising contract from Sprint, Case protested: the ad was too prominent, too visible.

"I don't like the fact that it's going to be such a big ad," he told Berlow.

"It's $5 million, Steve; they want a big ad," Berlow replied matter-of-factly.

"I don't mind giving them a big ad," Case continued, "but can't we put it someplace where the members won't see it?"

Berlow was floored. "Steve, you don't really mean that you want to put this in a place where our members can't see it?" But that really *was* what Case meant.

"I don't want our members to see the ads," Case said, "because they might get upset."

Again Berlow was almost fired. Losing his composure, such as it was, he said to Case: "Are you out of your fucking mind? Who the fuck is going to spend money on ads that you don't see?"

■ ■ ■

BY THE END OF 1996, CASE WAS STARTING TO PANIC. HE couldn't afford to walk the high road. In order to replace the millions of AOL members who were bolting to other, cheaper Internet providers, AOL had to spend more and more on marketing gimmicks and giveaways. Every new subscriber now cost AOL $270, up from $130 just a few months earlier. Meanwhile, AOL's stock price kept slipping; without new ways to make money, the company would be out of cash soon. Despite Myer Berlow's talents as a salesman, advertising had not really changed AOL's bottom line, mostly because major national advertisers were deeply suspicious of the Internet;

whatever money they spent online was a fraction of a fraction of what they spent on traditional media like television, newspapers, and magazines. In October 1996, only six months after putting Case on its cover, *Business Week* decreed ominously: "If those new sources of revenue don't materialize, AOL does not have many other tricks."

Bob Pittman had just arrived at AOL; he was cutting expenses, introducing strict budgets, firing people left and right, and reorganizing the company. But for all that, it became clear to insiders that AOL needed a radically new business model, fast. Then, all of a sudden, right in the nick of time, AOL was saved by a young hustler named Daniel Borislow.

A former cable TV installer with little formal education, but with tons of moxie and ambition and instinct, Borislow operated a tiny long-distance telephone company called Tel-Save Holdings. He had grand plans for Tel-Save: offering long-distance service for just nine cents a minute, he boasted that he would become as big as AT&T and Sprint. He had an ingenious idea: The easiest, cheapest way to sign on new long-distance customers was to tap AOL's subscriber base. To anyone reading this chapter, Borislow's plan may seem obvious. But it wasn't obvious in 1996. Back then, AOL seemed doomed to extinction, like the Dodo or like Jerry Levin's Full Service Network. According to investors and the media, the new World Wide Web, which offered an easy and painless way to navigate the Internet, had made AOL irrelevant. Why, AOL couldn't even handle the increase in traffic caused by its new flat-rate price plan! cried the media. But while some people predicted that AOL would be wiped out any day, Borislow saw opportunity. As the Internet kept growing, he intuited, it would become more and more chaotic—more fragmented and complex and demanding. Ordinary people, nontechies, would welcome the safe, simple haven provided by AOL. It was the perfect place to promote Tel-Save's long-distance service.

In January, 1997, Borislow showed up in Dulles with a $50 million check made out to AOL. "I got a call from a portfolio manager at

Putnam [Investments]; they were investors in Tel-Save," recalled Richard Hanlon, head of AOL's investor relations department at the time. "He said, 'We have this guy Dan in our office and you need to talk to him about this idea he has.' So I called Borislow. This man was passionate, if not insane, and he tells me he's about to jump in his car and drive down to Dulles, Virginia, with a check for $50 million. And for some reason I actually didn't think he was insane. I hang up, go down the hallway to Bob Pittman's office, and say, 'Bob, you won't believe the phone call that I just got.' "

By the time Pittman's top deal maker, David Colburn, was finished negotiating with Borislow, the initial $50 million had grown to an unbelievable $100 million, up front and in cash. In exchange for his $100 million, Borislow would have exclusive rights to sell long-distance telephone service to AOL's members. *One hundred million dollars.* It was the big deal AOL needed. Borislow's Tel-Save Holdings, a company with sales of only $20 million, paid $100 million for the rights; it also promised AOL at least half of all profits earned from the deal, plus stock warrants for as much as 15 percent of the company. Mortgaging the future of Tel-Save, Borislow figured that in the long run, AOL would bring him so many new customers that he'd earn back that $100 million and then some. It was a fantastic gamble. By the late 1990s, hundreds of other companies would adopt the same business model.

The Tel-Save deal wasn't advertising in the classic sense; it was an ambitious marketing "partnership" that embedded the company in every part of AOL. Aside from Tel-Save banners and pop-up ads, a special interactive software was available from AOL to help members choose the Tel-Save calling plan that was best for them. As well, AOL members would have their Tel-Save phone bills paid automatically, using the credit card already on file at AOL. Such marketing partnerships would come to be known as "portal deals"—deals in which companies gave away huge sums of money, and huge chunks of equity and future profits, for a "storefront" on AOL, the Internet's most exclusive real estate, with a stunning view of the planet.

Borislow had guessed right: the World Wide Web wasn't taking customers away from AOL after all; on the contrary, the more widespread the Internet became, the more people craved the relative ease of AOL. What's more, all the publicity about AOL's access crisis made them even more eager to join. If this thing called AOL was such a huge deal, who could afford to miss out?

Thanks to Borislow's arrangement with AOL, one hundred thousand new customers a month now rushed to get their long-distance service from Tel-Save. The impact of the AOL deal on Tel-Save's stock price was even more impressive. By early 1998, despite mounting losses of $21 million on sales of $300 million, Tel-Save was valued by the stock market at $2 billion, as much as Northwest Airlines. Borislow's personal stake in the company was an awesome $500 million, on paper. Now that Tel-Save was so successful, he boasted to *Fortune,* he was just about to sell it to a "very big company," thereby locking in that $2 billion valuation. Dazzled, analysts predicted that in 1999, Tel-Save's revenues would reach $1 billion.

Tel-Save's deal with AOL soon spawned a great Wall Street myth: The way to fame and fortune was to cut a portal deal with AOL. It was that simple. Shortly after the Tel-Save deal was announced, CUC International agreed to pay AOL $50 million to market its online discount-shopping services. Preview Travel paid $32 million to be AOL's online travel agent. For $25 million, 1-800-FLOWERS became AOL's exclusive vendor of fresh flowers. For $18 million, N2K was named AOL's exclusive music retailer. Autobytel paid $6 million to be affiliated with AOL. Cybermeals.com, which promised to transform the take-out food business by taking orders online rather than by phone, paid $20 million for the right to match AOL users with restaurants offering home delivery in their neighborhoods. Revising the meaning of the word *exclusive,* and offering an early glimpse of AOL's brazen negotiating tactics, both Amazon.com *and* barnesandnoble.com signed portal deals, for $19 million and $40 million, respectively; both were going to be the "exclusive" bookseller on AOL (one on AOL.com the Web site, the other on AOL's proprietary online service).

All those companies had something in common: they were upstarts, unfamiliar dot-coms, craving the credibility and exposure that came from being associated with AOL, the biggest, most powerful brand on the Internet. Doing a deal with AOL became the magic potion. The mere hint of a forthcoming deal with AOL could send the stock price of a public company soaring. Private companies, start-ups on the verge of going public, had even more to gain. Going into business with AOL became the surest way to attract customers or, in Internet-speak, to ensure that a company and its product (flowers, furniture, snacks, CDs, books, pet supplies, mountaineering equipment, coffee beans) had "first-mover advantage." In the dot-com frenzy of the late 1990s, what counted was trumping your competitors by being first to market. Everyone knew that. Profits were irrelevant; once a company had cornered its market, the thinking went, it would have the economies of scale needed to make a bundle of cash, and to cash out.

More and more, then, a portal deal with AOL was considered a rite of passage for young companies, especially companies looking to raise public money. Under pressure from their insatiable venture capitalists, start-up firms began appearing at AOL's Dulles headquarters, uninvited, pleading frantically to rent a storefront on AOL, camping out in the lobby on the slim chance they'd be granted a face-to-face ("f2f" in Internet-speak) meeting with AOL's omnipotent rainmakers. The companies may not have had much in the way of revenues, they may not have had a business plan (they certainly did not have profits), but in the view of Wall Street, hooking up with AOL and latching on to their coattails would guarantee investors a dizzying, unforgettable ride.

At the beginning, AOL didn't fully grasp the power it had over companies trying to go public. After all, until the late 1990s, hurdles were set high: a company wanting to go public had to have been in business for at least three years and it had to show four consecutive quarters of rising profits; that was the old rule of thumb. By the time Microsoft had its IPO in 1986, for example, it had been in business for eleven years, it was (very) profitable, and its CEO, Bill Gates, was widely known as a computer genius. In other words, Microsoft did not sell shares in itself until it had a solid, well-documented track record. Even AOL, on going public in 1992, had been in business for seven years; at the time, it boasted revenues of $20 million and was (modestly) profitable.

In November 1998, however, every traditional, accepted, sane rule of business was all of a sudden turned upside down. That month something called theglobe.com, an online community of chat rooms, stock quotes, news, shops, and personalized Web pages, went public. Tiny and unprofitable, theglobe.com was run by two kids who'd started the company in their dorm room at Cornell. Nonetheless, on the day of its IPO, theglobe.com's shares climbed from $9 to $97 before closing the day at $63.50. It was the largest first-day gain in the history of the stock market (606 percent). After that, almost any company selling almost anything related to the Internet could be taken public. America was in the middle of a technological revolution, the reasoning went; the world had changed utterly, and old business models no longer applied.

Like those seventeenth-century Dutch tulip bulbs you keep reading about, dot-com IPOs had unleashed a speculative mania. What's more, by the late 1990s, IPOs had become great "branding events," which is only to say that the hype that came with having the price of a stock triple on its first trading day was a more persuasive advertising tool than a thirty-second pitch aired during the Super Bowl. "The stock price broadcasts to the world that you're a hot company," noted Jon Bond, of the New York ad agency Kirshenbaum Bond &

Partners, at the time. "That becomes a self-fulfilling prophecy. And that's the whole point."

It was during their negotiations with N2K (acronym for Need to Know), owners of the online record store Music Boulevard, that AOL's deal makers understood, finally, that they weren't just selling advertising space on the Internet. For heaven's sake, they were selling the rights to a hot IPO! Based on the number of AOL users who were likely to shop at Music Boulevard, Myer Berlow had intended to charge N2K $6 million to advertise on AOL. Then, in one of their meetings with AOL, N2K's executives let slip the urgency of getting the portal deal done *before* their forthcoming IPO. In a flash, the scales fell from Berlow's eyes, and he saw the light. Excusing himself from the meeting, he pulled aside his colleague on the deal, saying: "Look, we've made a mistake: we valued this deal based on their business, not on the value we add to it." When he came back to the negotiating table, Berlow announced that N2K would have to pay AOL $18 million; that was three times more than Berlow's initial estimate and ten times N2K's annual revenues. N2K's executives didn't flinch. After all, compared to the riches they'd get from their impending IPO, $18 million was a trifle, a drop in the bucket. As N2K's founder later told a reporter: "When you see that 40 percent of all online traffic is coming through AOL, you've got to be there."

In October 1997, less than a month after announcing its deal with AOL, N2K had its initial public offering. Convinced that N2K's online store, Music Boulevard, would be selling millions upon millions of CDs to AOL's subscribers, investors demanded so many N2K shares that at the very last moment, both the number of shares offered and the price of those shares were jacked up. At the end of its first day as a public company, N2K was worth $284 million, despite having lost $19 million on minuscule sales of $1.7 million in its most recent fiscal year.

Like other companies that signed coveted portal deals, N2K had to hand over most of its IPO money to AOL. After that it was all downhill; overwhelmed by marketing costs that dwarfed revenues, N2K never earned a penny. Other Internet companies, with names like Preview Travel, Beyond.com, and Cyberian Outpost, died, too. As for Dan Borislow's Tel-Save, it was not bought by a "very big company" after all. By late 1998, with payments to AOL contributing to a loss that year of $221 million, Tel-Save's stock collapsed. And Borislow left the company, his doom apparently sealed by an investigative article written by Alex Berenson for TheStreet.com: "Borislow has a criminal record, lied to *Fortune* about whether he graduated from high school, and once concluded a business letter by telling its subjects to 'go back to the section of hell you came from. . . . ' More recently, he responded to a question with the retort, 'I hear you have a small dick. Is that true?' "

Just how much AOL knew about Borislow's background is unclear. Certainly Pittman found him unsettling, so much so that Pittman came to dread each confrontation with the wily head of Tel-Save. Keenly aware of the crisis at AOL, Borislow kept extracting more and more concessions from Pittman. Good grief, for $100 million AOL would have sold its soul: any section of hell had to be better than Chapter 11. "We sort of did the deal with the devil," is how one AOL'er who worked on the Tel-Save deal put it. "We had to make that deal work, and Borislow knew that, so he really pushed us. He was very concerned about his stock price and certain things that we needed to do to keep his stock price up. . . . He was an asshole, and here he was our largest client." In one meeting with Borislow, the AOL'er, who was present, recalls: "I remember looking at Bob [Pittman] and he looked harried. You know, he's always neat and tucked in. But that day his hair was out of place, his shirt was untucked a little bit. He was sweating."

The fate of AOL's partners didn't seem to concern Wall Street. As soon as the Tel-Save deal was announced, AOL's stock price took off. Within a year, it had climbed 231 percent. That was the beginning. As a sign of its absolute dominance of the Internet, AOL announced in late 1997 that it was buying CompuServe, its biggest competitor and the very company that only five years earlier had tried to buy out AOL, which now boasted more than ten million members.

In March 1998, Steve Case appeared on the cover of *Fortune,* wearing pleated khakis and a broad smile. SURPRISE! AOL WINS, read the cover. "Today AOL is the only brand that counts in cyberspace, an online Hertz with no Avis in sight," declared the nine-page article, fawning: "While most Internet companies are small-time startups awash in red ink, AOL has become the first new-media company on a grand scale, more comparable to *Newsweek* or a cable company like TCI than to Netscape." As if to prove that AOL was in the same league as old-line media companies with hard assets, a illustrative table compared the company's "circulation" and "prime-time audience" to NBC and *The New York Times,* among others. Concluding the article, Pittman was quoted: "Now the only question is, How big, how fast?"

■ ■ ■

AS TIME WENT BY, THE UNDISPUTED STARS OF AOL WERE ITS salesmen and deal makers. And David Colburn, a lawyer by training, was the toughest, most ruthless deal maker around. He was a legend, not only for negotiating the Tel-Save deal on behalf of AOL, but also for an earlier deal he'd pulled off during the Internet browser wars. At the time, AOL was trying to decide which of two competing browsers to license: Netscape's Navigator or Microsoft's new Internet Explorer. It was 1996. Netscape's browser, which had transformed the Internet by making it easy to navigate, or to browse, the World Wide Web, controlled about 80 percent of the market. And Microsoft's new Internet Explorer was lagging way behind.

It was widely assumed that AOL would choose to license Netscape's browser, and not only because Netscape dominated the market. In the early 1990s, Microsoft had tried to buy AOL. "I can buy 20 percent of you or I can buy all of you, or I can go into this business myself and bury you," Microsoft's Bill Gates had once said, famously. Turned down by Steve Case, Gates decided to bury AOL, launching Microsoft's MSN online service in 1994. Not surprisingly, Microsoft was the enemy at AOL: Case referred to Microsoft as "the beast"; he even compared Microsoft to Hitler once.

Sure enough, on March 11, 1996, AOL announced a deal to license Netscape's browser. Netscape's executives rejoiced greatly. AOL's announcement was so significant that Netscape's stock climbed by 16 percent that day. But there was a catch: AOL never promised Netscape exclusivity, a signal detail overlooked by Netscape's negotiators. In fact, even while AOL was announcing its licensing agreement with Netscape, Colburn was putting the topcoat on an even bigger deal with Microsoft.

The next morning, on March 12, AOL made an announcement: Microsoft's Internet Explorer would be its primary browser, appearing automatically whenever AOL users went to surf the Internet. In return, Microsoft would bundle AOL with its dominant Windows operating system, a system used by twenty million people. Netscape's Navigator would still be available on AOL, of course (a deal is a deal); however, AOL members would have to download the browser themselves. News of AOL's deal with Microsoft was a blow to Netscape, whose executives, Colburn admitted, "felt they were jilted at the altar." More to the point, as Colburn would later testify eloquently, "[Netscape] certainly had become a wounded duck because of us doing the Microsoft deal."

Netscape was not the only company that felt betrayed by Colburn. As a team, Colburn and Myer Berlow were unmatchable. First Berlow and his two hundred odd salesmen would lure the potential partners to AOL. Price was seldom an issue during the opening rituals. Instead, Berlow held out desirable bait to advertisers, often promising what couldn't be delivered—a special position on the

AOL site, for example. Or else he'd guarantee someone exclusive rights that were far from exclusive. Autobytel, for example, was granted the "sole and exclusive right" to sell cars on AOL. A short time later, a competitor, AutoVantage, was signed on by AOL. As it turned out, Autobytel's contract had effectively been negated by a legal sleight of hand: a new section of AOL, created through an acquisition, was not covered under Autobytel's contract, and that's where AutoVantage wound up. "They were the biggest prostitutes in the world," recalled Autobytel's founder, Peter Ellis, still angry at the way he was treated by AOL. "We had an exclusive agreement with them, and so did everyone else."

In Berlow's mind, he hadn't done a thing wrong: AOL was moving so fast, morphing, that deals were sometimes altered by accident. His intentions were good: "There was never a time that I looked across the table at somebody and said, 'You have this exclusivity,' when I knew it couldn't be done," Berlow insisted. As one of Berlow's salesmen, Randy Dean, unapologetically explained: "It's a sales technique: if somebody is ready to buy the car, but they want some option that they can't get on the car, Myer would say, 'Don't worry, we'll get you that option. We'll figure out a way to get it for you. Just buy the car.' He wasn't trying to bilk people, he was just prone to saying whatever needed to be said to get the deal done." Having started off with a profound mission, having dedicated themselves to using an incredible new medium to change the world, AOL'ers had turned into car salesmen.

It was the way of the new Internet world. Berlow made up the rules as he went along, he said, because there was no rulebook. If some partners didn't do as well on AOL as they'd hoped, well, Berlow had done his best. Wide-eyed, speaking in the soothing cadences of an encyclopedia salesman, Berlow explained, not insincerely: "One way to look at things is that we overpromised. Another way is that it was a vision that was being expressed that oftentimes didn't get delivered."

That kind of double speak was second nature to AOL's sales force. And Berlow was juggling so many deals at the same time that of course he messed up. Sometimes he'd arrive at meetings hours late, looking as though he hadn't slept in days, with bloodshot eyes and a three-day-old beard, his cell phone ringing madly; meanwhile four potential partners were waiting for him. "It was like you were entering AOL-land," recalled Martin Nisenholtz, who as head of New York Times Electronic Media Company frequently negotiated with AOL. "There was normal business and then there was AOL-land, which had nothing to do with logic or coherence or linear progression."

Having promised whatever had to be promised to get the deal under way, the fast-talking Berlow would turn over the potential partner (aka the victim) to Colburn's division, which was called business affairs, or "BA" for short. There seduction turned into sadism. "Myer dragged the elephants back to the cave and David skinned them," is how one former colleague described the tactics of the Berlow-Colburn team. During the negotiating sessions, Colburn shouted obscenities, made outrageous demands, and, on at least one occasion, punched his fist against the wall. If a partner happened to object, Colburn would threaten to do a deal with the competitor, then storm out of the meeting, leaving the bewildered victim alone in an empty room. If a partner tried to haggle, AOL's negotiators would refuse to do the deal, period; after all, there was no shortage of people eager to meet AOL's demands.

Colburn insisted that his reputation as a bully was myth. "We really go through great pains so that a partner feels good about the process," he swore. From all accounts, however, Colburn was delighted by his reputation as an unstable, unpredictable cowboy. He was unshaven; he was badly dressed. In meetings he'd lean way back in his chair, fold his arms behind his head, casual-like, and put his feet up on the table, cowboy boots in your face. He addressed everyone

with the same arrogant, sarcastic tone of voice. Everything was calculated to impress; even his volatility was apparently a tactic meant to in-
timidate and wear down the opposition. "It was theater," is the way
one AOL partner described it. Colburn was quick on his feet and endowed with a near photographic memory. Off the top of his head, he
could recall the most minute detail of any contract. He had an uncanny ability to identify his opponent's vulnerability, his Achilles'
heel, and then go for it. "On pure mechanics alone, he could outma-
neuver anyone on the other side of the table," said a colleague.
Rephrasing that, Randy Dean said: "David will look you right in the
eye and take your wallet out of your pocket."

Solitary confinement, psychological torture, verbal abuse, black-
mail: the more powerful AOL became, the more its deal-making sessions were like scenes from a gangster movie or *The Sopranos*. One
popular joke inside AOL put it this way: "The salesperson's job is to
strap someone down to a chair while someone in business affairs beats
the hell out of them." Or, as an AOL'er who worked for the company's
business affairs division quipped "These were win-win deals: we win
and then we win again."

Invariably, Colburn would outsmart and exhaust the partners,
until finally, overwhelmed, they'd agree to every one of his terms. The
transactions he drew up were so complex, so biased, that they were
known internally as "BA Specials." One executive whose company
signed a deal with AOL told the *Industry Standard:* "For weeks it was,
'You're great, you're great, you're great,' and then one day [we had to]
give them every last dollar we had in the bank and 20 percent of our
company or they threatened to go to our competitor."

Battered and bruised and humiliated, some partners emerged
from negotiations with AOL convinced they'd been robbed blind.
Autobytel, for one, sued AOL for misrepresentation. But lawsuits
were rare, perhaps because many companies were out of business by
the time it dawned on them that their deal with AOL had been one-

sided. "The reason those deals didn't deliver isn't because AOL over-promised," insisted Berlow, loyal to the end. "The reason they didn't deliver is because they were bullshit companies with no business plans."

The truth was far more complicated. Both sides were playing a dangerous game whose rules were being written by a speculative stock market that rewarded short-term results above anything else. Under pressure from Wall Street, rewarded for its aggressive deal making, AOL was doing whatever it took to ratchet up earnings. At the same time, desperate to prop up their initial or secondary public offerings with a signed AOL deal, young companies were glad to endure the psychological abuse. "Look," a senior AOL executive said wearily. "We were delivering to these people what they wanted. . . . They got their IPO. Then they were public companies and the Street tells them, 'Okay, you guys have to perform,' and all of a sudden they forgot that their goal was to get their IPO and they look back at the deal with AOL and start crying foul."

Where were Pittman and Case when all this was going on? Both men regarded Colburn as a harmless eccentric, apparently. Yes, Colburn's business practices may have been unconventional, but then again, AOL was an unconventional company.

Within AOL, Colburn was viewed as a kind of rock star, the Mick Jagger of Dulles, Virginia. Once a month, members of his division gathered to celebrate their latest accomplishments: Colburn would deliver a rousing speech; then he'd present that month's top performer with a Bammy award, the business affairs equivalent of the music industry's Grammy Awards. Top performers won luxurious weekend trips for two to New York City. Occasionally, to encourage his team to give something back to the community, Colburn would organize a trip to Anacostia, a poor African-American neighborhood in Washington, D.C., where AOL's dealmakers planted and harvested produce for the needy. There were spontaneous morale-boosting adventures, too, including one trip in which a group of AOL'ers took the company plane to San Francisco for an evening at the city's famous Gold Club strip joint.

In return for being a part of AOL's elite business affairs division, Colburn's people had to perform. He didn't tolerate imprecision or carelessness or sloth. As brutal as he was with partners, Colburn was even tougher with the people who worked for him. They were like his children, he said; he expected great things of them. He was famous for humiliating his troops publicly, chastising them, shouting and cursing, until time and again they'd break down crying, anguished, sobbing into their soup. "He would make these guys cry all the time—all the time: the toughest, most educated guys would cry," remembers a former AOL salesman. "He would get under their skin and he would do that until they cracked."

For all that, AOL's adolescent deal makers just worshipped Colburn. They wanted to be big and tough like him. Imitating Colburn, they too wore cowboy boots and T-shirts with their high-end Italian suits and mastered the art of the permanent five o'clock shadow. They flew into rages, mocked co-workers, told dirty jokes, and treated their partners horribly. In the words of one AOL'er: "It was a shit-kicking, hulking, bravado culture." That shit-kicking culture seeped into every corner of AOL.

■ ■ ■

NOT LONG AFTER PITTMAN ARRIVED AT AOL, HE ASKED ONE OF his colleagues what his direct reports thought about him.

"They think you'll be good for the stock," she said.

"Is that important to them?" Pittman asked.

"Nothing," she replied, "is more important to them."

At least the goal posts were in place. If AOL had once been run by missionaries spreading the good word, it was now run by mercenaries like Bob Pittman, whose mission was to get the stock price soaring. Working at AOL had never been financially rewarding. Salaries had been kept modest—for years, Steve Case himself had made just $200,000, a pittance for the CEO of a company the size of AOL. Support staff was thin; so were expense accounts. Offices were small and stripped down, and even senior AOL'ers sent out their own FedEx packages. The company did not pay for executives' country club memberships, nor did it offer a car service for employees who worked late. There were no executive dining rooms at AOL. Yet by the late 1990s, taking a pay cut to join AOL was typical for many people. Why? Because what AOL offered its employees was a lottery ticket in the form of stock options. In the late 1990s, the odds were very good.

In the olden days, with AOL's stock price languishing, few people had given much thought to those options. But now, all that mattered at AOL was the company's stock price, permanently displayed by AOL'ers in the bottom left-hand corner of their computer screens. Even the liquid crystal displays on printers were programmed to show AOL's rising share price. By 1998, AOL's stock price had became the group's mission, a sacred trust. Owning AOL stock was the fastest, surest way to get rich in the here and now. In the space of just two years, 1997 and 1998, AOL's stock surged from about $2 a share to $40. In other words, a $10,000 investment made at the beginning of 1997 was worth $200,000 at the end of 1998. So fast did the stock shoot up that in 1998 alone, AOL announced three two-for-one stock splits.

If you recall, Steve Case's mission statement went like this: "To build a global medium as essential to people's lives as the telephone or the television . . . and even more valuable." Every day AOL was more and more valuable. Why, you could estimate an AOL'er's net worth based on the number of stock splits he or she had been around for. Compulsively, everyone did the math. New AOL'ers weren't a bit envious of the wealth amassed by old-timers; on the contrary, new AOL'ers were inspired. "We were always talking about what our 'number' was," said Paul Baker, a lawyer in AOL's business affairs department, explaining how things worked. "By our 'number' we meant how much I need after tax to be happy. And we used to laugh because that number changed a lot between 1997 and 2000. Your number might have been $2 million when you started, then it moved to $5 million, and boy, before you knew it, you just couldn't live without $10 million."

Before you knew it, the Neons and Toyotas and Fords in AOL's parking lot had been replaced by Porsche Carreras, BMW roadsters, Mercedes-Benz coupes, Jaguars, and the occasional custom-made Ferrari. Everyone was upwardly mobile; everyone was entitled to $10 million, at least. By one count, more than two thousand millionaires were working at AOL by 1999. As you can imagine, motivating them to work hard became a serious concern; thus, the company's human resources department organized seminars with topics like "How Do You Handle Employees Who Are Already Millionaires?" Those millionaires didn't just want high salaries. Instead, as incentives, AOL'ers were given grandiose titles. Soon the company was flooded with so many senior vice presidents, then presidents, that someone had a bumper sticker printed that read: "Honk if you're an AOL President."

Whereas AOL's employees had once shared basement apartments in Herdon or Arlington, Virginia, they now built sprawling neo-Gothic manors and pseudo-Georgian mansions in two rich suburbs of Washington: Great Falls, Virginia, and Potomac, Maryland. So many AOL'ers moved to Great Falls that the local strip mall, the Village Center, became AOL's de facto social center. Roaring into Great Falls's Village Center on his Harley-Davidson, Pittman would join his colleagues at Gilette's Coffee Shop, AOL's unofficial off-site cafeteria.

Instead of talking about the weather, AOL'ers traded talk about who'd bought what, and where, and for just how much. Size wasn't everything, naturally. Inspired by ads for luxury real estate, perhaps, AOL'ers installed mahogany-paneled foyers, tiered bronze fountains, numerous en suites, ponds stocked with Japanese koi, full-size basket-ball courts, five-car garages, outdoor hot tubs, banquet-size dining rooms with exquisite moldings, lush landscaping, forty-seat home theaters, marble floors, antique fireplaces, wraparound slate terraces, all the amenities, and soaring Palladian windows. Every home had a breathtaking view.

By 1999, the Forbes 400 list of richest Americans included four AOL'ers: Steve Case ($1.5 billion), Barry Schuler ($750 million), Bob Pittman ($725 million), and Ted Leonsis ($675 million). The highest-worth AOL'ers owned their own planes, helicopters, yachts, vine-yards, contemporary art collections, charitable foundations, and professional sports teams. Meanwhile, the striving class of midlevel managers did their very best to keep up. Kathy Bushkin, AOL's spokeswoman, used $3 million worth of her AOL shares to start her own family foundation, handing out "genius" grants to promising en-trepreneurs. Her husband's full-time job was to run the foundation. Seeming to model themselves on Bob Pittman, AOL'ers like Barry Appelman and Mayo Stuntz not only bought planes but learned to fly them. Fractional ownership of corporate jets became the rage. For $772,500 up front, plus a monthly fee of $7,000 and an hourly flying rate of $1,870, companies like Flexjet and NetJet allowed anyone to own one-sixteenth of a Learjet 60—and many AOL'ers did just that.

It was disorienting, being an AOL'er in the late 1990s. You lost your moral bearings. Every day, it seemed, the stock climbed higher and higher. Every day, it seemed, AOL announced another multimil-lion portal deal. The only limits to what the company could accom-plish were dictated by the number of hours in a day. AOL didn't operate just at Internet speed; it moved at the speed of light, almost. "I used to refer to working at AOL as riding on a motorcycle as fast as you can until you lit your hair on fire. And that was what it was like every single moment," recalled Myer Berlow.

Steve Case was AOL's spiritual leader, the father figure. But over time he had come to represent the old AOL, the unfallen world, where something more than money had counted. At least everyone was getting rich together. Even Case no longer seemed bothered by the tacky pop-up ads, banners, buttons, and sponsors that had hijacked AOL. The tension between Case and Pittman had relaxed somewhat, smoothed over by Pittman's success at propping up the stock price. "Steve knew that Steve couldn't be Steve without Bob: at some point, the cult of Steve would have run out of gas because the commercial side, where AOL had to go, was not Steve Case," argued Mark Walsh. "Without Bob, Steve figured out he would have hit the wall."

■ ■ ■

BY EARLY 1999, AMERICA ONLINE WAS WORTH MORE THAN DISney and Time Warner, more than Philip Morris, Bell Atlantic, and even IBM. Those companies' revenues dwarfed AOL's—Time Warner alone was five times bigger—but in the view of Wall Street, nothing could compare with the promise of AOL's growth. Marking its coming of age, AOL was added to the S&P 500 stock index, joining the pantheon of such American blue-chip companies as Exxon and General Electric. To make way for AOL, the S&P 500 dumped from its index the Woolworth Corporation. Founded in 1879 by F. W. Woolworth, the venerable five-and-ten store had been replaced by AOL, a company less than fifteen years old. Make no mistake: AOL was no longer a start-up; it was one of America's most important companies, period. As measured by market capitalization, it now ranked among the twenty-five biggest companies in the world.

By June 1999, the end of its fiscal year, AOL had revenues of $4.8 billion, up from $1.4 billion three years earlier, just before Pittman arrived in Dulles. Even more impressive was AOL's cash flow (its earnings before interest, taxes, depreciation, and amortization): $866 million, more than a threefold increase from the previous year. And there wasn't a penny of debt on AOL's books! Some twenty million people now paid $21.95 a month to belong to AOL, and according to

Bob Pittman, they could be convinced to pay even more. "I am loath to predict the future," he told *The New York Times* with affected modesty. "But people pay 50 or 60 bucks a month for cable. I think people see us as comparable, so we have a lot of headroom to deliver value." Subscription fees from members still made up the core of AOL's revenue. But while advertising had accounted for just 1 percent of revenues back in 1996, it now accounted for 16 percent, and unlike subscription revenue, it was pure profit, gravy. The respected media analyst Tom Wolzien of Sanford C. Bernstein & Co. made a prediction: Within a few years, AOL would generate more ad revenue than either ABC or CBS.

Investors, analysts, and journalists reached for hyperbole to describe AOL's apotheosis. "When the history books are written about the high-tech revolution of the late twentieth century, AOL's name will be there with the likes of Microsoft, Intel, Cisco, and Dell," reported CNBC, the cable news network devoted to business. "America Online is a company so dominant in its space, a company growing so fast, that even as big as it's become, the best may be yet to come." Ryan Jacob, the acclaimed manager of Kinetics Internet Fund, stated: "These days, portfolio managers look at AOL in the same vein as a Coca-Cola or a Gillette." Henry Blodget, the infamous Internet stock analyst, declared unequivocally: "AOL is *the* Internet blue chip."

PART THREE

The Big Deal

AOL and Time Warner, 1999–2000

SIX

IN THE SPRING OF 1999, STEVE CASE WAS YOUNG (FORTY), FA-
mous, and very rich (worth $1.5 billion). America Online, the com-
pany he'd built in just fifteen years, was worth more than General
Motors and Boeing combined. Effortlessly, AOL had just swallowed
up Netscape, an icon of the Internet age, for $4.2 billion. Case's photo
had appeared on the cover of *Business Week* for the second time. In the
company of other media stars and historical figures, he was invited to
state dinners at the Clinton White House. At the World Economic
Forum in Davos, Switzerland, economists and business leaders hung
on his every word. Wall Street was breathless with adoration. Even
the youth of America looked up to him, apparently. "I had a school as-
signment where I had to pick one person I would add to Mount Rushmore," a sixth grader told *The Wall Street Journal* in March 1999. "I
was going to add Steve Case. But it had to be historical, like a president or something. So I added Harriet Tubman. I thought Steve Case
was better than Harriet Tubman."

Steve Case didn't want to be added to Mount Rushmore. He
wanted to stay low, out of sight. The success of AOL was breeding resentment and hostility and envy among his competitors; from his perspective, he was surrounded by enemies. Quietly, as 1999 began, Case
prepared for war. He knew how vulnerable AOL was to an attack by

Yahoo! and also by MSN, Microsoft's fast-growing online service. In itself, MSN's market share was tiny, a sliver of AOL's; but as Case warned his executives, Microsoft was lethal. Remember, in the face of an assault by Microsoft's browser, Internet Explorer, Netscape's share of the browser market had collapsed. The same kind of thing could happen to AOL if they weren't careful. Everywhere Case looked, people were plotting, setting traps for him. Microsoft had thrown out hints already: it would be willing to cut MSN's fees in order to build a larger audience, much of it, presumably, lured away from AOL. What if Microsoft decided to offer MSN gratis? What would happen to AOL?

Those were not empty questions Case was asking. By 1999, more and more Internet providers were turning up, many of them offering their services for free. Out of nowhere, a company called NetZero signed up nearly two million registered users for its free Internet service. AltaVista, FreeInternet.com, WorldSpy, and Freewwweb began offering free Internet access, too. NetZero, whose slogan was "Defenders of the Free World," had lost $15.3 million in its most recent, and only, year of business. Nevertheless, despite (and because of) its dismal balance sheet, NetZero was preparing to go public; more, its hotly anticipated IPO was being underwritten by the respected firm of Goldman Sachs. Profits didn't matter anymore. It was perverse: in the ongoing mania of the late 1990s, turning a profit suggested that the New Economy had eluded a CEO—that he and his company were stale-dated.

AOL may have been an Internet company, but Case was not really a New Economy guy. He was realistic and unsentimental: the minute Microsoft offered to give away MSN for free, AOL would be dead. Face it: Apart from its seventeen million members, what was AOL? The company had no hard assets—nothing tangible like a factory, a film library, a computer operating system, or a collection of cable networks. Cut through the rhetoric, forget the hysteria and euphoria on Wall Street, and, honestly, AOL was nothing but a bunch of people hanging out online and chatting about nothing much.

From Case's perspective, it was only a matter of time before someone noticed the lack of substance at AOL. He believed fully in the Internet revolution, but surely AOL's stock price couldn't keep rising; at some point, Case reckoned, Internet mania, like other versions of mania, would peak, and companies like AOL would deflate. To one another, Case and his top executives admitted the truth: Internet stocks were way overpriced. "We didn't use the term *bubble,*" said Barry Schuler, who was then president of AOL's interactive services group. "But we did talk about a coming 'nuclear winter.' We had currency in our stock and felt it was very important to use it to diversify our business and set the stage for our next round of growth so if the nuclear winter did set in, we'd be better able to survive." To survive the nuclear winter intact, AOL would need the financial equivalent of lentils, split peas, batteries, bottled water, power generators, blankets, and gas masks.

An attack on AOL could come from anywhere, at any time. If Microsoft didn't destroy AOL, the collapse of the stock market would. And without its high-flying stock, what would become of AOL? Case figured it out, step by step: his company's survival depended on hooking up with, merging with, a company with real assets—hard-core, solid assets that would not be vulnerable to an attack by Microsoft— assets that would hold their value even if the nuclear winter set in. In retrospect, the decision to favor hard assets over Internet assets seems obvious; but back then, Case's strategy was so conservative, so old-fashioned, that it was the kind of thing you'd expect from someone who kept cash under the mattress and a cow in the backyard. "Case always understood that this wasn't going to last forever; that the time to merge with a traditional company was then," someone close to Case remarked. "That was Case's biggest contribution."

Something else: By 1999, Case had grown tired of running AOL.

As he confided to someone close to him, he didn't want to come to the office every day. He wanted to devote more time to his family; he wanted his second marriage to last. Still, Case had no intention of leaving his company in the hands of Bob Pittman, who in Case's view was an operator, not the man to lead AOL into the next century. Pittman was a "wind-up CEO," in the words of another AOL'er close to Case.

■ ■ ■

IT WOULD TAKE CASE NINE MONTHS TO REACH THE DECISION TO buy Time Warner. In his typical, meticulous, unhurried manner, he brought together huge amounts of data and studied them; throughout 1999, he called meeting after meeting to weigh the options. With its giant market capitalization, AOL could buy anything it wanted, almost. The only question was *what* to buy. Miles Gilburne, a confidant of Case's and AOL's top strategist, made the first move. A Princeton grad and a Harvard-trained lawyer, Gilburne was in charge of overseeing acquisitions and joint ventures at AOL and thus of positioning the company's future.

Gilburne, forty-eight, was regarded as a genius in his own way. In January 1999, he started filling the giant whiteboard in his Dulles office with scribbles and doodles and diagrams and financial projections. Originally, AOL had defined itself narrowly as an Internet service provider; like the telephone and cable television, AOL was just another pipeline into the home. More recently, AOL had come to resemble a media and entertainment company, providing news and information to its subscribers. Finally, AOL was using new technology to change the way people received information, paid bills, shopped, and communicated with one another. Which of those identities did AOL want to commit itself to? In the long run, which one offered AOL financial security?

While Gilburne was developing AOL's broad strategy, Michael

Kelly, the company's chief financial officer (CFO), was focusing on details of getting a deal under way. In February 1999, Kelly got in touch with Eduardo Mestre, head of investment banking for Salomon Smith Barney. Salomon was an odd choice, and not only because AOL and Salomon had never worked together. For one thing, the firm was an also-ran in the mergers and acquisitions business. Whereas Morgan Stanley, for example, would advise on $1.1 trillion of M&A deals in 1999, Salomon would oversee just $455 billion worth of M&A deals. Furthermore, Salomon had little experience in the Internet sector, ranking a dismal eleventh in Internet IPO underwriting. "I don't even know the names of anyone over there," a baffled technology banker at a rival firm would later say, referring to AOL's choice of Salomon. Goldman Sachs had advised AOL on its $4.2 billion acquisition of Netscape, so it seemed the obvious firm to advise AOL on the next big deal. Nonetheless, Kelly bypassed Goldman entirely; maybe it was retribution for Goldman's leading NetZero's $160 million initial public offering, was the take of some Wall Street observers. But Kelly insisted he'd gone with Salomon for one reason only: Mestre was one of the most talented bankers in the business.

Certainly Mestre's low-key style was in sync with Case's. Unlike many of his competitors, Mestre was understated and discreet. Tall and slim, elegant and well featured, he tended to stoop, as if he wanted to hide his good looks. "Be humble, be bold, and never say never," was Mestre's guiding principle. Already fifty, ancient in the culture of the late 1990s, Mestre had lived through the excesses of the 1980s; he knew the dangers of being added to Mount Rushmore and sticking out. Born in Havana, Cuba, where his father and his uncles had founded and owned the country's principle broadcasting network, Mestre and his family relocated to Argentina after Castro took power. As a teenager, he was sent to boarding school in Connecticut; then he studied at Yale and at Harvard Law School. In 1977, after four years as an associate with the law firm of Cleary, Gottlieb, Steen & Hamilton in New York, Mestre joined Salomon Brothers.

By the late 1990s, Mestre was widely recognized as one of the top telecommunications bankers in the country. Known as the tactician who'd planned SBC Communications's $69 billion acquisition of Ameritech Corp, Mestre had also helped WorldCom outmaneuver GTE Corporation to buy the long-distance company MCI Communications for $37 billion, almost entirely in stock. That was in 1997. It was during the battle for MCI that Kelly (then an executive at GTE) got a firsthand look at Mestre's negotiating skills. In frustration and amazement, Kelly had watched as WorldCom, a Mississippi-based upstart, used its then overvalued stock ("this funny currency," in Mestre's words) to beat GTE's all-cash offer for MCI. From Kelly's perspective, Mestre was the banker AOL needed: he knew just how "funny currency" could be used to buy established companies.

On February 23, Mestre arrived in Dulles to meet AOL's senior team. By that time, Gilburne and Case had narrowed the field. There were three possibilities, they told Mestre, three paths to salvation: AOL could merge with a media and entertainment conglomerate; AOL could merge with a telecommunications company; or AOL could merge with another, established (that is, profitable) Internet company. From Case's perspective, merging with a media and entertainment company made the most sense; he liked the idea. And of the seven major media and entertainment companies, Time Warner, with its cable networks and its powerful branded content, was the most attractive candidate; only Viacom and Disney came anywhere close.

Good, so AOL was attracted to Time Warner; but it was unrealistic to imagine that an august, respected company like Time Warner would be interested in an upstart like AOL. What did Time Warner have to gain? What could AOL offer to Jerry Levin? Asked what he thought of AOL's chances of doing a deal with Time Warner, Mestre told Kelly: "To be honest, I can't see how it can be done. There's just no way they'll accept your currency."

Case wasn't ready to commit himself, not yet. He thought about making a deal with WorldCom. He thought about merging with eBay. He thought about merging with Citigroup. One after another, those companies were weighed in the balance and found wanting. At one point during the summer of 1999, AT&T's CEO, Mike Armstrong, was asked about doing a deal with AOL. He declined: AT&T was in too much turmoil to handle another distraction. Michael Eisner of Disney was approached, too; the idea was ludicrous, he thought. The more Case thought about it, the more he was drawn to Time Warner.

■ ■ ■

THAT SUMMER OF 1999, A HEAT WAVE HIT NEW YORK CITY. DAY after day, week after week, relentlessly, the thermometer climbed over one hundred degrees. There were widespread power failures. Subways stalled and summer schools were forced to close. You couldn't breathe, the air was so polluted. People suffered from heat stroke. In Harlem, people were sleeping on the sidewalks to escape sweltering apartments without air-conditioning and without fans that turned. It was a catastrophe. Mayor Rudy Giuliani lashed out at Con Edison for its failure to maintain the city's electric grid.

Jerry Levin didn't need the Weather Channel to know it was the hottest July on record. But being Jerry Levin, he had more urgent things to worry about than air conditioners and heat strokes and asthma attacks and sleepless nights. What about the future of Time Warner? Yes, when Levin evangelized at meetings, preaching the good word about the digital future, the company's division heads listened politely, then ordered their midlevel managers to devise clever Internet strategies and launch Web sites here, there and everywhere. But nothing much changed. In the spring of 1999, Levin had been forced to disband Time Inc's disastrous Pathfinder portal, but not before it had swallowed up something in the range of $80 million to $100 million. From its inception, no one had really grasped the reason for Pathfinder's existence, nor had anyone figured out how to make money from the portal. The magazines that were meant to provide Pathfinder's content offered as little cooperation as they could. The site's managers fought like street gangs on a long hot summer night. Like New York's electric grid, Pathfinder was a fiasco.

From Levin's point of view, his inspired, visionary plans for Time Warner were being undermined by the dull people around him. What enraged him most was not so much the $100 million they'd thrown away on Pathfinder (it wasn't the first time he'd wasted piles of money on a failed technology initiative). But it was the summer of 1999! By now, everyone who mattered on Wall Street had embraced the digital revolution or was riding on its coattails; yet in the small, blinkered minds of Levin's executives, the Internet barely figured. Some division heads didn't even use e-mail! "They were embedded in the analog world," explained Levin.

Earlier that same year, getting their acts together for Time Warner's big annual off-site strategy meeting with the board of directors, each of the company's divisions had presented Levin and Dick Parsons with their latest five-year plans. Sitting through endless tedious PowerPoint displays, slide shows, and strategic reports, Levin was overcome with despair. It was hopeless. None of Time Warner's divisions had come up with a convincing Internet initiative or strategy, not even the music division, which everyone knew was losing market share to free online music exchange services like Napster. Terry Semel's presentation, glitzy and fast paced, had tried to prove that Warner Bros. was on the cutting edge of the digital age. But when Levin asked Semel for specifics, there were none; Semel didn't have a clue. *What were these men thinking?* Levin asked himself. *What planet were they on?* He wanted to grab his executives by their overpriced collars and scream: *The Internet is here and it's real and it's passing us by! Don't you get it?*

In the sweltering summer of 1999, Levin decided to take matters into his own capable hands. And why shouldn't he? After all, he reminded himself, he'd always forged his own path; and more often than not, he'd been right. It was not for nothing that early in his career at Time Inc. he'd been dubbed the company's "resident genius"! He, Jerry Levin, had had the prescience to put HBO on satellite. He'd embraced cable before it became commonplace. And yes, he had also engineered the brilliant takeover of Turner Broadcasting. Now he'd lead Time Warner into the digital age. As a symbol of his absolute commitment to the Internet ethos, Levin ditched his suits that summer. From that time forth, he'd wear the prep school uniform of Silicon Valley: pleated khakis and open-collared shirts. "I was determined to transform the company—and to do it internally," he later explained. If his divisions couldn't get it together, he'd force the matter from headquarters.

In July 1999, Levin announced the creation of Time Warner Digital Media, a new centralized unit dedicated to funding and building and assembling the company's Internet assets. The job of running Time Warner Digital Media was given to Richard Bressler, Time Warner's chief financial officer. "Digital media is Time Warner's single most important growth area," Levin stated definitively at the announcement. "More than any other Time Warner executive, Bressler is uniquely qualified to lead our company through a revolution that is transforming both our content and distribution businesses."

By all accounts, Bressler, forty-one, was a fine manager and a good man. He'd grown up on Long Island, where his father sold men's suits at wholesale. After graduating in 1979 from Adelphi University in Garden City, New York, Bressler dedicated nine years to the accounting firm Ernst & Whinney, where he eventually became a partner responsible for the Time Inc. account. In late 1988, shortly before Time merged with Warner, Bressler joined Time Inc. as an assistant comptroller. Diligent, reliable, and unpretentious, he was soon noticed by Levin, who took the young accountant under his broad wing. By the time Bressler was named chief financial officer of Time Warner in 1995, he was one of Levin's most trusted confidants and one of his favorite protégés.

Bressler wasn't a visionary or an intellectual or a tech head. So what made him "uniquely qualified" to head Time Warner Digital Media? To many people, his appointment didn't make sense. In reference to Bressler's lack of technical background, a company insider told *Wired* magazine: "I could name 50 other people at Time Warner—well, maybe 25—who knew more about the subject." Another insider noted arrogantly: "His knowledge of new media seemed to be gleaned largely from reading *Fortune.*"

How much Bressler understood about the new media is conjecture. One way or another, though, his appointment exposed one of Levin's greatest weaknesses as a CEO. Convinced that only he, Gerald Levin, had the foresight to transform Time Warner and lead it through the revolution, he discouraged free-ranging debate among his executives and was hostile to ideas that undermined his own. Over the years, as Levin's power base had solidified, he'd become, in his own words, an "imperial CEO." Time and again, he'd assigned competent but uninspired executives to senior posts; many were courtiers, glad to be of use. What counted above all at 75 Rock was loyalty to the CEO. Levin didn't want to know about other people's dreams and visions; he wanted someone to execute his own. When it was time to put his Internet strategy in place, Levin believed Bressler had the right stuff.

Instead of gathering all Time Warner's content into one Web site, as Pathfinder had tried to do, the plan for Time Warner Digital Media was to organize that content into vertical "hubs," separate Web sites devoted to news, entertainment, sports, and finance. Right away, Wall Street speculated that the real goal of Time Warner Digital Media was to create an Internet division that could be spun off in a high-flying IPO. Already, Disney, Viacom, and NBC were working on spin-offs of their Internet assets.

■ ■ ■

JERRY LEVIN TURNED SIXTY THAT SUMMER OF 1999. PREDICTABLY for a man of his age and stature, his thoughts were turning to the legacy he'd leave to mankind. His son Jonathan had died in 1997; since then, he had known that his own life lacked a higher purpose. He didn't just want to be remembered as a CEO who'd improved the bottom line; he aspired to be known for so much more—integrity, for instance; high moral principles; and wisdom. Already Levin had introduced a company wide "Vision and Values" initiative, whereby Time Warner's five hundred most senior executives, guided by outside consultants, participated in day-long seminars and discussions about ethics, workforce diversity, compassion, reaching out, and making a difference. But there was more to do. "I've obviously been an idealist my whole life, and I guess it always bothered me—I didn't want to be a CEO, I didn't want to be a corporate type. But the way it worked out, I was satisfied to live through my son. What he was doing was the highlight of my life," he noted. "I thought at the time [of my son's death] I wasn't going to return to the company. And then I decided, 'Let's see if I can make happen through my position some pretty important things, and carry on in that way.' "

Levin couldn't help but measure himself against Henry Luce. Over the years, he'd read biographies of the great man; now, thinking about his own parting legacy, Levin sifted through Luce's speeches and letters cataloged in the Time Inc. archives. Luce had it all: he was an intellectual, a gifted writer (whose prose, Levin noted, possessed "Presbyterian muscularity"), an innovator, and a brilliant businessman. Even more, Luce was guided by a fine-tuned moral compass. "Luce insisted that it wasn't enough for business leaders to pursue efficiency and productivity," Levin noted in a speech he gave that August to the Aspen Institute. "Those who entered the executive suites of American business had to have a heightened sense of their responsibility to the common good. I share this conviction."

Levin didn't only share Luce's moral compass; he believed that, like Luce, he was ahead of his time. It occurred to Levin that just as Luce had harnessed new photographic technology to create the revolutionary *Life* magazine in 1936, so Levin would bring together media and the Internet to lead Time Warner through the digital revolution. "Organization that can't . . . incorporate a digital intelligence and learn to operate in 'Internet time,' that won't empower their people to pursue the myriad opportunities of this transforming technology, are doomed," Levin prophesied that summer. "For Time Warner, the promise of the digital future is rooted in Luce's legacy; in the tradition of journalistic integrity he created, in the enthusiasm for innovation he created, in the enthusiasm for innovation he instilled, in the commitment to values he insisted on. It's a legacy I embrace and a future I will do all in my power to make happen."

Committed utterly to Luce's values and to the digital revolution, Levin would use Time Warner as a platform. Like Luce, he would become an ambassador to the world, promoting democracy and a free press and insisting on corporate responsibility. It was a sacred trust. In homage to the old Time Inc. of Henry Luce, Levin hatched a plan: In the middle of September 1999, Time Warner's board of directors, top executives, and a handful of the company's most senior journalists would make an eleven-day tour of China. Back in the heyday of Time Inc., in the 1960s, the company had regularly organized two-week trips abroad known as "*Time* news tours"; during those trips, a select group of two dozen or so American executives and Time-Life correspondents would meet with foreign military and political leaders and take the pulse of the world. On the *Time* news tour of 1966, for example, the group had motored through the Iron Curtain, visiting Budapest, Bucharest, Warsaw, Prague, and Belgrade. In 1969, while the Vietnam War was on, the *Times* news tour had made a daring visit to Saigon as part of a sixteen-day tour of Asia. Levin's forthcoming trip to China would be the tour of tours. The summer of 1999 was devoted to planning every stage, every detail, of what he dubbed the "Time Warner News Tour."

On September 22, day number one of the Time Warner News Tour, two planes (the company's brand-new $40 million Gulfstream GV and a chartered Boeing 757) landed in far western China in the venerable Silk Road city of Kashgar. Among the twenty-eight Time Warner board members and executives who came along were most of the company's division heads (Don Logan, Roger Ames, Jeffrey Bewkes, Terrence McGuirk, and Joe Collins), many of the most senior corporate executives (Dick Parsons, Rich Bressler, Joe Ripp, Chris Bogart), and a handful of Time Inc.'s top managers and editors, including Norman Pearlstine, Walter Isaacson, John Huey, and Bruce Hallett. Of Time Warner's thirteen directors, twelve were present; conspicuous by his absence was Ted Turner, who reportedly, when he was told that spouses weren't invited, declared that he couldn't last that long without sex.

As the Time Warner people disembarked at the desolate Kashgar International Airport (which despite its name was receiving an international flight for the first and last time), they were saluted on the runway by a crisp formation of soldiers. In honor of Time Warner and its most distinguished representatives, a military band played the national anthem of the People's Republic of China ("Arise, ye who refuse to be slaves! / With our very flesh and blood, / Let us build our new Great Wall! / . . . Arise! Arise! Arise! / Millions of hearts with one mind / Brave the enemy's gunfire, / March on!").

First on the crowded itinerary was a visit to Kashgar's fifteenth-century Id Kah Mosque, the largest mosque in China, whose imam presented Levin with a ceremonial gown and cap. So proudly did Levin wear his white gown and cap that Dick Parsons started calling his boss "Imam," an honorific that pleased Levin greatly. From Kashgar, the News Tour made its stately way east, cruising down the Yangtze River, passing through the Three Gorges, visiting Buddhist temples, attending state dinners hosted by the governors of various Chinese provinces, and, together with the Carter Center, monitoring a mock "democratic election" in a rural village.

In every town and hamlet, Levin was received like a potentate. Police motorcades cleared the roadways for him; army troops stood by to protect him. Night after night, at yet another dinner hosted by one Chinese dignitary or another, elaborate speeches were made in praise of Levin and his extraordinary career. It was a privilege and a pleasure. "He loved it," recalled one member of the entourage, alluding to Levin. "He just drank this stuff up." One memorable evening, cruising slowly down the Yangtze River under a full moon, the air warm and soft and full of promise, Levin was serenaded (in Mandarin Chinese) by a lovely young woman with flowers in her hair. The scene evokes an old Warner Bros. movie. Before long, everyone on the News Tour was addressing Time Warner's imperial CEO as "Imam." "It was an unforgettable journey," Levin recalled nostalgically. "It was really something."

Levin's News Tour made its way to Shanghai, in time to coincide with the three-day Fortune Global Forum, whose stated topic was "China: The Next Fifty Years." As the Time Warner planes descended into Shanghai's airport, one of the company's directors marveled at the view; the thick, gray, noxious smog that usually shrouded Shanghai had vanished into thin air. Only later would the truth come out: In honor of Levin, his entourage, and the hundreds of executives attending the Fortune conference, the Chinese government had closed all the factories and ordered toxic gas–emitting cars off the roads. Gardeners had been ordered to uproot all the blackened shrubs and replace them with healthy shrubs and bright-colored flowers. Buildings had been repainted.

■ ■ ■

STEVE CASE AND HIS WIFE, JEAN, WERE ON THEIR WAY TO SHANG-hai to attend the Fortune Global Forum. Case wasn't all that interested in global business, but he was interested in Jerry Levin, one of the hosts of the Fortune Global Forum. On the long flight from

Dulles, Case had absorbed every detail of the Time Warner deal book prepared for him by Salomon Smith Barney, and he liked what he saw: the charts, the financial summaries, the projections looked good. In particular, Case coveted Time Warner's cable systems, the second largest in the nation. For some time, AOL had been fighting unsuccessfully to gain access to high-speed lines into the home. The future of AOL depended on cable access. So far, twisted-copper phone lines had served AOL's needs; e-mail and simple text documents travel easily over phone lines. But more and more, as AOL's users started downloading heavy-duty music and video clips, they'd be demanding high-bandwidth Internet connections. If Case could take control of Time Warner's cable lines, he reasoned, the future of AOL would be assured. By the time his flight touched down in Shanghai at the end of September 1999, Case was convinced that Time Warner was the right company for him. But was Levin the right man?

The two men knew each other, vaguely. In 1998, they'd been invited to the White House for a screening of the Warner movie *You've Got Mail* (in which Tom Hanks, playing the ruthless owner of a superchain bookstore, and Meg Ryan, the sympathetic manager of a small children's bookstore, meet in an AOL chat room and, despite their opposing view of capitalism, fall in love, hearts with one mind). As well, Case and Levin had served together on the board of the New York Stock Exchange. And in September 1999, a few weeks before the Shanghai conference, Case and Levin had co-hosted an ambitious one-day conference in Paris with the overblown title, "Global Business Dialogue on E-Commerce," whose grand mission was "the creation of a policy framework for the development of a global online economy." Back then, Levin had found Case to be self-important and cold.

That was then. Now Levin and Case were together in Shanghai, in the illustrious company of other corporate heroes of the late 1990s: GE's CEO, Jack Welch; Enron's Kenneth Lay; Jerry Yang of Yahoo!; Michael Dell of Dell Computers; Ford's Jacques Nasser; American

International Group's Maurice "Hank" Greenberg; Doug Ivester of Coca-Cola; Roger Enrico of PepsiCo; Viacom's Sumner Redstone; MIT Media Lab's Nicholas Negroponte; former secretary of state and Nobel laureate Henry Kissinger; former Secretary of the Treasury Robert Rubin; and onward. On the morning of September 27, Jerry Levin struck the giant brass gong at the Shanghai Stock Exchange. That evening, presiding at the gala dinner, Levin proudly introduced the keynote speaker—his "good friend" Jiang Zemin, president of the People's Republic of China.

On the first or second day of the conference (no one remembers quite when), Merv Adelson, a longtime Time Warner board member, pulled Levin aside. "Jerry," Adelson said to him urgently, "Steve Case just whispered something to me about how we should bring our companies together. Has he said anything to you?" Levin shrugged; he hadn't a clue what Adelson was talking about. *Maybe Adelson had misunderstood?* Levin was too busy to give it another thought.

Rushing from one event to the next, with every tight minute of every tight day accounted for in his itinerary, Levin had barely noticed Case. There were more important people to hang out with. But then, one damp, foggy evening in Shanghai, Levin saw Steve Case embracing his wife, Jean. It was moving, that scene, thought Levin. A man so loving toward his wife, so unafraid of expressing his love openly, in public, couldn't possibly be as cold and calculating as Levin had imagined. He must have misread Case, misjudged him. He has a human side that people don't see, Levin thought, feeling a sudden warm connection to the founder of AOL.

It was reciprocal: Case was dazzled by his host, Jerry Levin. "Jerry had a prominent position there. He was greeted by officials in China basically as an equal," explained an AOL executive who accompanied Case on that fateful trip. "He handled himself at that level—with heads of state—with aplomb, and he was treated as a head of state by the Chinese government."

Following the conference in Shanghai, Case and Levin went on to Beijing, where they attended celebrations for the fiftieth anniversary of communist rule in China. On October 1, 1999, as eleven thousand soldiers paraded in Tiananmen Square like eleven thousand wind-up toys, flanked by rows and rows of tanks and hundreds of bright patriotic floats, Case came to a decision: Jerry Levin would be his business partner. Now, at the turn of the millennium, they'd change history. Everything augured so well: when Case looked up in the sky that day, he marveled at the gorgeous streaks of red, blue, and gold made by a formation of Chinese jets. That night, apocalyptically, Beijing was illuminated by fireworks, smoke, and mirrors. It was blinding.

■ ■ ■

Two weeks later, the phone rang in Levin's office at 75 Rock. "Steve Case is on the line," Nan Miller, Levin's longtime secretary, told her boss. As Levin later recalled, Case didn't waste time with small talk; he went straight to the point: "Jerry? I've been thinking: we should put our two companies together. What do you think? Any interest?"

Levin was caught off guard. Of course he was interested, but he knew better than to respond to such a question over the phone. The law was clear on such matters: if Case *did* offer to buy Time Warner, Levin could be forced to disclose the offer publicly, or at least disclose it to his board of directors. Levin replied cautiously: "I don't think so, Steve. But I'll think about it."

Case wasn't a bit discouraged; he was always a step ahead of Levin. Knowingly, he threw out the bait: If America Online and Time Warner came together, he promised, Levin would of course be CEO of the new giant company, while Case would be chairman. "I'm not interested in being an operating guy," Case told Levin confidingly.

"You understand this business, Jerry. If we merge our companies, you should be the man in charge. I work better at this sort of strategic level."

Levin didn't bite the first time round. "We're not doing a deal Steve," he repeated as if he really meant it.

In retrospect, offering Levin the position of CEO was the deciding factor in the creation of AOL Time Warner. "If he'd said anything else, there's no fucking way I would have gone ahead," Levin would later tell me, remembering the substance of that October phone call from Case. "There was no way AOL was going to run Time Warner." But Case had called his bluff. Having made one painless concession to Levin's ego, Case would now take him to the cleaners. Armed with months and months of meticulous research, Case and his advisers knew how to build the perfect trap. In the words of Kenneth Novack, AOL's vice chairman and Case's closest advisor: "We believed that the only basis on which Time Warner would be prepared to do a merger with us was if Jerry was CEO and it was perceived as a merger of equals."

As soon as he was off the phone with Case, Levin summoned Dick Parsons, Richard Bressler, and Christopher Bogart, Time Warner's deputy general counsel, into his office. Levin was intrigued by Case's offer. It was the perfect solution to Time Warner's lack of digital strategy! America Online wasn't only a successful Internet company; it was a real business. The men who ran America Online didn't play foosball at the office or allow employees to bring dogs and parrots to work; they had MBAs and wore Italian suits. What's more, Levin observed, AOL had a "blue-chip" board of directors that included some of the very people he'd hoped to recruit to Time Warner's board—people like former general Colin Powell and Marjorie Scardino, CEO of Pearson PLC, publishers of the *Financial Times* and Penguin books. Still, Levin was not naive. After all he'd gone through, fending off Paramount in 1989 and dealing with Seagram's creeping takeover attempt in the early 1990s, he was cautious, conditioned to assume that Case was secretly planning a takeover. Let's face it: America Online was worth so much more than Time Warner that a takeover attempt, either friendly or hostile, was a distinct possibility. Levin would not hand over Time Warner to just anyone, he vowed, especially not to a parvenu like Steve Case. Thinking out loud, he said to his advisers: "Time Warner is not for sale." Parsons, Bressler, and Bogart nodded solemnly in agreement.

Still, the men agreed, a battle plan had to be drawn up at Time Warner; otherwise Case might catch them unawares. He was wily. It was very unlikely he would make a hostile bid: Time Warner had a "poison pill" in place to prevent that. But what if Case attempted a friendly takeover of Time Warner? On paper, Parsons said, noting the obvious, America Online was worth way more than Time Warner; if America Online offered a big enough premium to Time Warner's shareholders, how could Levin play down the financial benefits of such a deal? More, if Levin tried to prevent such a takeover, his actions could constitute a breach of his fiduciary responsibilities to his shareholders.

Levin and his sophisticated advisers were pretty confident they could prevent a takeover. They'd start their line of defense by arguing that America Online's market value, while *apparently* larger than Time Warner's, wasn't sustainable; it was an optical illusion. Clearly it was not in the best interests of Time Warner shareholders to exchange their high-grade shares, shares grounded in proven, concrete assets, for stock in a disembodied entity. That would be Levin's rhetorical defense against a takeover. If Case was still determined to do a deal, then the only option was a merger—"a merger of equals." And so it was agreed: Levin would hear Case out; he'd listen to him and digest whatever he had to say. But on no account would he say or do anything that might encourage Case to mount a takeover.

A few days later, on Monday, October 25, Levin called Case back. "I've given your proposal some thought, Steve, and I just don't see it," he began casually. "But maybe you and I should get together,

not to talk about a deal, but just to talk about what you're trying to accomplish, what your values are, and to get to know each other." A
week later, Case flew to New York to meet Levin for a private dinner.
To avoid being spotted together, they booked a suite at Manhattan's
Rihga Royal Hotel, right around the corner from Time Warner's
headquarters, and ordered room service.

It was an unforgettable evening, that dinner of November 1,
1999. Getting to know each other, Case and Levin talked the night
away. They had so much in common—a love of fine wines, for example. More crucially, they were on a common mission. Business was not
just about making money, they agreed; it was about integrity, and values, and the greater good, and making a difference. Both men steered
their courses by a moral compass. With conviction, Case described the
AOL Foundation, whose purpose was to empower the disadvantaged
and disenfranchised and dispossessed by means of the Internet. He described an AOL-funded venture called Helping.org, whose purpose
was to connect volunteers and donors with nonprofit groups. AOL's
My Government was out there, too, helping ordinary citizens connect
to their elected officials. More and more, Case told Levin, America
Online could help people control their destinies and change their lives.

That kind of high-minded talk resonated big with Levin. He too
was determined to serve humankind and to make a difference. By
using the new technology to give people access to news and information, and to one another, Time Warner could reduce ignorance, intol-
erance, and injustice. "I've been building networks all my life," Levin
boasted.

As they uncorked a bottle of red wine, Levin felt a deep kinship
with the young man seated across the table. He told Case about the
painful depression he'd gone through after his son was murdered in
1997. Over time, he explained to Case, it had occurred to him that devoting his life to others was the best way to serve his son's memory—
and what better way to effect change than from his platform as CEO

of the world's most powerful news and entertainment company? "Henry Luce never apologized for being a businessman, and neither do I," Levin said to Case. "Making profits is not incompatible with making a real difference in our society." Case would toast to that.

Over dessert and after-dinner drinks, Levin raised the subject of Luce's will, his final testament, in which Time Inc. was identified as "a journalistic enterprise operated in the public interest." Intending perhaps to discourage Case from making a hostile bid for Time Warner, Levin focused on the wording of Luce's will: it had been central to the outcome of a lawsuit initiated by Paramount Communications in 1989 to prevent the merger of Time and Warner. In the opinion of Delaware Chancellor Allen, Time Inc. was under no obligation to make a business decision based on financial advantages alone. That court decision was so important to Levin that he had memorized Chancellor Allen's conclusion: "The mission of the firm is not seen by those involved with it as wholly economic."

Case was impressed. Levin wasn't only a powerful man worldwide, treated as an equal by such leaders as Jiang Zemin, president of the People's Republic of China. In Case's eyes, Levin was also a sensitive man, a man of integrity. Case marveled at Levin's breath of knowledge: he could quote Greek and French philosophers and passages from the Bible. For his part, Levin was attracted to Case's brilliance, his original mind, and his youthful enthusiasm. Despite the age gap, Levin felt that he and Case shared a common worldview, and now their paths had crossed. How could it have taken so long for two such like-minded people to come together?

By the end of the evening, Levin and Case were of one mind. Together they could create the world's most powerful and respected Internet-driven media and entertainment company. They'd make the world a better place.

■ ■ ■

SO MUCH FOR LOFTY IDEALS AND SENTIMENT. IF CASE AND LEVIN were to bring their companies together, they would have to agree on terms. Sorting out management issues seemed easy enough: the new board of directors would be split equally, with eight members from AOL and eight from Time Warner. Case would be chairman; Levin would be CEO; and the position of chief operating officer would be shared by Dick Parsons and Bob Pittman. Agreeing on the merger's strategic rationale was simple, too: together, America Online and Time Warner would create "the world's first fully integrated Internet-powered media and communications company."

When it came to subject of ownership, however, the two sides weren't even talking the same language. Yes, Case and Levin had agreed that it would be a "merger of equals," but what did that phrase mean? Were the two companies equal in size, in value, in power? Time Warner, with revenues of $27 billion, had seventy thousand employees. By contrast, America Online was tiny, with less than $5 billion in revenues and fifteen thousand employees. In another era, a less manic one, Time Warner might have swallowed up America Online without blinking. But the late 1990s were not normal times, and from the perspective of the stock market (what other perspective mattered then?), America Online, a company with one-fifth the revenues of Time Warner, was worth almost twice as much as Time Warner: $175 billion versus $90 billion. Those two numbers are not equal.

AOL was a "concept company," which is to say its stock price reflected abstract promises of a digital future. Simply put, in 1999, shareholders were ready to pay more for AOL's potential growth than for Time Warner's proven and dependable cash flow. Compared to AOL, Time Warner was considered old world: unhurried and complacent and going nowhere fast. Time Warner's revenues and cash flow were huge; but look how slowly the numbers were growing! AOL, meanwhile, was practically doubling in size every year. As soon as you extended the companies' growth rates out five years and plotted the numbers on a graph, the future was obvious. Before too long,

AOL would produce just as much money as Time Warner—and then more.

AOL's bankers were perfectly clear on what the figures meant. If the two companies combined, AOL would account for 65 percent of the new company, whereas Time Warner would account for 35 percent. Even without a slide rule, you know those percentages are not equal. But Levin wouldn't buy the math. From his perspective and that of his advisers, the deal's exchange ratio—the number of shares a shareholder of one company would receive in the new combined company—should be based, at least partly, on revenues or cash flow. In which case Time Warner's shareholders would have as much as 85 percent of the new company. The difference between AOL's proposed ratio and Time Warner's seemed insurmountable.

Back and forth, back and forth, they went, making the smallest possible concessions to each other each time. On November 9, as the skaters moved round and round the Rockefeller Plaza ice rink below them, Rich Bressler, Miles Gilburne, and Ken Novack had a three-hour meeting at Bressler's office on the twenty-eighth floor of 75 Rock. Over the next few days, Novack and Bressler spoke by phone about half a dozen times. One week later, on November 16, the men got together again. Still, no real progress was made. "It was like trying to mate a horse with a dog," said one of the participants.

A week before Thanksgiving, on November 17, 1999, Case was in New York; first he met with Ted Turner, then with Levin. As Time Warner's biggest individual shareholder, with about 10 percent of the shares, Turner had to be sold on the deal. But Turner was unimpressed. It's not that he was opposed to the concept of merging Time Warner and AOL, but he was suspicious of Internet valuations; besides, he had other priorities. Enraged because Viacom had managed to buy CBS, a deal announced in September 1999, Turner was far more interested in bidding for NBC than in merging with AOL. "If we're going to be big, then let's be big and own one of everything," Turner said loudly and publicly on the general subject of Time

Warner's future. "I want one of the broadcast networks. But I also want us to have a greater presence in the Internet world. I want one of everything." Levin, as usual, didn't pay a lot of attention to Turner, but even he was starting to think that a deal with AOL was impossible. No matter how badly he wanted to merge with AOL, he would never take less than half of the new combined company. "The deal's off," Levin told Case. "I'm sorry."

Frustrated, Case returned to Dulles. He couldn't possibly give Levin half their combined companies. That would be like telling AOL shareholders that their high-flying stock was equal in value to Time Warner's anemic stock. It was out of the question. There'd be a revolt; AOL shareholders would go nuts; there'd be lawsuits. Privately, Case may have feared that a nuclear winter was about to set in; he may have told himself that AOL's stock price was dangerously overvalued. But he couldn't admit all that publicly. Back in Dulles, Case's advisers suggested they return to the drawing board. If a deal couldn't be done with Time Warner, maybe it was time to reconsider their other options. But even as he went through the motions of reexamining other merger candidates, Case became more determined to wait out Levin. He, Case, had never failed to get what he wanted in business; why should this time be any different?

■ ■ ■

ON NOVEMBER 29, WITH MUCH FANFARE, TIME WARNER DIGITAL Media launched phase one of Richard Bressler's new Internet strategy for Time Warner: Entertaindom.com. Using video streaming and Flash technology to display short films and animation, Entertaindom was meant to be a kind of cutting-edge TV network for the Internet. Desperately, pathetically, it tried to be hip and cool. In one cartoon, two figures, God and the Devil, were cast as talk show hosts who interviewed guests such as Keith Richards, Charlton Heston, Santa Claus, John Wayne, and Gandhi (Gandhi promotes a body-building tonic that transforms him into Arnold Schwarzenegger). At the end of each show, online polls were taken to encourage Internet interactivity. Viewers were to decide whether that episode's guest should be sent to heaven or to hell. Entertaindom.com also featured a 3-D version of the *Superman* comic series and classic Looney Tunes cartoons; it ran a live webcast of *The Drew Carey Show*.

Even on its first day of business, you knew Entertaindom.com had to fail. Unequipped to handle the traffic streaming to its site, the Web site's home page flickered and displayed slowdown notices. "Due to the unprecedented popularity of this feature presentation, we cannot accommodate your request," it read.

As the days grew shorter and fall turned to winter, AOL's stock price climbed higher and higher. In the two months since Levin's return from his tour to China, AOL's stock had climbed yet another 50 percent. Meanwhile, just as though its gears were stuck in neutral and rusting, Time Warner's stock had barely moved. Bressler's Entertaindom was a write-off. More and more, Levin viewed his company as an obsolete enterprise. AOL was now worth twice as much as Berkshire Hathaway; it was almost three times as valuable as Walt Disney Co. It was more valuable than McDonald's, Philip Morris, and PepsiCo combined. Everywhere, almost everyone agreed that old media was dead. Even Yahoo! was now worth more than Time Warner.

As the days passed, Case's offer for Time Warner appeared more and more generous to Levin, even gracious. Every little upward tick in AOL's stock price made Levin gasp. From trading for less than $2 a share just three years earlier, in late 1996, AOL's stock was now approaching $90. As AOL itself boasted in a press release, a shareholder who'd paid $11,500 for one thousand AOL shares at the company's initial public offering in 1992 would now own AOL shares worth about $8 million.

It was incredible, AOL's valuation. AOL was unlike anything anyone had ever seen before. The Internet was real, it was huge—and it was passing Levin by. If somehow the two sides could ignore market valuations just for a moment, a deal between Time Warner and AOL could alter the course of history and define the new millennium. Levin would leave his competitors in the dust; his reputation as a visionary would be sealed, his legacy assured. It was too good to drop, the deal with Case. That November, at an investor conference devoted to the Internet, Levin was asked how he planned to get his company's stock price moving again. "I have to do a transforming transaction," he answered indiscreetly.

Levin's indiscretion may have set it off, or leaks may have sprung in Dulles. Or maybe it was only natural, given AOL's stock price, to assume that Case was hunting big game. By December 1999, rumors were flying: something was going on between AOL and Time Warner. Money manager Gordon Crawford, whose Capital Research & Management was one of Time Warner's biggest shareholders, got wind of it. Right away he called Levin. "Listen, Jerry, I'm hearing rumors that AOL is looking to launch a bid for Time Warner. You'd better watch your back." Levin didn't give Crawford the time of day. As for Crawford's prescient warning of a potential takeover, Levin was too focused on the glorious future and his legacy to watch his back.

Meanwhile, emboldened by his rising stock price, Case decided to make another run at Time Warner. On Wednesday, December 8, having received orders from Case to make the deal work somehow, Ken Novack called Richard Bressler. Relieved that Case had come back to him after their brief parting, Levin responded with open arms. Two days later, like reunited lovers determined to prove their commitment to each other, two hearts with one mind, AOL and Time Warner entered a confidentiality agreement, standard practice for companies thinking of merging.

On the morning of December 13, another negotiating session took place in New York. Now, Levin was offering to make the deal a clean 50/50, a real "merger of equals." In response, Case had lowered his former demands, but only slightly. Unlike Levin, Case didn't have his back against the wall: AOL's stock was worth more than ever. Case proposed a 60/40 split. "I was prepared to pay a premium," Case recalled, "but there was only so far I could go."

From Mestre's perspective, Case's offer of 40 percent was much too generous. There were huge implications for AOL: "If we give them this giant premium, the market will think we think our stock is air!" Mestre declared to Novack. "It's like admitting that AOL's stock isn't worth anything."

Maybe AOL's stock *was* air. Maybe it was form without substance. A small but growing number of skeptics thought so. In August 1999, *Upside* magazine rated AOL as one of the nation's twenty most-inflated tech stocks. Clear-minded, intelligent people were starting to say that the mania for Internet stocks was the biggest bubble in history, bigger than the British and American railroad stock speculation of the late 1800s.

It was easy to compare the stock market boom of the 1990s to the boom of the 1920s. Back then, people swore that America had entered a brand-new era of unlimited prosperity, of unequaled opportunity, of democratic vistas, of international understanding, and so on. The automobile and radio and talkies had revolutionized the way people communicated with one another and received information. Productivity was soaring in the 1920s. *Barron's* wrote optimistically about a "new era without depressions." Everyone wanted a piece of utopia with its diamonds and pearls. Celebrities like Irving Berlin and Groucho Marx became stock market speculators, buying thousands of shares on margin. The old ways of valuing companies had gone out of date, it was alleged way back then. Between 1921 and 1929, the value of Radio Corporation of America's stock climbed from $1.50 to $114. In 1927, after Charles Lindbergh's solo flight across the Atlantic, shares in new speculative aircraft companies went crazy.

Was history repeating itself, neurotically, compulsively? Were Internet stocks the radio and aircraft shares of the 1990s? Even Barbra Streisand had turned herself into a stock expert, according to a June

1999 interview in *Fortune:* "She studies business publications like *Barron's* and watches CNBC religiously. She has installed a real-time stock-quote service at home. And she wakes up at 6:30 every morning to catch the opening of the East Coast stock markets."

In the fall of 1999, speaking at a conference, Steve Ballmer, president of Microsoft, had dared to say it out loud: "There's such an overvaluation of tech stocks, it's absurd." He was right, of course. But so what? Mesmerized by the vast fortunes being made, many investors believed they had no choice but to go along for the ride. They were afraid to let go. "It's nuts," conceded one stock trader I spoke to in late 1999. "Everyone knows it, even the believers. But no one seems to care." We're in the middle of a technological revolution, the thinking went. The world is upside down, old models don't apply, it's a whole new game. Either you get it or you don't. Echoing the popular view, Roger McNamee, one of the best-known tech investors in the country, noted with resignation: "You either participate in this mania, or you go out of business. It's a matter of self-preservation."

Jerry Levin was torn. On the one hand, a deal with AOL was a matter of self-preservation. On the other, Levin wasn't a sucker. Case would have to pay a massive premium for Time Warner's shares; he, Levin, would take AOL for all it was worth. No matter how much he wanted to do the deal, he would never ever take less than half of the new combined company—it was an affront, an insult to his intelligence, asking him to accept 40 percent!

■■■

ON DECEMBER 14, ONE DAY AFTER TIME WARNER'S LATEST stalled talks with AOL, Levin sent out a companywide memo that seemed designed to let AOL know he would not be intimidated. Rambling on in single-spaced type for three pages, without mentioning his secret discussions with AOL, Levin assured his employees that he had "set in motion a digital makeover of *all* of Time Warner to ensure a digital focus is integrated into every aspect of the company's operations." On the face of it, the letter seemed a bold defense of Time Warner's Internet strategy. On closer reading, however, it became clear that Levin was trapped.

"Dear Colleague," the letter started off; "Time Warner's robust growth, which should be right in the double-digit range we projected for 1999, reflects our overall strength. But the dynamic consistency of our operating performance shouldn't obscure the fact that the global communications industry is in a period of radical transition. In a breathtaking brief time, a huge digital marketplace has come into being and is expanding exponentially. The technology that defines and drives this new networked community is evolving minute to minute."

The rhetoric betrayed Levin's bitterness: he'd been left out of the "huge digital marketplace." The "period of radical transition" was taking place without him. "We all feel a degree of frustration at the failure of the market to value our company in a way that approximated its superior worth," he continued, using understatement. "It's not my purpose to compare Time Warner to a dot-com company. By whatever measure you use—consistent performance growth, free cash flow, range of content, media savvy, and creative talent—we're so much more."

Coincidently, just as Levin was writing that memo, AOL's stock price hit its all-time high of $95.81: in the past twelve months, AOL's shares had climbed a staggering 329 percent. Steve Case had never been more powerful.

■ ■ ■

As Christmas approached, it seemed to the companies' negotiators that the two sides would never reach an agreement. On the morning of December 23, one final negotiating session took place, this time at Novack's office in Boston. Reflecting the absolute seriousness of the talks, Bressler and Novack were joined by all the top brass: Dick Parsons; Time Warner's banker, Paul Taubman; AOL's chief financial officer, Mike Kelly; and AOL's banker, Eduardo Mestre.

In terms of the exchange ratio, AOL and Time Warner were now closer than ever to finalizing a deal. But as with all negotiations, the final concession is the hardest one to make, and no one would budge. Levin and Case might just as well have been at the beginning of their discussions. Negotiations had ground to a halt. Case was immovable. Levin had to decide: Either give up or make another concession to AOL.

■ ■ ■

LEVIN SPENT THE CHRISTMAS HOLIDAYS IN VERMONT, IN HIS nine-thousand-square-foot country house, built of thick wooden beams hewn from old barns and decorated in southwestern style by his wife, Barbara Riley. Surrounded by Navajo textiles, rustic furniture, vintage cowboy boots, Mexican fiesta masks, decorative moccasins, Native American baskets, folk art, and nineteenth-century tobacco pouches, Levin tried to think clearly. Mostly, like Thoreau at Walden Pond, he spent his days alone. He took long walks in the woods behind the house. In the afternoons he retreated to his small, book-lined study.

Almost every day, he spoke with Rich Bressler by phone. Time Warner's fourth-quarter results were coming in, and they didn't look especially good. Already, Time Warner's stock had fallen nearly 17 percent from its 52-week high in April; it would go lower still when these earnings were released, Levin had to assume. His company's traditional lines of business were slowing down, and for all its hype, Time Warner Digital Media was going nowhere. It could not have escaped Levin's notice that *The Wall Street Journal,* calculating that

AOL's stock had climbed nearly 80,000 percent in the past decade, had just named AOL the "Biggest Gainer of the '90s," easily beating out Microsoft and General Electric among many others.

The situation was obvious: To salvage Time Warner and to leave a meaningful legacy, Levin had to do something bold; and the boldest act of all was to merge with AOL. No matter how Levin looked at it, owning less than half of a combined AOL Time Warner had to be worth more than owning 100 percent of a sinking Time Warner. What other choice did he have? He'd have to accept less than half of the combined company; otherwise he was in danger of getting nothing. From the point of view of eternity, details were irrelevant. They were trifles. Alone in his study, Levin made up his mind. He would take 45 percent of a combined AOL and Time Warner and nothing would stop him. In the long run, who would remember that he had accepted less than half of the new company?

Over and over, Levin rationalized his decision. His vision would drive the new company. After all, he'd been promised the job of CEO. And consider the gigantic 71 percent premium AOL would be paying for Time Warner's shares: for every share that Time Warner shareholders now owned, they would receive 1.5 shares in the new company, whereas AOL shareholders would received just 1 new share. Officially, on paper, if you cared to study the numbers, AOL may have been buying Time Warner; but as far as Levin was concerned, the deal was unquestionably a merger—a merger in which Jerry Levin personally would wind up on top. "I realized that it didn't matter what the numbers were because we were equals," is how Levin would later recall things.

At midnight, December 31, 1999, as the champagne corks popped, Levin made two resolutions for year 2000: He'd shave off the mustache he'd worn for thirty-five years, and he'd become Steve Case's business partner. It was a new millennium, and Jerry Levin was a new man.

SEVEN

MONDAY, JANUARY 3, 2000: THE FIRST WORKING DAY OF THE NEW millennium. It was unusually mild in New York City, somewhere in the mid-fifties. Riding the elevator up to the twenty-ninth floor of 75 Rock, Jerry Levin felt easy for the first time in months. His company would merge with AOL. It would be the defining moment of his career, the "transforming transaction" he'd spent his whole life chasing. All roads, even detours, had led him to AOL. And honestly, whether he wound up with 50 percent or 45 percent of the combined company was irrelevant, Levin told himself, whistling in the dark. Yes, he'd pacify Steve Case by giving him a bigger piece of the new company's pie, if that's what it took to get the deal done. But in truth, he, not Case, would wind up running the combined company. After all (Levin kept reassuring himself and others), as chairman, Case would have no official operating role; his job would be largely ceremonial, cosmetic. Case would preside over the board of directors and make the occasional speech.

That day, meeting Dick Parsons, Rich Bressler, and Chris Bogart, Time Warner's newly named general counsel, for their weekly lunch in one of Time Warner's executive dining rooms, Levin declared himself. "We're going to do this deal," he said once they were seated. "I've thought about it and I'm prepared to accept less than half." Logic and high school mathematics didn't apply to this ground-breaking deal, Levin explained. What he was proposing was the biggest corporate merger in history, and there was no way he'd let it fall through because of an inconsequential 5 percent here and 5 percent there. The crucial thing to remember was this: He would be CEO of the new company, and fully half of the new board of directors would be his own people. He, Jerry Levin, would be left alone to execute this bold vision and control the mammoth company. Everything else was a red herring.

■ ■ ■

THREE DAYS LATER, ON THURSDAY, JANUARY 6, LEVIN AND Bressler took the Time Warner plane from New York to Virginia for a dinner meeting with Steve Case and Ken Novack. Now that Levin had agreed to accept 45 percent of the new combined company, Case had to be convinced to accept the remaining 55 percent. Neither Bressler nor Levin was convinced that Case would meet their terms, but they'd do everything in their power to sway him.

Sitting around Case's living room, the four men glided on social surfaces; they chatted about hockey and *The Sopranos.* Then they moved to the dining room, where dinner was served. Before long, when the timing was right, Levin made Case a firm offer: Levin was prepared to settle for a 45 percent stake in the new company, but not a fraction less. Case was delighted. Recognizing that Levin had just made the ultimate concession, he retreated to his wine cellar and brought back a rare bottle of 1990 Château Léoville-Las-Cases. It was just after midnight when the men finished their chocolate mousse and shook hands. The deal was done.

■ ■ ■

AT ONE A.M. ON FRIDAY MORNING, JANUARY 7, CHRIS BOGART heard the telephone ring. He rolled over in bed, grabbed the receiver on his night table, and heard the voice of Jerry Levin, calling from a cell phone on his way to New York from Dulles. "Chris? It's Jerry. I'm sorry to call so late, but we've got a deal." *Holy shit!* When Bogart had gone to bed, he'd assumed that Case and Levin hadn't managed to reach an agreement. Yet here it was. Like a machine on automatic, Bogart jumped out of bed, pulled on his clothes, drove to the office, hit his speed dial, and summoned Time Warner's legal team. Faiza Saeed, a partner at Time Warner's law firm, Cravath, Swaine & Moore, heard from Bogart at two A.M. "We've made a deal with AOL," he told her. "How soon can you get to the office?"

At six A.M., Saeed broke the news to Robert Kindler, head of Cravath's twelve-lawyer team on the deal. Kindler was on vacation in Anguilla. Chartering a plane to New York, he went straight from the airport to the Cravath office; it would be another three days before Kindler made it back home to suburban Westchester. And on it went, one phone call after another; by the time the sun rose on Friday, January 7, 2000, teams of high-powered lawyers and bankers were hard at work drawing up the documents needed to merge AOL and Time Warner.

Levin and Case were determined to sew up the deal as quickly as possible, before word could get out. Once news of the merger leaked somehow, the damage could be irreparable. For one thing, their companies' stock prices would go wild, thereby undermining the agreed-upon exchange ratio. And more: Levin and Case wanted total control in shaping media coverage of the merger. As soon as the media got even a hint of the deal before the official announcement, second-guessing would start. Levin and Case still needed their deal to be approved by their boards of directors and by their shareholders; federal regulators too would have to sign off on the merger. With those hurdles ahead, they couldn't afford to give anyone time to sabotage their official spin. "This was friggin' Time Warner," Bogart explained. "Everything oozes out of the walls into the hands of the press. We couldn't work on a deal for two weeks and not have it show up in the paper."

Just after nine A.M., Bressler called Novack. The two men had agreed to sleep on the deal—to make sure it hadn't been the wine talking the previous night. "Is there anything that has changed since we talked last night?" Bressler asked.

"No, nothing at all," answered Novack.

That morning, first thing, an e-mail went out at 75 Rock, summoning every senior officer from Time Warner's corporate headquarters to a "must attend" meeting at ten A.M. in Steve Ross's old conference room on the twenty-eighth floor. "I knew it was something big," recalled one person who received the e-mail. He had no idea how big it was. "To be honest, I thought it would be that Ted Turner was selling his shares and stepping down from the board."

To appreciate the reactions of some of Time Warner's top people, you have to know something about Levin's strategy and stealth. With the exception of Parsons, Bogart, Bressler, and Rob Marcus, who worked for Bressler, no one at Time Warner, no one at all, knew anything about the ongoing talks with AOL. The first time a select group of Time Warner employees heard about the imminent merger was that Friday morning at ten A.M.

"We've agreed to a merger with America Online," Chris Bogart announced to the two dozen Time Warner executives gathered around the massive mahogany conference table. "That's the good news. The bad news is that you're all sequestered here until Monday. We've got three days to put this deal together, and until we do, you can't tell a soul what's going on, not even your families."

They weren't prepared for Bogart's announcement. On the one hand, the news was awesome. This would be the biggest deal in history, it was all being done in a weekend, and the people sequestered in that room were part of it. On the other hand, "We were shocked, shocked," one attendee told me, still shaken by the memory of that January meeting. "Never, ever would I have guessed. I barely knew AOL. I mean, if the deal had been with Disney or with any other media company, I might have understood. *But AOL?*"

People who did know AOL were no less shocked. Timothy Boggs, Time Warner's top lobbyist, had spent the past year fending off AOL's demands that regulators force Time Warner to open access to its cable systems. "I was stunned at the news," he said. "I knew the AOL people well; we were in battle with them. They were slippery and very aggressive. These were not people of quality, not in my mind. I was stunned."

Edward Adler, head of Time Warner public relations, and Joan Nicolais Sumner, head of investor relations, sat together during the meeting. They were speechless. *This giant deal, this monumental deal, has been unfolding for months and no one told us about it?* Joe Ripp, the company's chief financial officer, was numb. Levin hadn't consulted him! A no-nonsense numbers man, Ripp had devoted his entire career to Time Inc. and then Time Warner. In 1975, soon after graduating from Manhattan College and joining the accounting firm Ernst & Whinney, Ripp began working on the Time Inc. account. Named assistant comptroller of Time Inc. in 1985, over the next fifteen years he'd worked his way up to chief financial officer of Time Warner. The company was his life. And though he'd never been close to Levin personally, he had regarded himself as a core member of Time Warner's brain trust. To Ripp, the news of a deal with AOL proved that he wasn't part of Levin's inner circle after all. Like almost everyone else assembled in that room on January 7, Ripp had been one of Levin's pawns.

Then there was Peter Haje, one of the most accomplished and respected corporate lawyers in the country, whose legal career had been devoted to Time Warner. Back in the 1960s, fresh out of Harvard Law School, Haje had started working for Steve Ross, helping him assemble his empire, piece by piece. In 1990, Haje, then a partner at Paul, Weiss, Rifkin, Wharton & Garrison, joined Time Warner as general counsel. In his decade of service to the company, Haje had proved to be a brilliant legal adviser; he was also known for his absolute discretion and loyalty. On hearing about the AOL deal, Haje was enraged. Even more, he felt sickened by Levin's lack of respect for him. True, Haje had announced his retirement and on January 1, 2000, he'd been succeeded by Chris Bogart. But still, all through 1999, when the AOL deal was brewing, Haje had been the company's top lawyer. Why would Levin have frozen him out? If in the past Haje had ever had reservations about Levin, if he'd ever questioned Levin's abilities as CEO (and he had), Haje had always kept his thoughts to himself. No longer. Now Haje told friends that the AOL deal was a disaster in the making; he wished only the worst for Levin.

If it ever occurred to Levin that executives like Haje and Ripp would feel betrayed, he probably assumed that the damage would be short-lived. Levin had never been a consensus builder. As one of his executives phrased it, Levin was the company's "switchboard": he maintained control at Time Warner by controlling the flow of information, like a miller with control of the dam. Over the years, determined to get what he wanted on his terms, Levin had figured that the best way to get things done was to do them himself. He didn't need others getting in his way, wasting his time, sowing confusion by dropping in ideas about this and that. By the time Time Warner's division heads were told about the AOL deal, it was too late: the train had left the station, the ship had sailed, the gate was closed. Given more time, could Don Logan, Jeff Bewkes, Joe Collins, and other senior people at Time Warner have altered the deal with AOL? Could they have talked Levin out of it, or at least demanded better terms? Possibly. But at the same time, they could have wrecked the deal; and Levin couldn't afford to take that risk. After all, this merger of equals was the defining moment of his life.

If suppressing other people's views and voices had worked for Levin in the past, it was a major tactical error this time round. To make the AOL deal work, Levin needed the active cooperation of his top executives. But why should they promote the megavision of someone who had humiliated and betrayed them? Someone who had treated them with contempt they didn't deserve? Levin couldn't have known it then, but from the time the AOL merger was announced publicly on January 10, scores of Time Warner executives would do everything in their power to derail it.

Chris Bogart outlined the terms of the AOL deal in full during the fateful meeting. The more he spoke, the more questions he raised in the minds of the Time Warner people gathered in that room. "Why exactly are we doing this? What's the point?" asked one of the VPs in the room. "How long have the discussions with AOL been going on?" asked another. "Will we lose our jobs?" "Who's going to be running the company?" "How long will it take for the deal to close?"

At last, someone asked the overwhelming question: "You're telling us this is a merger, but it doesn't sound like a merger to me. It sounds to me like AOL is buying us. How could that possibly be good for us?" The question hung in the air like a swarm of gnats. Then the moment of recognition: *Levin has sold us out.* For reasons they could not fathom, Time Warner had been betrayed—double-crossed by its own CEO.

■ ■ ■

EDUARDO MESTRE, AOL's BANKER, GOT WORD OF THE IMPEND-ing agreement as he was getting ready for bed on Thursday night, January 6. Mike Kelly called him at home: "How fast can you get your due diligence done, Eduardo?" There were mounds of documents to plow through; data to be sorted; meetings with executives to be scheduled. Proper financial forecasts had to be made. Mestre also needed to write up his bank's fairness opinion on the deal. In order to help AOL's directors vote on the proposed merger, he would have to make a convincing presentation to the board.

"We need a week, Mike; maybe ten days."

"Forget it," said Kelly. "We're announcing on Monday. You've got three days."

Three days! Mestre called Michael Christenson, Salomon's lead tech banker. "Mike, the deal's a go. We've got till Monday. Get to work. Now."

Salomon's media bankers, Kate Brown and Terry Kawaja, got word next. "You're not going to believe this," Christenson told them. "They've agreed to a deal." It was just before midnight.

"You're kidding me!" Kawaja replied. "Holy shit!"

Kawaja hopped in the shower, got dressed, and went straight to the office. For the next ninety-six hours, none of the investment bankers went home. When they did sleep, it was for no more than two or three hours at a time.

■ ■ ■

"SURREAL" WAS THE WORD MOST PEOPLE USED TO DESCRIBE THE atmosphere that Friday morning in AOL's "Malibu" conference room in Dulles, where two dozen of the company's top executives had gathered. Was this really happening? Were they actually buying the world's largest and most powerful media and entertainment company? In the words of one senior vice president who attended the meeting: "I was floored. It was wild. I'm, like, 'Wow!' "

Mike Kelly conducted the briefing on the deal; as if he were planning a military invasion he mapped out each piece of the strategy to complete the due diligence. "All of you in this room are leaving for New York first thing tomorrow morning. You can pick two of your best people to help on this stuff, but don't let them breathe a word to anyone. Got it?"

On Saturday morning, January 8, at eight A.M., two Gulfstream IVs packed with AOL executives took off from Hawthorne, the private airport near Dulles. David Colburn, Myer Berlow, and other top AOL'ers, overstuffed briefcases in hand, were on their way to New York to complete the biggest corporate acquisition the world had ever seen. They were pumped. They were psyched. *We're buying Time Warner!*

■ ■ ■

For three days, from Friday, January 7, to Monday, January 10, about fifty Time Warner executives, bankers, lawyers, and accountants took over the forty-eighth and forty-ninth floors of Cravath, Swaine & Moore's New York office on Eighth Avenue and 50th Street. To feed the troops day and night, Cravath's cafeteria staff worked round the clock. Meanwhile, across town, AOL had set up shop on the top two floors of Simpson Thacher & Bartlett at Lexington Avenue between 43rd and 44th streets. To prevent leaks, secretaries typing documents were given code names to identify the two companies: "Black" for AOL and "Blue" for Time Warner.

Three days. There was no way on this earth that proper due diligence could be done in such a limited time. "If you do a deal over a weekend, you take shortcuts," one of the bankers on the deal told me later, acknowledging privately what he could not say out loud. "In hindsight, it was sloppy."

Some people didn't need the benefit of hindsight to understand that the weekend was more about rubber-stamping the deal than about doing due diligence. "It really was a joke," one AOL lawyer remarked. "It was a done deal. We were just going through the motions so there wouldn't be any lawsuits. I got the feeling that no matter what I uncovered, this deal was going to happen."

The amount of paperwork to be completed was huge. Not only did the core merger agreement have to be written; all the accompanying documents had to be written up as well: employment contracts, deal termination agreements, breakup fees, exchange procedures, accounting methods, pension plans, press releases, capital structures, charters and bylaws, appraisal rights, exchange procedures, and on and on, with clauses and subclauses. And all in just three days.

Investment bankers for both AOL and Time Warner spent the weekend working on their so-called fairness opinion, a written assurance to their respective boards of directors that the terms of the deal were fair to shareholders. If the fairness opinion wasn't grounded in logic—if the financial projections of merging AOL and Time Warner weren't based on real evidence—the directors would leave themselves open to shareholder lawsuits.

From the perspective of Salomon Smith Barney, AOL's bankers, the fairness opinion was a breeze, relatively speaking. Sure, if someone really, truly believed in inflated Internet valuations, it wasn't so easy to persuade him that AOL, whose valuation was twice Time Warner's, should be winding up with just 55 percent of the new combined company. But to almost everyone else, it was pretty obvious that the deal was good for AOL; for one thing, AOL was exchanging its airy, unanchored, fantastic stock—its "currency," in banker-speak—for real assets. As one of AOL's bankers put it to me: "We were paying with Brazilian cruzeiros and they were accepting them as British pounds."

For Time Warner's bankers, Morgan Stanley, drafting a fairness opinion was more complex, to put the matter delicately. On the one hand, AOL was paying a massive 71 percent premium over Time Warner's current stock price. How could that not be fair to Time Warner's shareholders, whose limp stock had appreciated by only 6 percent in the past twelve months? On the other hand, in order to justify the deal and deem it fair to shareholders, Morgan Stanley would have to argue that AOL's stock price was real—that Time Warner wasn't being paid in devalued Brazilian cruzeiros or a mess of potage. That assurance to shareholders required a leap of faith, a suspension of disbelief, and a crystal ball: Morgan Stanley would have to insist that AOL's historic upward growth rates would continue into the foreseeable and not-so-foreseeable future.

In short, bankers acting for both AOL and Time Warner had to make the deal sound perfectly rational on paper, sober and well considered. The wording of their fairness opinions had to suggest that exact science, not hocus-pocus, had made the numbers work. Then again, the bankers' responsibility was only to convince the boards and shareholders of their companies to vote in favor of the proposed deal. What happened afterward wasn't their business, legally. The two bankers, Morgan Stanley and Salomon Smith Barney, were highly, hotly motivated to get the AOL Time Warner deal done, despite anyone's reservations. Huge, obscene banking fees were at stake. That was the bottom line.

How huge were those fees? Salomon's Terry Kawaja would soon find out. Late Saturday night, January 8, Kawaja approached Mike Kelly of AOL: "Mike, listen, I've got to talk to you about our fee."

Kelly was rushing down the hall madly, moving from one meeting to another, documents in hand, cell phone ringing. "All right," he said to Kawaja. "But let's do this quickly. How much do you want?"

"Sixty million," Kawaja blurted out. *$60 million!* It was a number so inconceivable, so inflated, that Kawaja couldn't believe he'd had the nerve to ask for it.

Kelly glanced at the document Kawaja was holding out, a sheet filled with figures justifying a $60 million fee. "Look, Mike," Kawaja continued boldly, "based on fees paid on other deals, we could justify asking $70 million, but—"

Kelly interrupted the sales pitch. When it came right down to it, he didn't give a shit what the fee was; it was a drop in the bucket; it was meaningless, absolutely fucking meaningless. Here he was, in the midst of negotiating a $160 *billion* merger, a merger bigger than the GDP of Portugal, and he, Mike Kelly, was wasting his time haggling over $60 *million*?! It was a gnat on the elephant's tail. He'd had enough; the meeting was over. "All right," Kelly said, pushing the paper back into Kawaja's hand. "Sixty million." As Kelly disappeared

down the hallway, Kawaja stood there in disbelief. Then, with Kelly
out of earshot, he pumped his fist in the air. "Yes, baby!"

"It was the biggest fee and the shortest negotiation I've ever
had in my entire life," Kawaja would later marvel. "You know, $60
million . . . that's a lot of money." In total, the AOL Time Warner
deal would earn Salomon Smith Barney and Morgan Stanley $120
million—$60 million for each firm.

■ ■ ■

AS PUBLIC COMPANIES WITH ANNUAL REPORTS AND NUMBERS
out there, America Online and Time Warner had disclosed most of
the financial information needed to complete the required due diligence. Still, both sides had to be sure they understood each other's
businesses, and more, that assumptions being made about their future
together were based on concrete evidence and real numbers. Typically, that sort of information is written down and studied at
someone's leisure; in this rushed case, however, most of the due diligence was conducted orally. Back to back, day and night, dozens of
sessions were held in which AOL executives interrogated their counterparts at Time Warner, and vice versa. The pressure was intense, as
you can imagine. Time was running out, and there were still vast
quantities of information to process. Mental and physical exhaustion
set in.

As the weekend wore on and people wore out, the two sides
bickered openly. Like a general, AOL's Mike Kelly barked out orders
to his troops. Faster, faster. What a prick, people on the Time Warner
side whispered to one another. Treated like a servant by more than
one AOL'er, Rich Bressler was struck by the crudeness of it all. David
Colburn and Myer Berlow were busy making locker-room jokes—
anything to get a reaction from the uptight, plodding, well-mannered
Time Warner executives, who for their part were offended by the
AOL team's lack of decorum.

Meanwhile, it occurred to more than one member of the Time Warner team that the tension building that weekend might be a sign of things to come—that, after all, the AOL Time Warner partnership might be unworkable. Had they witnessed the fight that took place between Jerry Levin and Steve Case on Sunday afternoon, their suspicions would have been confirmed.

It was shortly after noon on Sunday, January 9, less than two hours before Time Warner's board was scheduled to vote on the merger with AOL. Despite the pressures and time constraints, Bressler and Novack were still on the phone, haggling over details in yet another draft of the merger agreement. In particular, Novack was focusing on one key aspect of the document: the job descriptions of top management in the new company. Pointedly, Case was being described as "non-executive chairman."

"Is this right, Rich?" Novack asked, his Boston twang especially pronounced.

"Absolutely," replied Bressler. "That's what Jerry and Steve agreed on."

"Really? It doesn't sound right to me. Let me talk to Steve and get back to you."

Novack called Case at home. "They're saying you're going to be a non-executive chairman, Steve. Did you agree to that?"

"What the . . . ?!" Case exploded. "That's bullshit! I never agreed to that. You tell Bressler that if Jerry wants me to be non-executive chairman, the deal's off."

Case had never agreed to be a non-executive chairman, he insisted loudly. Why would be have agreed to that? To have no role in the combined company other than presiding over board meetings? The situation was unthinkable. It was crazy for Levin and Bressler to imagine it! AOL was Case's baby, his company, his genius; he had conceived of the merger with Time Warner! Sure, Case wanted to spend more time with his family, he didn't want to report to work every day, and he was glad to leave the day-to-day operations to Levin.

But he wasn't stepping down; no way! He intended to play an active role in seeing his strategy put into operation. He was going to be involved. What sort of crap was Levin trying to pull, anyway? Case instructed Novack: "There's no way I'm going to be some figurehead, Ken, not in a million years. You tell them that."

Novack called Bressler back: "Listen, Rich. I just spoke to Steve. We've got a problem, and if it can't be resolved Steve says the deal's off. He's not backing down on this."

"Okay," said Bressler. "I'll call the old man and get back to you. But I'm warning you: I don't think this point is negotiable."

Levin, "the old man," was furious when Bressler called him. Where did Case get off trying to change the rulebook at the eleventh hour? Up and down Levin swore to Bressler: Case had agreed to be non-executive chairman, period. That was the premise on which the deal had been made. Those were the conditions. Remember that phone call back in October, when Case had promised to make Levin CEO? That's when the two men had agreed that Case would *not* have an operating role in the new company, Levin explained to Bressler; he was absolutely sure of that. Otherwise, he, Jerry Levin, would never have moved forward.

The clock was ticking, the sand was running out, and Time Warner's board was scheduled to meet in less than an hour to vote on the merger with AOL. Novack waited to hear back from Bressler. He wasn't sure the deal would even happen; he'd known Case long enough and well enough to realize that Case wasn't going to back down, not an inch.

By the time Levin and Case actually spoke to each other by phone, Time Warner's board was assembling; it was just before two P.M. "Go take a jog, Steve," Levin blurted out, his head pounding. "You agreed to take a non-executive role." Levin's carefully devised scheme was crumbling. To make this deal work, Case had to be convinced to take a non-executive position; how else could Levin maintain control of the new company? Sharing power was not an option, as

Levin knew from hard experience. He shuddered at the memory of Steve Ross and Nick Nicholas battling for control of Time Warner in the early 1990s. Yet what could Levin do at this point? He was in a corner, trapped. In his heart and soul and ego, the AOL deal was done. Levin was fully invested in it.

To anyone who knew the two men, what happened next was entirely predictable. Case stood his ground, stubborn and unshakable. Convinced as always that he was right, he told Levin that he would not take a non-executive role; unless his conditions were met, the deal was off, *now*. And he meant it. Levin, by contrast, despite his tough, smart, New York talk, withered in the face of this last minute confrontation. He had way too much to lose. Attempting to bully Case into submission, Levin had started off aggressively. ("You've got to have brass balls," was the crude expression favored by Levin and his closest associates when discussing their negotiating tactics.) Then, as soon as he was challenged by his calm and determined opponent, Levin had to back down. The stand-off between Levin and Case lasted only a few minutes. As it turned out, Case would *not* be a non-executive chairman after all. Far from it. He'd have specific operating duties in the new company, as well as areas of authority that included global public policy, technology policy, venture-type investments, philanthropy, and "future innovations." Those weren't the only concessions that Levin agreed to at the last trump. In a most unusual arrangement for a company's chairman, Case would have a handful of top executives reporting directly to him and bypassing Levin, including AOL vice chairman, Ken Novack, George Vradenburg III, senior vice president for global and strategic policy, and chief technology officer, William Raduchel.

If for a fleeting moment Levin had ever imagined he'd sideline Case and maintain total control of the new company, he should have known better. AOL was buying Time Warner: that was the reality of the situation. It was one hell of a way to begin a marriage of equals.

■ ■ ■

IF JERRY LEVIN HAD LITTLE RESPECT FOR TIME WARNER'S EXEC-
utives, he had even less respect for Time Warner's board of directors.
He didn't go out of his way to seek their advice. For the most part, giving them as little information as he could get away with, he generally
made it clear that his decisions were a fait accompli—that they, the directors, were well-paid rubber stamps. Levin confided in no one.
Even directors who had been on Time Warner's board during his entire tenure as CEO didn't feel close to him. He regarded them as "a
necessary evil," in the phrase of one director I talked to.

In turn, most of the Time Warner directors were cowed by
Levin, who wouldn't tolerate dissension on the board. In the event a
director dared to speak his mind, it was pretty clear he'd be attacked
or treated with condescension by Levin. Once, when someone did op-
pose Levin, the director in question was taken aside after the meeting
by a longtime board member. "You may not know this yet," he told his
new colleague kindly, "but you either do it Jerry's way or you don't
stay on this board."

Any director who took on Levin had little chance of winning. To
be fair, that was partly because Levin, with his deep knowledge of
every aspect of his business, was a tough and informed opponent. But
there was something else, too: Time Warner's thirteen directors did
not operate as a team. Directors who quarreled with one another were
not likely to form a substantial block against Levin. "Divide and con-
quer": that sums up the way Levin ran his business and his board. It
summed up his corporate and personal strategy.

The Time Warner board comprised at least four separate fiefs,
the largest of which was controlled by Levin. Of the thirteen directors, six could always be counted on to support him. There was Levin
himself, of course, and then Dick Parsons. Of the outside directors in
Levin's fief, the staunchest advocate was Francis "Fay" Vincent, who,
despite a brief tenure as CEO of Columbia Pictures in the late 1970s,

was best known as the former commissioner of Major League Baseball. Of all the directors, Vincent, sixty, considered himself closest to Levin; still, as he conceded, that didn't mean much. "Even though we are very close, he doesn't call me up just to chat," he noted. "I can't say we're chums." A strapping six-footer who'd attended Williams College on a partial football scholarship, Vincent invariably stood by Levin. As did John Danforth, sixty-two, the earnest, retired senator from Missouri, and "pro-life" Episcopal minister, whose main contribution to the Time Warner board was delivering pious sermons about corporate values. In fact, Danforth's deepest allegiance was to Vincent, with whom he'd attended law school; Vincent had recruited Danforth to the Time Warner board.

At seventy, Merv Adelson and the former opera diva Beverly Sills Greenough were Time Warner's oldest directors. Cronies of the late Steve Ross, they represented the last vestiges of the Ross era, and both were staunch backers of Levin. Sills Greenough (née Belle Miriam Silverman) didn't feel especially close to Levin personally, but as chair of the Lincoln Center for the Performing Arts, she was grateful for his charitable contributions. Adelson had been a Hollywood mover in his heyday. Having sold his television production company, Lorimar Telepictures, to Steve Ross for $1.3 billion in 1989, he had settled into a peaceful semiretirement. Divorced from Barbara Walters since 1992, Adelson was utterly devoted to his new (fourth) wife, the 37-year-old Thea Nesis; the couple had just adopted their first child.

Of the seven remaining directors, Reuben Mark was the thorn in Levin's side, the stone in his shoe, the fly in the ointment. The longtime CEO and chairman of Colgate-Palmolive, Mark, age sixty, was smart, opinionated, critical, and quick to challenge Levin. A gruff, tough-talking, no-nonsense New Yorker, Mark was not well liked by his fellow directors; thus, he rarely made any headway as Levin's opponent. The objections he did make were drowned out by Vincent, then by Ted Turner, who would jeer, only partly in jest, "Reuben, you make toothpaste! What do you know?"

Turner, being Turner, was probably the least predictable director on the Time Warner board. Sometimes, on a whim, he'd vote with
Levin; other times, losing his temper and his cool, he'd launch into a
long, loud rant about Levin's errors and omissions. With few allies on
the board, however, Turner was generally seen as a loose cannon, his
one loyal supporter being J. Carter Bacot, sixty-seven. Back when he
was CEO and chair of the Bank of New York, Bacot had supported
the cable industry by approving massive loans to Turner Broadcasting
and to John Malone's Tele-Communications Inc. After Turner
merged his company with Time Warner, he was given two seats on
the board: one he took for himself, and, on the advice of his friend and
adviser John Malone, he elected Bacot to the other.

That left just four directors. Gerald Greenwald, sixty-five, and
Stephen Bollenbach, fifty-seven, had joined the Time Warner board
in 1997. At the time, it was thought that they would shake up the insular Time Warner board, which, in a singular honor, had just been
named by *Business Week* as one of America's twenty-five worst boards.
Greenwald was very able. As the retired CEO and chairman of UAL
(United Airlines's parent company), and as the former vice chairman
of Chrysler Corporation, where he'd helped bail the auto company
out of bankruptcy, Greenwald had years of experience to offer Time
Warner. He didn't seem to be all that devoted to his work on the
board, however. Busy starting a private equity fund, he didn't appear
to follow the details of Time Warner's business, nor did he challenge
Levin. On the other hand, Bollenbach, president and CEO of Hilton
Hotels Corporation, did live up to his promise. A well-regarded deal
maker, financially sophisticated, and able to build consensus, Bollenbach was perhaps the best of the Time Warner directors. Carla Hills,
the former U.S. trade representative, and Michael Miles, former chair
and CEO of Philip Morris, were first-rate, too. But on a board of thirteen, three directors couldn't be expected to make much of an impact.
All in all, the Time Warner directors were no match for Jerry Levin.

In brief, the board of Time Warner was railroaded into approving the deal with AOL. Given only a few days' notice of the special board meeting that Sunday, members had little information. How could they have been expected to make an informed decision? Then again, let's imagine for a moment that the thirteen directors *had* been given time to consider the AOL deal thoroughly, line by line, implication by implication. It's doubtful things would have turned out differently. It's unusual for corporate boards to vote against their CEO.

Despite the last minute summons, twelve Time Warner directors attended the board meeting in person. The one director who could not be present, Carla Hills, spent the whole meeting connected by phone from China, where she was traveling on business. Beginning at two P.M. and lasting seven hours, the meeting was exhausting. From all accounts, it was like a country fair, complete with salespeople promising eternal life, a buoyant stock market, and cures for everything under the sun. The most dazzling performance was put on by Mary Meeker, Morgan Stanley's celebrity Internet analyst. Like someone leading a religious revival, Meeker implored the thirteen directors of Time Warner to embrace the digital age. Preaching the glories of a future life with AOL, Meeker ridiculed financial metrics that valued concrete assets over the world to come. They had to have faith, she told the directors. Redemption was at hand, and Time Warner would be saved by AOL. She concluded with a commonplace of high drama: "Henry Luce and Steve Case were separated at birth." After a series of hardships, shipwrecks, and mistaken identities, Steve Case and Henry Luce (reincarnated as Jerry Levin, I guess) had recognized each other by the marks on their signet rings, or whatever.

Meeker's inspired and not disinterested speech was followed by an impassioned presentation by Paul Taubman, the lead mergers and acquisitions banker in Morgan Stanley's media and telecom department. Taubman was followed by the indomitable Jerry Levin. One director recalled: "Looking back, it occurred to me that there must have been a few dress rehearsals, because they all sang from the same hymnbook. I felt uncomfortable at the lack of thoroughness."

Lasting only two hours, the AOL board meeting was less memorable and less dramatic. The only board member who opposed the deal, slightly, was Franklin Raines, chairman and CEO of Fannie Mae, who questioned the logic of buying Time Warner rather than another, cheaper media and entertainment company. "Michael," he said, addressing Mike Kelly, who had just finished his presentation, "what I don't understand is why you picked Time Warner. It's the most expensive one. It's got the highest multiple. It seems to me we've overpaying." Raines couldn't know that his question was way off the mark; AOL had bought Time Warner for a song.

Even though the AOL board meeting had started much later than Time Warner's, it was adjourned so quickly that AOL's top executives and advisers had to sit around for hours, waiting for news from the other side. For some people the delay was nerve-racking. What if the Time Warner board voted against the deal? It was unusual, but not unheard of, for a deal to collapse at this late stage. Eduardo Mestre, for one, was unsettled, anxious. Waiting in his Manhattan apartment to hear the outcome, he convinced himself it wouldn't happen. *This is too good to be true.* This is too good to be true, he kept telling himself, until the phone rang.

Finally, when it came time to vote, all the Time Warner directors were in favor of the deal. Any reservations they may have had were not voiced that Sunday; exhausted, they voted the way Levin wanted them to vote. So joyless were the proceedings, however, that Ted Turner demanded a repeat vote. "Don't you think we ought to vote more enthusiastically?" Turner asked them. "You might as well go out of the locker room at halftime with everybody giving high fives." And so it was that Time Warner's board of directors voted a second time, wholeheartedly approving the sale of their illustrious firm to an Internet company not yet fifteen years old—a company with a single product and with one-fifth the revenue of Time Warner. It was, as the media would soon report, a historic moment.

■ ■ ■

DESPITE ALL THE EFFORTS TO KEEP THE NEWS UNDER EVERY-
one's hat, rumors of a deal between AOL and Time Warner finally
leaked out. Shortly after one A.M. on Monday morning, only a few
hours after the Time Warner board had voted for the deal, Peter
Gumbel, Los Angeles bureau chief for *The Wall Street Journal,* got a
phone call at his home in Pacific Palisades. It was ten P.M. in Los Angeles. On the line was one of Gumbel's best sources in Hollywood:

"I've got a big scoop for you, Peter. There's going to be a deal announced tomorrow morning between Time Warner and America
Online."

"Some sort of merger?" asked Gumbel.

"That's how they're presenting it, but it's really an acquisition."

"What?! Really? Who's buying whom?"

"Who's got the best currency?" the source answered rhetorically.

Gumbel, who'd been covering Hollywood for *The Wall Street
Journal* since 1996, trusted his source. Still, he couldn't believe what he
was hearing. AOL was *buying* Time Warner? If it was true, it would
be the biggest scoop of his career. Frantically, Gumbel called every reporter in *The Wall Street Journal* empire who'd ever covered any part
of AOL or Time Warner. On the East Coast, where it was now nearing one-thirty A.M., he dragged colleagues out of bed: "Call all your
sources, now. We need to find out if this is true."

Kara Swisher, who covered Silicon Valley for *The Wall Street
Journal* and had written a book about AOL in 1997, went online immediately. As her instant messaging program opened up, her "buddy
list" revealed that dozens of her AOL sources were online. She knew
something very big was up; it was the middle of the night. But the
minute she began sending messages to her sources, asking them to
confirm the rumor, they logged off, avoiding her. Meanwhile, in New
York, Martin Peers, who'd covered Time Warner for many years, was

madly calling his sources. Amazingly, one of the top public relations officers at Time Warner actually answered his cell phone: he wasn't asleep; he was in a meeting! It was just before three A.M. in New York.

"We've just heard that AOL is buying Time Warner. Can you confirm?" Peers asked quickly.

"Yes, it's true—but don't quote me," came the response. Bingo!

Gumbel called the night editor at Dow Jones Newswires (whose parent company owns *The Wall Street Journal*). "I've got a huge scoop coming your way any second. It's going to knock your socks off, but it's not a hoax. We've got it all confirmed." At exactly 3:00 A.M. EST, an unbelievable headline rolled across the Dow Jones Newswires: "Time Warner in Pact to Merge with America Online—Sources." Two minutes later, at 3:02 A.M., two more headlines rolled across the wire: "AOL's Steve Case to Be Chairman of New Company"; and "Time Warner's Gerald Levin to Be CEO of New Company."

CNBC Europe, which is co-owned by Dow Jones and NBC, picked up the story almost immediately. Bloomberg News followed twenty-two minutes later. By 3:38 A.M., Gumbel had added a story to the headlines. Appearing simultaneously on the Dow Jones News-wires and *The Wall Street Journal*'s Web site, the item was 212 words long:

LOS ANGELES (Dow Jones)—Time Warner Inc (TWX) and America Online Inc (AOL) are expected to announce a stock-for-stock merger early Monday, according to people familiar with the situation.

Details of the deal weren't immediately available.

America Online Chairman and Chief Executive, Steve Case, is expected to be named chairman of the merged company, while Time Warner's Chairman and Chief Executive Gerald Levin will be chief executive.

People briefed on the transaction said AOL share-holders are likely to hold a majority stake in the merged company of just over 50%. AOL currently has a market capitalization that is about twice that of Time Warner, but the deal's terms are unlikely to value AOL as highly, according to these people.

AOL has a market capitalization of about $164 billion, while Time Warner has a market capitalization of $83 billion.

By uniting a major media conglomerate with a leading Internet company, the transaction is likely to have major repercussions on both industries. It comes at a time when many big media companies are struggling to figure out how to harness the power of the Internet, and when Internet companies are increasingly looking to put entertainment and other content on their Web sites to attract more customers.

By the time America woke up on Monday morning, January 10, the news was everywhere. It was incredible, crazy news. And nothing else on the planet mattered that day. This was the biggest merger ever! An Internet company, AOL, was buying the world's biggest and most important media and entertainment company! For $165 billion! Was it really true? Could it be true?

Driving to work that morning and hearing on the radio that their company was buying Time Warner, more than one AOL'er reported nearly driving his high-end car off the road. In New York, getting dressed or eating breakfast, Time Warner employees froze in front of their television sets, in shock. Everyone was caught off guard. Jack Haire, president of Time Inc.'s Fortune Group, heard about the deal when he phoned his office from an American Airlines flight somewhere in the air between Denver and Detroit. "So, what do you think of the merger?" his secretary wondered.

"What merger?" he asked.

"With AOL," she said.

"Who are they merging with?" asked Haire.

On Wall Street, astonished stock traders were glued to CNBC's *Squawk Box.* It was unreal. In London, where the markets had been open for hours, the stocks of both Time Warner and AOL had already surged wildly. Meanwhile, executives at competing media and entertainment companies felt their throats tighten, as if they were under attack. "My first thought was, 'Oh, my God,' " recalled Edgar Bronfman Jr., head of Seagram, which controlled Universal Studios and Universal Music Group. Driving into Manhattan from his country house, Henry Luce III answered his cell phone: the company his father had founded in 1929 was being bought by an Internet upstart, he was told. For Luce, it was as if John F. Kennedy had just been shot. As if the *Challenger* shuttle had just exploded into smithereens. It was a tragedy.

To announce "the first global media and communications company of the Internet century," the official press conference was held at ten A.M. that Monday morning in the Equitable Center's five-hundred-seat auditorium in midtown Manhattan. Coincidently, as Jerry Levin noted, it was ten years to the day since Time and Warner had come together.

Notebooks in hand, reporters crowded inside the auditorium. News cameramen jostled one another to get a clear and unimpeded view of the proceedings. Yet the press conference felt more like a choreographed awards ceremony than a news briefing you'd take seriously. Financial matters were barely addressed. Up on the big stage, illuminated by spotlights and the ongoing bursts of flashbulbs, Jerry Levin and Steve Case hugged each other and high-fived. This was a merger of equals, they assured the assembled throng; theirs was a partnership made in heaven, a love affair brokered by fate. "Jerry and I have become close friends over the past year," the 41-year-old Case confided. Glowing with pride, Levin concurred: "You can look at body language up here and see the interaction and the relationships that already exist: we've become a company of high fives and hugs."

Signalling his firm commitment to the New Economy, Levin, age 60, wore a recognizable Silicon Valley outfit—rumpled khakis and an open-collared shirt. Case wore a conservative dark suit. Behind the two men, seated in a row of wood-and-canvas director's chairs, and looking ecstatic, were the top executives of both companies, including Mike Kelly, Bob Pittman, Dick Parsons, and Ted Turner. Expressing his unalloyed support for the deal, Turner raved: "Shortly before nine P.M. last night, I had the honor and privilege of signing the piece of paper that irrevocably cast a vote, the first vote taken, a vote of my one hundred million shares more or less, for this merger. I did it with as much or more excitement and enthusiasm as I did when I first made love some forty-two years ago."

Levin went further than that. Asked by someone how he could justify accepting AOL's stock as legitimate currency, he proclaimed in circular logic: "I accept the market capitalizations in the Internet space because I think something profound is taking place. While most people may have some difficulty with those valuations, in fact, to me, it's really quite simple: it's a belief that the present value of future cash flow is so significant that that's how you justify it." You justify the future by the future. Later on, he elaborated, telling a reporter: "The new media stock-market valuations are real. . . . [AOL's] valuation is real, and I am attesting to that."

The next day, AOL Time Warner's forthcoming merger made the front page of every newspaper in the country. The banner headline in the usually reserved *New York Times* took up three lines and was an inch and a half high:

AMERICA ONLINE AGREES TO BUY

TIME WARNER FOR $165 BILLION;

MEDIA DEAL IS RICHEST MERGER

In addition to its front-page story, *The New York Times* ran fourteen articles about the deal that day. *The Washington Post* ran fifteen articles; *the Wall Street Journal,* twenty-one. Every nuance of the deal's conception, gestation, and birth was examined under microscopes and dissected. The deal was an "awesome megadeal" and "a fusion of guts and glory"; it was "the deal of the century" and "a mega-marriage of earth and cyberspace"; and so on, in giant-speak. Beneath a tall, clever headline that read, YOU'VE GOT DEAL, the *New York Post* devoted its whole cover to a photograph of Levin and Case posing as the happy couple; the subhead read, "Ted Turner: It's Better Than Sex."

The AOL Time Warner merger made the cover of all the major weekly magazines. Breathlessly, *Business Week* proclaimed that the deal was evidence of a new world order. "The pattern is clear," the magazine's cover story read. "The digital will prevail over the analog, new media will grow faster than old, and the leaders of the Net economy will become the 21st century Establishment." Roger McNamee, the well-known Silicon Valley venture capitalist and investor, attested to *Time* magazine: "Let's be clear: This is the single most transformational event I've seen in my career."

There were skeptics, of course; there always are, and they inevitably put a damper on things. One skeptic was Nick Nicholas. Nearly a decade after he was betrayed and then deposed by Jerry Levin as CEO of Time Warner, Nicholas gave *Wired* magazine his opinion of the AOL Time Warner deal. "It's a brilliant deal for Steve Case. From the view of a Time Warner shareholder, I just don't get it," he answered matter-of-factly, a man of experience. "Case is using inflated Internet wampum to buy real assets."

Likewise Carol Loomis, an editor-at-large for *Fortune* (a Time Warner publication), who may have been the most outspoken critic of the AOL deal. In the forty-eight years she'd worked at *Fortune,* Loomis had earned a reputation as one of the canniest, most independent business journalists of her time. Accounting was her specialty; and to Loomis's keen eye, the hyped-up numbers of the AOL Time Warner deal didn't make sense. They were a sleight of hand. Line by line, in an article for *Fortune*'s issue of February 7, Loomis untangled

and unraveled the math, concluding that the chance of the deal working as promised was as likely as "pushing a boulder up an alp."

No one listened to *Fortune*'s Cassandra; besides, it was too late.
Most people out there didn't pretend that stock market valuations
were based on real math and bottom lines. Why were Nick Nicholas
and Carol Loomis focusing on numbers? That sort of approach was,
like, so two years ago! Acknowledging the fuzzy math behind the
AOL Time Warner deal, an analyst for J. P. Morgan spoke for many
on Wall Street when he stated: "Frankly, it is difficult to predict the
true potential of this new entity, but we know it's big."

On the day of the AOL Time Warner announcement, stock
trading was frenetic. The Nasdaq composite index posted its biggest
single-day gain ever: a 167-point increase that pushed the Nasdaq up
over 4000. Time Warner's shares went wild, soaring on January 10 by
almost 40 percent to close at an all-time high of just over $90. You'd
think that Time Warner was a hot Internet stock if you didn't know
otherwise! Levin was triumphant. Turner was in the clouds: in one
day, the value of his Time Warner holdings rose by $3 billion to
around $10 billion.

AOL shareholders were more restrained. Fervent believers in
the glorious New Economy and things to come, they couldn't understand why Steve Case had hitched his high-flying cart to a lame horse.
Their beloved AOL stock was trading at fifty-five times cash flow! By
contrast, Time Warner, an old, slow media firm, was trading at just
fourteen times cash flow. Based on AOL's market capitalization,
AOL's shareholders should have received 68 percent of the new combined company; instead, they were getting a mere 55 percent. Why on
earth would Case have paid such an outlandish premium for a
broken-down nag?

Whether or not you admired the deal, one thing was certain: It
was a "transformational event." Everyone agreed on that. In Internet
chat rooms and trading floors, speculations began: Who would be
next? Internet analyst Henry Blodget thought that AOL would now

go after Wal-Mart. Others said Yahoo! would buy Disney. Some said
Microsoft would take out Viacom. In response to the unfounded rumors, Disney's stock jumped 15 percent on January 10, the News Corporation 19 percent, Seagram 11 percent, and Viacom 9 percent.

Within the media and entertainment companies themselves, un-
certainty and doubt set in. Rupert Murdoch, chief executive of News
Corp., explained: "You suddenly realize, from being a reasonable-
sized company you are pretty much a minnow in a pool with a very
big fish in it." In the face of this megamerger of AOL and Time
Warner, a company on steroids, could traditional entertainment companies survive? Responding to that question, and reflecting a widely
held view, pundit Peter Huber wrote apocalyptically: "For the old
media, now it's go digital or die." Concurring with Huber, an
investment banker told *The Wall Street Journal:* "Everyone [in the
media and entertainment business] is trying to figure out where they
go next. There's not a communications or media company that isn't
trying to figure that out."

Overnight, it seemed, everything had turned upside down. It
was a new world. The combination of AOL and Time Warner would
apparently transform American business as it once was. "By assembling more assets and audiences and advertisers for the new digital
marketplace than anyone has previously even thought of, [AOL Time
Warner] sees a chance to move so far ahead that others won't catch up
for years," *Business Week* informed its readers. AOL boasted thirty
million subscribers and the most powerful brand on the Internet. Its
partner, Time Warner, the world's biggest and most powerful media
and entertainment company, had assets that included Warner Bros.
Pictures and New Line Cinema; the Warner Music Group; and Time
Inc., the country's largest consumer magazine publisher. It also
owned Time Warner Cable, the country's second-largest cable system; Warner Bros. Television (which produced *ER, The West Wing,*
and *Friends*); Warner Books; the cable networks CNN, HBO, TNT,

and the Cartoon Network; the WB Network; and even a baseball team, the Atlanta Braves.

The marvelous future envisioned for the combined AOL and Time Warner was a sure thing. The new company would fulfill every promise of the digital revolution, all the wonders foretold by sooth-sayers. Overnight, by tapping into AOL's network, Time Warner would reach deep into the homes of tens of millions of new customers. As for AOL, it would use Time Warner's high-speed cable lines to de-liver Time Warner's branded magazines, books, music, and movies. As soon as Time Warner's creative content was converted from ana-log to digital, consumers would access that proprietary content in all sorts of unforeseen ways: through their cell phones and computers, their PalmPilots, and their television sets. Together, as one, with an awesome 130 million "subscription relationships" in total, AOL Time Warner would be unstoppable. "We're at the cusp of what we think will be a new era as the television and the PC and the telephone start blurring together and the promise of the Internet—the promise of in-teractive personalized services—really moves out to the world at large," Steve Case said. "And that's really what's exciting about this company. We think we have a unique opportunity to really improve people's lives."

Consumers weren't going to be the only beneficiaries of those grand promises; shareholders of the company would be rewarded greatly. Levin and Case were quite sure of that: in 2001, AOL Time Warner's first year as a combined company, its cash flow would climb by a remarkable 30 percent to $11 billion. Moreover, Levin assured re-porters and Wall Street, cash flow would continue to climb by 25 per-cent a year thereafter. Case stretched his elastic imagination, too, prophesying that within five years, AOL Time Warner would be the world's biggest company—bigger than Microsoft and General Elec-tric, among others—as measured by stock market value. According to AOL's Bob Pittman, the man who would become co–chief operating officer of the new company, the slow-moving Time Warner would from this time forth take off at Internet speed: "All you need to do is put a catalyst to [Time Warner] and in a short period you can alter the growth rate. The growth rate will be like an Internet company."

Pittman was right. AOL Time Warner, like other Internet companies, was doomed.

PART
FOUR

"Surviving is Winning"

AOL Time Warner,
2000–2003

EIGHT

FAMOUSLY, BACK IN 1941, HENRY LUCE HAD CALLED THE TWEN-
tieth century "the American Century." In January 2000, announcing
the takeover of Time Warner, Steve Case called the twenty-first century "the Internet Century."

To some observers, the AOL Time Warner deal was a social and
political allegory: rising out of nowhere in just fifteen years, a bunch of
Internet cowboys from Dulles, Virginia, had taken over one of the
grandest institutions in America. "A company that isn't old enough to
buy beer," marveled *The Wall Street Journal,* "has essentially swallowed an ancien régime media conglomerate that took most of a century to construct."

The upstarts had triumphed. In the raging bull market of the
late 1990s, everyone and his uncle could dream of becoming the next
Steve Case, the next Internet billionaire. In early March 2000, two
months after the AOL Time Warner deal was announced, the Nasdaq composite index, driven by Internet stocks, closed above 5000 for
the first time ever. Just four months earlier, in November 1999, the
Nasdaq had closed above 3000—an inconceivable benchmark then.
The Dow Jones Industrial Average peaked in early 2000, stopping
just short of 12,000. Americans were in the grip of stock market
mania, and everyone was in on the act, watching CNBC, reading *Bar-*

ron's, tracking stock tickers, getting stock tips, and making money. Owning stocks became the ultimate expression of democracy in America.

One of the hottest-selling books of late 1999 and early 2000 was *Dow 36,000: The New Strategy for Profiting from the Coming Rise in the Stock Market* by James Glassman and Kevin Hassett. The market was still undervalued, and stocks were no riskier than bonds, the book argued. "It is impossible to predict how long it will take for the market to recognize that Dow 36,000 is perfectly reasonable," Glassman and Hassett wrote in good faith. "Our own guess is somewhere between three and five years, which means that returns will continue to average about 25 percent per year."

The best was yet to come, the Emerald City was ahead—and not only in the view of Glassman and Hassett. To quote one of Wall Street's own fortune-tellers, Ralph Acampora of Prudential Securities: "Now that we've closed above 5000, I think we can see Nasdaq 6000 in the next 12 to 18 months."

Acampora made that heady prediction on March 10, 2000. As it happened, that very day marked the peak of the market. Within the space of three weeks, from late March to mid-April 2000, the Nasdaq composite index lost one-third of its value.

■ ■ ■

BY THE TIME SHAREHOLDERS OF AOL AND TIME WARNER GOT around to voting on the merger, in late June 2000, AOL's stock had fallen precipitously, from $94 to $53. The stock market was exhausted. Underfinanced dot-coms were folding their tents, pulling up stakes, and leaving town. Investors cared about financials again—not just revenues, but actual profits. Stocks of hot new tech companies could no longer be expected to double or triple on the first day of their IPOs; in fact, there *were* no more IPOs of tech companies. Pets.com had been the last pom-pom waver of dot-com IPOs. In its first few days as a public company, in February 2000, shares in Pets.com lost a third of their value; nine months later, the company was out of business.

The stock of AOL was like a dog chasing its tail: if Internet companies were in trouble, they wouldn't be spending money on advertising; if they weren't spending money on advertising, what would happen to companies like AOL? Analysts like Holly Becker (Lehman Brothers), Henry Blodget (Merrill Lynch), and Andrea Williams Rice (Deutsche Bank Alex. Brown) suggested that any company that depended on online advertising—AOL and Yahoo!, for instance—could slow down.

Baloney, was Steve Case's response. He couldn't attest to the shape Yahoo! was in, of course; but as far as AOL was concerned, it was a thing apart, a company unlike other Internet companies. In Tysons Corner, Virginia, where more than five hundred AOL shareholders gathered on June 24 to vote on the impending merger with Time Warner, Case explained away AOL's tumbling stock price: "What's happening really has less to do with AOL and less to do with the merger and more to do with what's happening in the sector," he assured his constituency, implying that AOL had little in common with garden-variety Internet stocks. "Almost every company we compete with, ranging from Yahoo! to Amazon to Microsoft to AT&T, is down substantially more than we are." Shareholders believed every word. In June 2000, 99 percent of Time Warner's shareholders and 97 of AOL's shareholders approved the terms of the AOL Time Warner deal.

A few weeks later, AOL reported record results for its fiscal 2000; true to Case's promise, business was better than ever. Revenues were up 43 percent to $6.9 billion; net income was up 59 percent to $1.2 billion. What's more, AOL's advertising and commerce sales had *doubled* to $2 billion. "To put this in perspective," Bob Pittman boasted during a July 20 conference call with analysts and investors, "we are getting more advertising dollars than any single U.S. advertising vehicle except for the top four broadcast networks."

The most impressive, reassuring part of AOL's year-end results was the company's advertising backlog—money coming to AOL in the near future from contracts that had already been signed. The backlog was $3 billion, a figure so immense that it suggested AOL was immune to a downturn in the advertising market. "Our backlog at the end of fiscal 2000 is equal to our total revenues for 1998," advised Mike Kelly, AOL's chief financial officer. In the event people were concerned about the quality of that backlog (worried it could depend on contracts with shaky or impoverished dot-coms), Kelly added: "As we've shown our ability to deliver for our advertising and commerce partners, we've attracted more of the traditional blue-chip names. Today, these are the kinds of companies that account for the vast majority of our backlog." In other words, the $3 billion wasn't coming in from fly-by-night operations like Tel-Save or N2K. "The vast majority of our agreements are with companies that have been around for decades," Case told investors.

Way back in 1999, Case had been afraid that AOL would lose out to free Internet service providers like NetZero. Now it seemed his fears had been unjustified. Along with the other glowing news released by the company, AOL boasted 23 million subscribers worldwide. During the past year, it had been adding subscribers at a faster pace than ever, having signed up a record 5.6 million new AOL members in 2000.

And Jerry Levin? He was smitten with Steve Case. For AOL to prosper in a booming stock market was one thing; but to be running ahead of the pack in a downturn—that was something else!

■ ■ ■

THE AOL TIME WARNER DEAL WASN'T OFFICIAL—IT STILL HAD to be approved by regulators. But since it had already been approved by shareholders, the two companies could make their first tentative steps toward working as one. First the senior management team had to be appointed. From the beginning, Levin had wanted Time Warner people to be more like AOL'ers: modern, young, adaptable, digital, and quick on their feet. The surest way to shake up Time Warner's old order, Levin figured, was to appoint AOL'ers to top positions throughout the new company. "We did the AOL merger because we thought we could get digital by injection instead of by evolution," is how Dick Parsons explained it.

And so it came about that almost every senior corporate position in the newly merged company went to an AOL'er. The job of general counsel went to AOL's top lawyer, Paul Cappuccio, not Time Warner's Chris Bogart. The job of CFO went to AOL's Mike Kelly, not Time Warner's Joe Ripp. Ed Adler, Time Warner's head of corporate communications, reported to AOL's Ken Lerer; and Joan Nicolais Sumner was replaced as head of investor relations by AOL's Richard Hanlon. AOL's George Vradenburg was put in charge of overseeing public policy, displacing Time Warner's Tim Boggs. Even Richard Bressler, Levin's loyal and trusted protégé, was shunted into a minor non-executive role and told to report to Steve Case. Before long, Bressler would be gone completely, forced out by Case, who considered him a lightweight, according to Levin. "Not one of the Time Warner executives survived: we were fired outright or pushed aside," reported one victim of the Levinist purges. "Levin didn't fight for his people."

The new company was owned 55 percent by AOL shareholders. Called AOL Time Warner and run by AOL's top management team, it would be known as "AOL" on the New York Stock Exchange. If despite those signs anyone doubted that the so-called merger of equals was in reality a takeover of Time Warner by AOL, those doubts vanished when Bob Pittman's job description was made public.

Early on in their negotiations, Case and Levin had agreed to split the position of chief operating officer between Pittman and Dick Parsons. Now it was clear that Pittman would be the more equal of the two men. Granted control of the new company's most important divisions—AOL, the Time Inc. magazine unit, Time Warner Cable, Turner Broadcasting, HBO, CNN, and the WB Network—Pittman would oversee 80 percent of the firm's cash flow. The heads of those divisions, people who had reported directly to Levin, would now report to Pittman, who overnight had become the second most powerful person at AOL Time Warner, just behind Levin. Before long, it was rumored, Pittman would topple Levin. "He's probably measuring Jerry Levin's office for curtains right now," quipped one insider.

Parsons, by contrast, had been left to run a portfolio that included the Warner Bros. and New Line studios, Warner Music Group, and Warner Books. Behind his back, people called him Pittman's "water boy." Publicly, Parsons accepted his new role with dignity. Privately, however, he was stung by Levin's lack of gratitude, his lack of loyalty. Parsons's wife, Laura Ann Bush, encouraged her husband to start looking for a new job.

As for Ted Turner, the man Levin had once called "my colleague, best friend, and new partner," he was being eased out, stripped of his responsibilities for the company's Turner Broadcasting division, and forced to hand over his beloved CNN to Bob Pittman. After the AOL Time Warner merger was announced in January, Turner had been kept out of discussions about how the new company would be organized. Then, in May 2000, Turner received a five-page fax at his 580,000-acre ranch in New Mexico.

The fax included an AOL Time Warner press release listing the company's new management team. Reading it through carefully, "Ted went white," according to John Malone, who was with him that day. Turner's role in the new company would be nominal; he would be vice chairman and "senior adviser." Reeling from Levin's treachery, Turner told *The New Yorker* he felt suicidal; he even compared himself to Job. Alluding to his new, empty role, Turner remarked: " 'Vice chairman' is usually a title you give to somebody you can't figure out what else to do with."

Like Steve Ross, Nick Nicholas, and Michael Fuchs before him,

Turner had underestimated Levin. Or perhaps Turner had overestimated Levin, taking for granted he'd adhere to certain unspoken rules of personal and business conduct. Had Turner been suspicious, he could have protected himself back in January; for one thing, his vote on the AOL merger could have been made contingent on a binding employment contract.

Levin, for his part, implied that the wording of Turner's job description was irrelevant. "It doesn't make any difference what our prosaic reporting lines are," he said. "What really matters is that [Ted] is there and that he is a transcendent figure." Steve Case concurred, telling reporters: "Ted Turner has been a hero of mine for 25 years and he and I are basically going to be joined at the hip."

Turner was no fool, and he wasn't moved by their flattery. Not long after his demotion, speaking at a cable industry trade show, he recalled the day Levin called him his best friend: "I said, 'I'm your best friend? Jerry, I've never even been in your home. If I'm your best friend, who's your second-best friend? Nick Nicholas?' "

■ ■ ■

ON MONDAY, JULY 10, 2000, THE BOARDS OF AOL AND OF TIME Warner flew to Atlanta, Georgia, for their first ever joint meeting. A dozen or so top executives from each company were asked to come along. As conceived by Levin, the three-day get-together included a series of meetings, ceremonies, self-congratulations, and outdoor activities, culminating in a group outing to baseball's "Midsummer Classic" All-Star Game at (Ted) Turner Field. Now that the deal was all but finalized, the two companies had to figure out just how to work as one, how to blend their cultures, and how to meet the giant numbers promised to Wall Street. In other words, the most important steps for ensuring a successful merger had been left for last.

With temperatures hovering above one hundred degrees, Atlanta was oppressive and muggy. Few of the Time Warner executives wanted to be there at all. "The trip was universally unpopular," said one person who attended. "People tried hard to cancel the thing. There was a lot of anxiety: that we weren't ready for this, that it wasn't going to go well, that we weren't far enough into the commingling of our businesses to articulate plans for how this was going to work."

Of all the Time Warner divisions, Time Inc. was probably the most hostile, not just to the meeting in Atlanta, but to the impending merger with AOL. When Dick Parsons first told Time Inc.'s CEO, Don Logan, about the AOL deal way back in January 2000, Logan exploded. "You've got to be fucking kidding!" he shouted. "That's the dumbest thing I've ever heard in my life. I hope you're joking."

Disbelief may have been natural in a division composed of skeptical journalists. But aside from that, the deal with AOL had struck an old chord: it resonated with the merger of Time Inc. and Warner Communications back in 1990. Like the deal between AOL and Time Warner, the merger of Time and Warner had been announced with a flourish of promises; ultimately, it was accepted with resignation. Even now, ten years later, Time Inc.'ers were angry about the terms of the Warner deal.

The parallels were hard to ignore. Once again, ten years later, Time Inc.'ers were convinced they'd been sold out by headquarters. Just as they'd held their partners in contempt back in 1990, so they were contemptuous of AOL'ers now. Bob Pittman they found repulsive; he made their skin crawl. In 1995, when Pittman was running Time Warner's Six Flags, he'd been fired by Levin. Now, having landed at AOL by way of Century 21, Pittman was on top of the heap again, crowing, the co-COO-in-waiting of AOL Time Warner. And Time Inc.'ers were enraged. "I'm not sure who was supposed to be the Cassandra, but somebody should have told Steve and Jerry, 'Hey, the last time we checked, Pittman actually got fired from Time Warner,' " a senior executive told me sarcastically. "I mean, he wasn't just a fox in the henhouse, he was a fox with a machine gun in the henhouse."

Was there a hidden subtext to Time Inc.'ers' resentment? First of all, Pittman was rich, and Time Inc.'ers were not. Since leaving Time Warner and joining AOL, Pittman had made at least half a *billion* dollars, personally. A risk-taking, motorcycle-driving member of the Forbes 400, he owned a Falcon 20 jet and a Bell helicopter. He collected Harley-Davidson motorcycles. He had four houses— showplaces: in Manhattan; Great Falls, Va.; Telluride, Colorado; and Round Hill, Jamaica. Meanwhile, the people at Time Warner hadn't accumulated much. To be sure, company executives earned respectable salaries and had sizable 401(k) accounts; their jobs were secure. Now and then they'd actually made some money on Time Warner stock options. But compared to the obscenely rich AOL'ers with their getting and spending, they were losers, small-time company men who mowed the lawn on weekends. It was enough to make Time Warner executives feel stupid for sticking around, doing the right thing, trying to please Jerry Levin. On July 10, AOL'ers arrived for the meeting in Atlanta on their private jets. Time Warner's executives and directors flew commercial.

The joint board meeting highlighted the cultural differences between the two companies. Traditionally, Time Warner's board meetings had been proper, serious affairs, run formally by Levin as chairman and CEO. There was a seating plan as well as a printed agenda that people followed ritually, item by item. Each director's place at the table was staked out with a black leather portfolio embossed with his or her initials. Before the elegant three-course lunch, uniformed waiters, balancing sterling salvers, served Scotch and sherry in crystal glasses. Outsiders were rarely invited; if a senior executive had been summoned for some reason, he waited in an anteroom until the appointed moment; once he was finished speaking to the board, he was escorted out.

That July, however, Levin was not running the board meeting in Atlanta; Case was. For the first time in Levin's decade as CEO of Time Warner, he was sharing control. AOL board meetings had al-

ways been chaotic: despite the agenda, directors spoke up and broke
in when the spirit moved them. Just about any AOL executive who
wanted to be there was welcome. The boardroom table was littered
with bags of Cheetos and Pringles, and AOL'ers drank Snapple iced
tea straight from the bottle. Some of the meetings turned into scream-
ing matches.

The joint meeting in Atlanta was an awkward attempt to fuse
the two cultures, and Levin was taken aback. "I didn't particularly
care for it," he said, describing the Atlanta board meeting. "It went on
endlessly, and it was like a fraternity party with people shouting out.
This was not what I was used to. . . . There was a lack of discipline
and decorum." Something else struck Levin about that meeting: "I
started to get a gnawing concern that the AOL directors didn't have a
clue, not a fucking clue, about things like the movie business or the
cable business," he recalled.

Time Warner executives had other gnawing concerns. Internally, they'd been working on their budgets for the year 2001; and for
divisions that depended on advertising, the numbers weren't looking
good. Thus, when Bob Pittman made his presentation in Atlanta,
Time Warner executives knew which end was up. In his best radio
voice, Pittman gave a marvelous performance. Impeccably dressed,
oozing charm and confidence, he outlined the many many ways AOL
would propel the new combined company to dazzling heights. By
charging more for branded Time Warner content online, Pittman explained, AOL would increase its monthly revenues from $20 a sub-
scriber to as much as $150. As well, by adding new services, the cable
division could sharply increase revenue, to as much as $200 a month
per subscriber.

As for AOL's advertising revenue, its growth was just starting to
take off. Presuming that historical growth rates would continue unin-
terrupted (and he did presume that), then by 2005, Pittman promised,
AOL alone would bring in $7 billion in advertising and commerce
revenue, up from $2 billion in fiscal 2000. As props, he'd brought

along charts, with thick colored lines leading straight to heaven. That's the way AOL's business had been accelerating since 1996; that's how it would go on accelerating when the Time Warner merger was completed.

Meanwhile, as Pittman was making his pie-in-the-sky forecasts, AOL's and Time Warner's top executives were looking on quietly. Like the audience at a small off-Broadway show, the executives were seated in three rows of chairs, all facing the directors' long rectangular table. Don Logan, head of Time Inc., was present. A onetime mathematician and computer programmer for NASA, Logan, fifty-six, was known for his levelheaded, no-nonsense approach to business and life in general. He's the sort of person who likes his facts and figures to be real and verifiable, and so he'd always refused to take new media seriously. Back in 1995, when Time Warner was throwing away tens of millions of dollars on Pathfinder, its failed Internet initiative, Logan had called it a "black hole." Since then, his cynicism about the Internet had only increased.

Listening to Pittman's fantasies that morning in Atlanta, Logan could hardly control himself. Growth rates like that are impossible, he said to himself. Turning to Norm Pearlstine, Time Inc.'s editor in chief, who was seated on his left, Logan raised his eyebrows knowingly. According to Pearlstine: "Don and I looked at each other and wondered what Pittman was smoking and how we could get some. You just could not take him seriously."

In Logan's view, Pittman's financial targets were wild and irresponsible. Nor was Logan persuaded by Levin and Case: once the two companies were working together shoulder to shoulder, they predicted, revenues would grow to $40 billion and cash flow would increase by an amazing 30 percent to $11 billion. Logan had been running Time Inc. since 1994, shrewdly turning the division into the nation's biggest and most profitable magazine group, and in his view there was no way on God's earth that the numbers Levin and Case were throwing out could be met. To meet the numbers promised by

Pittman, AOL would need to increase its ad sales by an amount that equaled the combined value of Time Inc. and Turner Broadcasting's current ad revenue.

Other Time Warner division heads agreed with Logan: in their view, the AOL deal was based on false premises and conjuring tricks. Joe Collins, the fifty-six-year-old chairman of Time Warner Cable, was a typical Time Warner division chief. Defiant and independent, Collins ran his business like a personal fief. Refusing to take orders from headquarters, he operated for the most part as if the other Time Warner divisions didn't overlap with his. Time and again, Ted Turner had complained about Collins's refusal to carry Time Warner's own programming. The company's CNNfn financial channel, as well as CNNSI, its sports network, had been pressuring Collins, trying to increase their distribution. *Forget about it.* Turner Broadcasting couldn't convince him to carry Boomerang, its new children's network, or Turner South, its regional sports channel. "Of all the cable operators, Time Warner is my worst customer," cried Terry McGuirk, the man in charge of Turner's cable networks. "You want to know how many subscribers they give us for Boomerang? None. You want to know how many they give us for Turner South? None."

With revenues of $6.1 billion, and more cash flow by far than any other Time Warner division, Time Warner Cable didn't need any help from relatives. That was Joe Collins's view, and he wasn't going to change his mind. A former navy officer and Harvard MBA, invariably described in the media as "burly," "gruff," and "physically imposing," Collins knew that AOL needed Time Warner Cable more than Time Warner Cable needed AOL. In the past five years, he'd spent $4 billion upgrading his cable systems and installing a hybrid network of copper and fiber-optic cable able to deliver streams of high-capacity data. Already Time Warner Cable's high-speed Internet access service, Road Runner, boasted one million customers; every week another twenty thousand were signing on. Meanwhile, in the years prior to the AOL Time Warner merger, Collins had been in a fierce battle with AOL over the question of open access. Leaning hard on Washington's regulators, AOL wanted to get access to the pipes Time Warner was running into American homes; Collins refused. His boss, Levin, had made a deal with Case, but Collins viewed AOL as the enemy.

Then there was HBO's Jeff Bewkes, forty-eight, who at the drop of a hat would launch into a tirade against AOL. He loathed their top executives. It was insulting to be told that AOL was going to "turbocharge" Time Warner. He and the company were doing fine without AOL, thank you. Nor did Bewkes regard the Internet as a threat to HBO's business. Like Logan and Collins, Bewkes was credible and experienced. Single-handedly he'd reinvented HBO by creating some of the hottest programming on TV—shows like *The Sopranos, Sex in the City,* and *Six Feet Under.* Bewkes had taken over HBO in 1995, and since then the number of HBO subscribers had increased by almost a third, to thirty-eight million, and operating profits had tripled. At the meeting in Atlanta, sitting in the back row with Collins and Warner Bros.'s Barry Meyer, Bewkes just kept shaking his head.

None of the Time Warner division heads supported the merger of AOL and Time Warner. The men may have felt threatened personally: they resented the conspicuous wealth of Pittman and his henchmen, and they were furious at Levin for keeping them in the dark while the deal was in the planning stages. But beyond that, they didn't share the utopian vision being promoted by Levin and Case. The more time Time Warner's division heads spent with their counterparts at AOL, the more doubts they had about the glories of the digital future.

On the evening of July 11, after two days of meetings and indignation, AOL and Time Warner's directors and executives made their way to Turner Field to watch the All-Star Game. Up in the bleachers, 51,323 die-hard baseball fans were tearing off their T-shirts and pouring water over their heads to cool down. The heat was unbearable. Out on the field, Baseball Hall of Famer Hank Aaron threw the ceremonial first pitch. The game dragged on and on; it was like one of those morality plays, where sinners are dropped into the fires of hell for eternity. Absurdly, people from the two soon-to-be-merged companies were trying to make small talk. "Wretched," is the adjective used by one Time Warner executive to describe the event. "Really horrible." Of all the All-Star Baseball Games that were ever televised, going way back to 1967, this one posted the lowest ratings ever.

■ ■ ■

IF PEOPLE LIKE DON LOGAN, JEFF BEWKES, AND JOE COLLINS doubted Pittman's forecasts, it was because they'd never had bosses who'd forced them to think big or control expenses. That, in a nutshell, summed up the studied opinion of AOL'ers, whose counterparts at Time Warner were said to be (pick an adjective and double it) lazy, plodding, complacent, boring, washed-up, middle-class, out of date. "It was a loaded, fat organization that you could cut until you were blue in the face and still not hit a bit of bone or muscle," Myer Berlow mouthed off.

"The Time Warner guys were never pushed to cut expenses, they were never pushed to perform," added another AOL executive. "They always had excuses—you know, like their business wasn't predictable, this movie didn't make it, or this star flaked out—and every quarter was a bag of excuses. That's why their stock never did anything: because they didn't deliver to the Street."

So that was the secret: the AOL guys delivered to the Street. Like acrobats in the Cirque du Soleil, they performed for stock analysts, jumping through hoops, swallowing daggers, juggling torches, and walking on stilts. Steve Case walked on water. AOL'ers had always done the impossible, of course: that's how Case had started the company, by pulling off one amazing, incredible, spectacular, stunning, awesome, mind-boggling, unbelievable feat after another. Remember, AOL was a product of the myopic 1990s, and what mattered then was not a company's balance sheet, but the flashy, short-term performance of its stock. In the greatest speculative market of all time, the whole point was to make money in a hurry: get in, get out, move on. Smart companies learned fast that the object of the game was to "pop" their stock; and when it came to getting a quick pop, few companies were as skilled as AOL.

One sure way to pop your stock was to beat Wall Street's "consensus estimate." Stock analysts focused on quarterly earnings—the financial results tabulated by companies every three months. Guided by a company's executives, whom they'd consult regularly, research analysts would try to predict the quarterly results. The average of their numbers was known as the "consensus estimate." In turn, the consensus estimate became the benchmark for judging a company's performance. If a company's quarterly earnings per share fell short of the consensus estimate, well, its stock would tank. If a company managed to beat the consensus, even by a penny, its stock would soar.

That confidence game was called "earnings management," and everyone knew how it was played. In 1999 alone, 278 companies on the S&P 500 index managed to beat their consensus estimates by exactly one penny. Here's a skill-testing question: You're responsible for earnings management, and your company's numbers aren't looking good. Between you and me, how would you go about beating the consensus? Correct answer: You'd employ one or more of the following tricks: 1) Encourage analysts to set targets that are sufficiently aggressive to impress Wall Street but low enough to be beaten; 2) Use accounting gimmicks to inflate a quarter's revenues or push current expenses forward, postponing them to a later date; 3) Scramble madly at the end of each quarter to make the numbers, even if it meant you had to undermine long-term, long-range sales by unloading merchandise or advertising it at cut-rate prices. (It's the oldest established permanent floating crap game in New York.)

Time Warner played the game badly, without enthusiasm. To be sure, the company cared about its stock market performance; but since employees were paid in hard currency rather than stock options, they weren't all that motivated to beat the consensus and juggle numbers. Time Warner people cared about outdated concepts such as job security and pension plans and balance sheets.

AOL, by contrast, had the earnings management game down cold. To the penny, every AOL employee knew exactly what the stock was trading at. Secretaries celebrated when their shares hit new all-time highs. It was a culture of stock options and short-term goals; and AOL'ers were speculators, living in and for the moment. Their livelihood, their very near future, and their egos depended on delivering to the Street. As soon as the company failed to deliver, as soon as things slowed down, even for a minute, the stock would sink, and AOL'ers would sink with it. To get rich and stay rich, all they had to do was make sure the stock was trading above the level at which they'd been granted their stock options.

Back when AOL had been a small, unpromising enterprise, it was a cinch to beat Wall Street's expectations—its consensus estimates. As the company grew, however, and investors took AOL's exponential growth rates for granted, it kept getting harder to deliver to the Street. That's where Bob Pittman came in. He'd set outlandish numbers—so-called stretch targets; then he'd force his employees to do whatever it took, anything, to make them. That was Pittman's job, to hit impossible targets. And every single quarter since he'd arrived at AOL, he'd pulled it off miraculously. "Bob Pittman told David Colburn, Myer Berlow, and the others, 'Go out and bring back what I tell you to,' " a senior AOL executive explained. "It's like the flying monkeys coming out of the fucking castle in *The Wizard of Oz*. You know, they'd send the flying monkeys out every quarter and they brought back Dorothy, and without that you don't have AOL and a market cap of $200 billion plus."

The pressure was intense, but that was AOL. The last few days of every quarter had always been a mad rush: AOL'ers worked through the night, faxing documents back and forth, frantically sign-

ing off on last minute deals, checking the fine print, bleary-eyed. Anyone who could handle it got rich. Anyone who couldn't left. "We went
through fire drills all the time," one AOL'er recalled. "We were used
to stretch targets that, every quarter, at the beginning of the quarter,
felt impossible to make. For five years it was always like that." To
quote Paul Baker, then a top lawyer for AOL's business affairs division: "There was pressure to hit the numbers and pressure to get the
deals done: it was just a pressure cooker all the time. It was always,
'Microsoft is going to kill us' or 'We have to beat earnings by two
cents.' "

Right after the AOL Time Warner deal was announced, in early
2000, the stock market started to deflate. Advertising was slowing
down. And at AOL the pressure was getting unbearable. Don't forget, the Time Warner deal hinged on AOL's extraordinary growth
rates: if AOL couldn't make its numbers—if it couldn't beat the consensus estimate every quarter—the deal might be exposed on Wall
Street as a house of cards. What's more, AOL'ers had tens of thousands of stock options riding on the Time Warner deal; as soon as it
closed, most of those options would be fully vested. What would happen if the deal didn't go through?

■ ■ ■

BY THE FALL OF 2000, THE NASDAQ COMPOSITE INDEX WAS
trading around 3000, down 40 percent since March. Up and down
Wall Street, investors and research analysts were nervous about the
advertising market. Things weren't good. It wasn't only dot-coms
that were cutting back on ads; traditional companies, aware of the
shaky economy, were cutting back, too. "The worst is yet to come,"
warned Henry Blodget, alluding to the online advertising market.
Holly Becker agreed: "Our contacts suggest that the environment
continues to worsen."

On Tuesday, October 17, the day before AOL and Time Warner

were scheduled to release their latest earnings reports, shares of both companies fell sharply. Anticipating bad news, investors drove down AOL's stock by 17 percent. Time Warner's dropped 16 percent. But once again, it appeared investors had overreacted. On October 18, both companies reported record results. AOL looked especially strong. For the three-month period through September 2000, AOL's advertising and commerce revenue had jumped an amazing 80 percent to $649 million over the same period a year earlier. Pittman's flying monkeys had done it again.

Determined to calm Wall Street's rattled nerves, Levin and Case spent all day on October 18 talking up their companies and the wisdom of the merger. First there was a two-hour meeting with analysts, then lunch with journalists, then an hour-long conference call with investors, then numerous live television interviews. Each step of the way, Levin and Case kept insisting on one big thing: Despite the gloom on Wall Street, their future together was bright as a button. "The postmerger planning, the integration [of the two companies] is actually going—and I have some experience over several transactions—better than anything I've ever experienced," enthused Levin. Case added: "We feel terrific about the way the new company is coming together, and we are convinced we'll meet the financial targets we have set."

Case and Levin seemed to be reading from the same note cards, singing from the same hymnbook. From the perspective of AOL and Time Warner, there *was* no economic downturn. "This is a kind of nervous Nellie, manufactured issue that's been given a name, 'the dot-com shakeout,' " Levin argued, as if the "manufactured issue" didn't exist. Case was smart, too: far from hurting AOL, he said, the so-called dot-com shakeout was encouraging advertisers to spend more money on AOL. "There's a lot of swirl about the advertising market, [but] AOL's advertising growth is right on target," Case told everyone. "The current advertising market benefits us because it drives a flight to quality." Repeating the noun *swirl,* Levin echoed Case: "There's been a lot of swirl around the advertising market, particularly related to the so-called dot-com shakeout. I don't get it and I don't buy it."

Drawing from the scripted "talking points" used by Levin and Case, other senior executives of AOL swore it up and down: as far as they could tell, the ad market was not slowing down. "I want to separate the swirl from reality," said Mike Kelly, AOL's chief financial officer. "Based on our reported revenue and numbers and our backlog numbers and based on what we're seeing in our business today and looking forward, AOL's advertising commerce business is very healthy. I can't say that strongly enough." And Bob Pittman, was he by chance feeling the impact of a weak ad market? "For this company, I don't see it, and I don't buy it. Business looks great to us."

All day on October 18, reporters, analysts, and investors kept baiting Levin and Case. One television reporter asked incredulously: "Everybody has been hurt by the crashing dot-com advertising. You have not?"

Case replied: "Maybe we're a little bit different than everybody else. We've always felt that we were, maybe, a cut above. I don't say that arrogantly, but we have been doing this for over fifteen years and we've kind of emerged as the blue-chip. And we have a little different business model—a different approach. I think we benefit from that."

■ ■ ■

No one knew it then, but by 2003 the assurances given by Levin and Case on October 18, 2000, would become key evidence in dozens of shareholder lawsuits filed against AOL Time Warner. There were other things we didn't know then. By the fall of 2000, AOL's business affairs division (home of the flying monkeys) was holding weekly emergency meetings to discuss the "swirl about the advertising market." It was serious, and it was real, the slowdown. Running out of money, dozens of AOL's "partners" were threatening to pull the plug on their multimillion-dollar portal deals.

AOL's "pipeline report," a confidential document listing advertising deals in the pipeline, detailed the status of every AOL advertiser: money paid so far, money owed, and the likelihood of collecting the debt. Page after page, the report named companies that were deadbeats or were likely to become deadbeats. For example, an outfit called Living.com owned AOL $1.2 million. "They are out of $, wanted to look at a new deal but then backed out completely," noted one AOL report. "Not solvable," was someone's frank assessment of the deal with Living.com.

For months now, AOL had been keeping up appearances, delivering to Wall Street by restructuring long-term deals into short-term agreements that brought in quick cash. The restructurings seemed good for both parties: by paying AOL a breakup fee, struggling dotcoms were freed from their long-term obligations; at the same time, by booking those breakup fees as regular advertising revenue (rather than as onetime gains), AOL managed to disguise its weak advertising sales. It was a conjuring trick. In effect, AOL was moving money from its advertising backlog to cover the current shortfall in sales. Taking a page from Borislow's operating manual for Tel-Save (rule number one: Mortgage the company's future), AOL was betting that by the time anyone realized what had happened, the advertising market would be on a sharp rebound and AOL's pipeline would be flowing with new advertisers.

Much later, in the summer of 2002, a stunning exposé in *The Washington Post* would reveal that AOL had had other, dazzling tricks up its sleeve in 2000–2001. Desperate to beat the consensus estimate, the company had been shifting money from one part of its ledger to another; booking barter deals as though they were cash; and converting unpaid legal settlements into advertising revenue. Here's one example of AOL's ingenuity. For years, Wembley PLC, a British firm that owned greyhound racing tracks in the United Kingdom and the United States, had owed AOL about $27 million. In September 2000, frantic to make the numbers for the quarter, someone at AOL figured out how Wembley could clear up its debt and, at the same time boost AOL's advertising revenue. It was simple: in the twinkling of an eye, the $27 million owed to AOL would be changed to ads for 24dogs.com, a greyhound gambling site Wembley was about to launch.

In the last days of September 2000, with less than a week left in the quarter, AOL scrambled to run as many of Wembley's ads as possible. All at once, thousands of banner and button ads for 24dogs.com popped up on AOL. Everywhere you looked, packs of anxious, panting greyhounds were racing madly across the pages, fleeing to quality. Sometimes as many as three or four 24dogs.com ads would be featured on a single page. Overwhelmed by the traffic coming from AOL, the 24dogs.com site crashed. Never mind. The numbers were all that mattered: by the end of September, by a whisker, AOL managed to book $16.4 million worth of 24dogs.com ads.

The money involved in these transactions wasn't huge, relatively speaking; nonetheless, it was just enough to help AOL beat Wall Street's "consensus estimates" by a penny a share for two quarters in a row in 2000. In turn, beating the numbers meant that AOL's share price didn't keep falling.

So far, by hook or crook, AOL had been able to meet its quarterly numbers; but how much longer could investors be fooled? What if advertising didn't rebound? By early October 2000, less than two weeks *before* Pittman and Case assured Wall Street that AOL had not been affected by the advertising downturn, that it "was right on target," AOL's advertising executives had concluded that the company was at risk of losing at least $140 million from shaky ad deals. David Colburn and Myer Berlow were losing their grip. In meeting after

meeting, they tyrannized their salesmen, demanding they find ways
for their delinquent partners to pay up. *Why can't you get this deal
closed? Why can't you?*

The forecasts from New York didn't look much better than
those from Dulles, Virginia. Time Warner was embellishing its numbers, too. In its October 18 earnings announcement, for example, the
company claimed its cash flow had jumped 13 percent in the first nine
months of 2000. Once you focused on the fine print in its SEC filings,
however, you realized that some of Time Warner's growth was derived from unusual onetime gains that should have been booked sep-
arately. The true growth figure was closer to 10 percent.

Meanwhile, by October 2000, senior executives at various Time
Warner divisions were quietly scaling back their projections. Time
Inc.'s magazines were being hurt by a drop in advertising. CNN was
losing viewers to Fox News. Profit margins in the cable systems division were narrowing. And the music division was falling far behind
Vivendi Universal, the industry leader. As for the film division, one of
its big movies of the season, Adam Sandler's *Little Nicky,* had run way
over budget and was opening to scathing reviews. "The movie doesn't
have one genuine moment of imagination, good timing or comic in-
spiration," one reviewer wrote. And another: "*Little Nicky* is a movie
for people who find pop-up books too intellectually demanding." And
a third: "Poorly conceived, poorly produced, terribly edited. [*Little
Nicky*] just sucks on all levels." That flop would rack up a loss of about
$50 million.

■ ■ ■

IT WAS NOVEMBER. SINCE THE ANNOUNCEMENT OF THE AOL
Time Warner deal in January, AOL's stock had fallen by 50 percent.
Whatever enthusiasm Time Warner people may have felt about the
deal back then was waning. Anyone with a calculator could run the
numbers. Had the AOL Time Warner deal been negotiated only a

By 1944, when this photo was taken, Henry Luce, age 46, was already a media baron: one in every five Americans was reading a Time Inc. publication. Power motivated Luce, but money did not. In his will, he stated: "Time Incorporated is now, and is expected to continue to be . . . an enterprise operated in the public interest as well as in the interest of its stockholders."

Yousuf Karsh/Camera Press/Retna Ltd.

Jerry Levin, age 33, and his then boss, Dick Munro, celebrate the launch of HBO in 1972. It was, Levin would later note, "an electrifying kind of experience." Before long, with the success of HBO, Levin would become the company's "resident genius," and Time Inc. would be changed forever. Henceforth, Luce and his gentlemen editors would be replaced by "market-oriented" men from the company's cable and video group.

Courtesy of Gerald Levin

Time Inc.'s directors were deeply opposed to merging with Steve Ross's Warner Communications. In their view, Ross and his executives were not "their kinds of people." Ross, pictured here in the late 1980s, had his hair blow-dried every day. He was an intimate friend of Hollywood stars. He was glamorous and sophisticated. Rumor had it he and his company had links to the Mob and organized crime.

After the Time Warner deal in 1990, Steve Ross, left, shared the title of co-CEO with Nick Nicholas, right. Though Time had acquired Warner, Ross took control—and Nicholas rebelled. Soon, the two men were barely communicating, and Jerry Levin stepped in to fill the vacuum. By the end of 1992, Nicholas had been pushed out, Ross was dead, and Jerry Levin was named chairman and CEO of the world's biggest media and entertainment company.

Ron Galella

On announcing Time Warner's acquisition of Turner Broadcasting in 1995, Levin described Ted Turner as "my best friend." Years later, after he was stripped of his responsibilities at Time Warner, Turner recalled that day: "I said, 'I'm your best friend? Jerry, I've never even been in your home. If I'm your best friend, who's your second-best friend? Nick Nicholas?' "

Sonia Moskowitz/Globe

By 1990, Bob Pittman and his first wife, Sandy Hill ("the socialite everyone loves to hate")—here attending a "hoedown for literacy"—were New York's "couple of the minute." A cofounder of MTV and a protégé of Steve Ross's, Pittman was then a rising star at Time Warner. But in 1995, he was abruptly fired by Jerry Levin. Years later, after the AOL Time Warner merger, Pittman had clawed his way back up: as co-chief operating officer, he would become perhaps the most hated executive at the new company. "He wasn't just a fox in the henhouse," remarked one insider, "he was a fox with a machine gun in the henhouse."

In its early days, America Online was "not just a company, it [was] a religion." For Steve Case, pictured here in 1996 at the age of 38, AOL was part of something as profound, as meaningful, as the Industrial Revolution. Back then, he would have been just as happy running AOL as a not-for-profit organization.

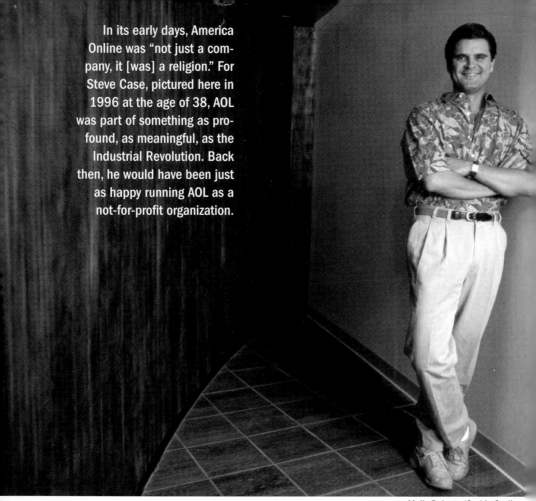

Molly Roberts/Corbis Outline

Andrea Renault/Globe

By the late 1990s, AOL's stock price had become the company's mission. Steve Case, here greeting his fans at the 1999 launch of AOL 5.0, was worth $1.5 billion. As for America Online, it was now worth twice as much as Berkshire Hathaway, nearly three times as much as Disney, and more than McDonald's, Philip Morris, and PepsiCo combined.

Steve Case and Jerry Levin embrace at the press conference announcing their historic merger on January 10, 2000. "I accept the market capitalizations in the Internet space because I think something profound is taking place," said Levin.

On stage at the announcement of the AOL Time Warner deal, from left, Steve Case, Jerry Levin, Ted Turner, and Bob Pittman. Expressing his unalloyed support for the deal, Turner boasted that he voted in favor of the merger "with as much or more excitement and enthusiasm as I did when I first made love some 42 years ago."

After Jerry Levin quit to rediscover "the poetry" in his life, Dick Parsons was named CEO of AOL Time Warner. This photo was taken on May 16, 2002, Parsons's first day on the job. "Surviving is winning," he noted. "There's a certain amount of luck involved in anything in life, but I never had a doubt about how this would all work out."

Kathy Willens/AP/Worldwide

Misha Erwitt

Since leaving AOL Time Warner, Levin has a new life and a new vocation devoted to the healing arts. Living with his fiancée in Marina del Rey, where this photo was taken in early 2003, he's divorcing his wife, writing a self-help book called *Soul Communion,* and starting a holistic mental health institute called Moonview Sanctuary. "I don't have any regrets," he said on the subject of the AOL Time Warner deal. "I'm not defensive about it either. It is what it is."

few months later, Time Warner shareholders could have wound up with 65 percent of the combined company. But here they were, stuck in a downturn, holding 45 percent of a shrinking asset.

Urgently, a few of Time Warner's most senior executives at 75 Rock talked about breaking off the deal. They still had time, they told one another—the deal had not yet been approved by Washington's regulators. According to the companies' merger agreement, Time Warner could pull out if there was a "material adverse effect" on AOL's business or financial condition. Did the collapse of the New Economy constitute a "material adverse effect"? No doubt that argument could be made. Then again, if Time Warner made that sort of claim, AOL would sue for breach of contract. And then what? Over the years, in reaching their decisions on similar battles, the courts had usually been unsympathetic to companies with buyer's (or seller's) remorse. Still, even if they couldn't win a legal case, the threat of Time Warner's backing out might force AOL to renegotiate the terms of the deal: that option appealed to a few people. "It was a risky legal strategy," concluded one Time Warner executive who weighed the options. "But it was a credible one."

A less risky option, in the view of Time Warner's strategists, was to take advantage of another clause in the merger agreement: in the event the deal was not closed by May 31, 2001 (the "drop-dead date"), either of the two parties, AOL or Time Warner, could back out of the deal without penalty. It was late 2000, and the deal was expected to close soon. Having spent most of the year studying the antitrust implications of the AOL Time Warner deal, the Federal Trade Commission (FTC) and the Federal Communications Commission (FCC) were on the verge of approving the merger. Certainly the approval of the FTC and FCC would hinge on some tough conditions: they'd insist that AOL Time Warner give competing Internet service providers access to its cable lines, for example.

If in late 2000 Time Warner had wanted a foolproof way to get out of its deal with AOL, the company could argue (disingenuously, but not improbably) that the government's conditions were onerous. Time Warner could say that the AOL Time Warner deal raised no antitrust issues, and then the FTC would have sued to block the merger. Any such lawsuit would drag out for months, well beyond the deal's drop-dead date. In which case, regardless of the suit's outcome, Time Warner would be free to cut loose from AOL.

One way or another, Time Warner could have backed out. But whereas Dick Parsons, Rich Bressler, Chris Bogart, and most of the company's division heads would have been glad to call the whole thing off, Jerry Levin was determined to move forward. In casual conversations and in meetings with Levin, various senior Time Warner executives, including Parsons, suggested that the best course of action might be to pull out. But Levin didn't seem to hear them; or else, not wanting to be difficult, they backed down. "Jerry would not even entertain the argument," explained an insider. "It was a moral issue to him. He felt he was morally bound to the agreement with AOL." It was Jerry's deal; everyone else was just along for the ride.

That's not Levin's remembrance of things past. "I think that's an overstatement," he said. "I don't think a) that a lot of people [inside Time Warner] wanted to renegotiate; and b) that it was a moral issue." He was not advised to call off the deal, he suggested in so many words, and my sources were busy rewriting history: "I would have walked away from the deal, but I just don't recall that there was a big movement [to do so]. In people's minds there might have been; I just don't recall."

Maybe it wasn't a moral issue. Maybe Levin clung to the deal with AOL because he continued to believe in it—to believe it would be the defining moment of his life. One division head conceded that he never opposed the deal openly because he knew Levin had already made up his mind. "I knew Jerry wanted it to go down and that he would do just about anything to make sure it happened," this division head explained. "Once Jerry so strongly believes he has a vision, he's willing to pay any price to get there." Levin's commitment to his vision, his failure (or refusal) to back out of his deal with AOL, would cost his shareholders some $200 billion.

Selling his shareholders short, Levin made another blind error: He neglected to put a "collar" on the deal. Corporate acquisitions, especially between companies in different industries, normally include a collar. It's like an insurance policy. A collar protects the acquired company (Time Warner) from a drop in the stock price of its buyer (AOL). If the buyer's stock falls below a certain level (called "a floor"), the deal is renegotiated. In this case, there was no collar, and Time Warner wasn't protected. Even though AOL's stock had fallen in half since January 2000, the terms of the deal—the exchange ratio—could no longer be changed.

Incredibly, Levin claimed he hadn't wanted a collar in the first place. As late as October 2000, when he was interviewed before a public audience at Manhattan's 92nd Street Y, Levin stated: "With a collar, the implication is that you are not really sure—your commitment to the valuations is somewhat insecure, and you need this kind of protection. I wanted to make a statement that I believe in it. It will be good for Time Warner shareholders, it makes sense for AOL. In other words, no collar . . . means a total commitment to the deal come hell or high water."

NINE

BY EARLY 2001, THE SIGNS AT AOL TIME WARNER POINTED TO disaster. Two years later, as shareholder lawsuits started making their way through the courts, one question would become crucial. Exactly when (day, month, year) did the company's top executives realize that the fantastic numbers they'd promised to Wall Street couldn't be met? Were shareholders of AOL Time Warner intentionally misled? Jerry Levin and Steve Case swore that their first inkling of a shortfall came late in 2001, like a bolt from the blue. You could have knocked them over with a feather.

This much we know: By the time the AOL Time Warner deal was approved by regulators on January 11, 2001, executives at every division of AOL Time Warner were starting to panic. The targets were out of reach. There was no way the company's cash flow could be increased by 30 percent in a single year. Nor was it likely that revenues would jump by 10 percent to $40 billion, as Levin and Case had promised. "I don't think there was a divisional CEO who wasn't in favor of revising downward," I was told by one division head.

From Levin's vantage point at AOL Time Warner's headquarters, twenty-nine floors above the crowd, things apparently looked fine. Naturally his people would complain about the numbers. What manager isn't looking for easy targets? Levin had no in-

tention of revising downward. Determined to run the combined
company the way AOL had been run, he'd force his managers to
perform. The new stretch targets would "turbocharge" the company
and shake up complacent division heads. In the words of an AOL
executive, the aggressive projections would "kick these guys into high
gear."

Buoyant whenever he'd meet the press, Levin insisted that AOL
Time Warner was fully capable of meeting its (impossible) goals.
"Our company rides above normal market dynamics," he stated in
April 2001, as though the company were airborne. Case went further,
assuring analysts in early 2001 that AOL Time Warner was on track
to achieve his personal long-term goals: revenues of $100 billion and a
market capitalization of $1 trillion.

To demonstrate their commitment to the company publicly,
Case and Levin initiated what's known as a "stock buyback," agreeing
to spend as much as $5 billion of the company's money on buying
AOL Time Warner shares on the open market. For investors, the
news was inspiring. Stock buybacks imply that from the point of view
of management, the company's shares are undervalued. Levin used
just those words, unambiguously, at the announcement of the buyback program in January 2001: "We believe our shares are undervalued."

Levin's beliefs were shared by Mary Meeker, Morgan Stanley's
celebrated Internet analyst, whose first report on the new AOL Time
Warner, released on January 19, 2001, referred to the company as "our
best moneymaking idea." (She was not, apparently, alluding to the
$60 million fee earned by Morgan Stanley for brokering the AOL
Time Warner deal.) In Meeker's considered opinion, the company's
stock would be hitting $75 within a year, up about 50 percent from
where it now stood. She rated AOL Time Warner a "strong buy"; of
all the companies Meeker followed, it was the only one to receive that
stamp of approval in early 2001.

■ ■ ■

BOB PITTMAN WAS UNWAVERING IN HIS OPTIMISM. IN HIS TIDY mind, there was no room for ambiguity or negativity: there was a job to be done, and he was in charge of doing it. Simple. "The company must hit the numbers expected of it," he told *Business Week* matter-of-factly.

Already Pittman had set to work, forcing the new AOL Time Warner to adopt AOL's centralized and interactive and flexible culture. No more personal fiefdoms. Under the Pittman regime, Time Warner's division heads had meetings every few weeks to discuss ways they could work in tandem. Some of them had never spoken to one another before; now, suddenly, they shared a common goal—making the numbers promised to Wall Street.

Before the AOL deal, under Levin, Time Warner divisions had reported their financials to headquarters every few months or so. Aside from that, almost nothing suggested that they were part of a bigger company, under the same umbrella. The autonomy of his division executives had always grated on Levin, yet in the decade he'd been running Time Warner, he could never manage to change them; finally, he'd given up. Now, thanks to Pittman and his strong-arm tactics, divisions would be forced to cooperate with one another. Levin may not have liked Pittman personally (everyone noted that he always addressed him impersonally by his surname, as in, "How's it going, Pittman?" rather than, "How's it going, Bob?"), but like Case, he recognized that Pittman's frantic ambition and love of money were useful. Pittman was a hustler.

They were polar opposites, the two men. As Levin himself admitted, he suffered from a "charisma bypass." Pittman was charming; innately he knew how to manipulate people, even bully them, if it came to that. Levin avoided confrontation; Pittman thrived on it. It got the adrenaline pumping. Another crucial distinction: Levin affected a disdain for money, as though he were living on top of a mountain, counting prayer beads instead of dollars. For Pittman, however, business was about making money, period; it wasn't about making a difference and changing the world. "He personifies southern charm, but when it comes to business, he switches to a different DNA. He's cold-blooded," remarked news anchor Tom Brokaw, talking about his friend Pittman.

Describing how Time Warner's divisions had been run before he took over, Pittman noted with condescension. "They were managed quite well by their industry standards, but we're trying to get more out of them." Now division heads had to produce detailed weekly financial reports tallying revenues, profits, ad sales, subscribers, ratings, and so on. Pittman tracked their progress obsessively. He ordered them to cut costs sharply, by $1 billion in total, and to boost revenues by at least 10 percent. At an early meeting of the various divisions, one executive, alluding to the economic climate (the dark clouds and the gathering storm), was cut short by Pittman, who got straight to the point. "Are you going to make your numbers?" he demanded impatiently. Any division head who failed to make his numbers would receive a hostile phone call from the chief financial officer, Mike Kelly, demanding an explanation.

To align the goals of each Time Warner division with the larger goals of the combined company, long-term incentive bonuses based on the performance of individual units were eliminated. Now, instead of cash bonuses, executives were given AOL Time Warner stock options. As for the rest of the company's eighty-five thousand employees, their generous profit-sharing plans were replaced with stock options, grandly known as "founders' options."

The official line went something like this: Stock options would inject the new company with all of AOL's winning qualities—grit, commitment, hustle. That sounds good. But there was a more practical, more immediate reason for replacing cash bonuses with options. Unlike salary and bonus, stock options aren't booked as an expense on a company's income statement. They're like free money. By replacing bonuses and profit-sharing plans with stock options, the company would save $100 million in 2001 alone, according to Mike Kelly. More money could be saved if pension benefits for new employees were dumped altogether.

Rashly, Pittman promised Wall Street $1 billion of so-called synergies. That's how much money the company would save by dumping bodies (live ones), closing magazines, eliminating unprofitable ventures, getting rid of perks and benefits, shutting overlapping back offices, and slashing and burning. It was rough. When he was planning for the merger back in 2000, Pittman had come up with a list of about $700 million in synergies. As for the balance of savings he'd promised to Wall Street, "we figured we'd somehow find another $300 million," remarked a senior AOL'er offhandedly.

After the AOL Time Warner merger closed in January 2001, more than 6,000 employees lost their jobs. That alone saved $250 million. Another 3,200 workers were dumped (made redundant, eliminated) in 2001 when the Warner Bros. retail stores were closed. Five hundred longtime Warner Music executives, many of them holdovers from the Steve Ross era, were forced into early retirement. About a hundred employees of Time Warner's New Line Cinema were let go. Other employees were threatened: Accept severance packets or be fired outright. "To put it in plain-speak, we now have more folks on some parts of the staff than we need," read a memo of March 22, 2001, delivered to *Fortune*'s staff. If not enough "volunteers" came forward, all of them would be in dire straits: "While the details vary with each individual, you should know that job-elimination severance is more generous than performance management or cause severance."

History was being eliminated, along with jobs. At Time Inc., the magazine division's cherished library—known as the "morgue"— was closed down, its thousands of biographical and topical files, some dating back to the 1920s, hauled off to oblivion. On the Friday before Memorial Day weekend in 2001, employees of the morgue, some of whom had dedicated their entire working lives to Time Inc.'s library, were abruptly called into a conference room and fired en masse by a total stranger, a middle manager they'd never met before. "People were bawling at the meeting—it was horrible," I was told by a long-time librarian, a victim of the purge.

In the company's rage to save $1 billion, minor expenses became an issue. At *Money* magazine, fountains of free soda were replaced by coin-operated vending machines; at *Time,* writers and editors who worked late getting the magazine to press could order two free dinners a week, not three; at *Sports Illustrated,* the number of free pizzas brought in on late night closings was reduced to nine from fourteen, thereby saving the company $2,500 a year. All across Time Inc., vouchers for car rides home were cut back; employees who worked late were encouraged to take public transportation or taxis. Stung by the loss of their longtime perks (people had taken them for granted), a group of editors and art directors at *Time* staged a small act of civil disobedience, producing a mock issue of the magazine called "In Memoriam." Written in plain-speak, it included such helpful articles as "Ten Tips on Hailing Cabs" and "Need a Lift?" One after another, the cutbacks continued. In one fell swoop, the entire mailroom staff at the Time-Life Building was laid off and replaced by an outside contractor.

■ ■ ■

CONSOLIDATING PARTS OF THE COMPANY INTO A GREAT WHOLE, Pittman described his mission as a "jihad." Single-handedly he'd change Time Warner's insular and divisive culture. People would learn to work as a team. He'd done it at AOL, and he could do it again: Time Warner would turn into a money machine.

Encouraged by Levin and by the murmurs of approval he thought he heard from Time Warner's division heads, Pittman emerged from each meeting convinced he was making headway. "Bob really believed he could *will* them to work together," a friend of

Pittman's explained. In fact, Time Warner's executives didn't take Pittman or his agenda seriously, nor did they respect him. Despite all the talk about communal ideology and the "culture" of AOL, business at Time Warner went on more or less as usual in 2001. "It was clear to me that no one was playing along," said one executive who attended the division head meetings. "People were nodding their heads at Bob and then going off and doing what they wanted to do. One way to know the meetings weren't working was that a month later we'd still be discussing the same things, which suggested nothing had changed. The meetings were a disaster."

Big cross-divisional projects were proposed and discussed, memos were typed up, one meeting after another was held, but nothing much happened. Some people meant well. In early 2001, one mid-level AOL manager was instructed to have her department build Web sites for several Time Warner divisions. But as the months went by and work continued on the sites, no one in her department actually met anyone at Time Warner face-to-face to discuss the project. Six months later, the two sides still hadn't spoken to each other. Finally, the project was dropped. In another early 2001 meeting held with top editors from *Fortune Small Business,* an AOL'er laid out a bold plan to build a $3 billion business-to-business (B2B) portal focused on small companies. John Huey, who back then was in charge of Time Inc.'s business publications, dismissed the plan outright. "That's insane," he said, noting that $3 billion was more than AOL's entire ad revenue. "What are you talking about?" Refusing to back down, the AOL'er replied: "It's not insane! This is how we do things at AOL." And that was the end of that. Neither Huey nor anyone else at *Fortune Small Business* heard another word about the $3 billion B2B.

People at Time Warner were doing everything they could to avoid change. That was the general view of AOL'ers, who liked to accuse Time Warner of "obstructionist behavior." "I'd call for a five P.M. meeting on a Friday and I'd get back e-mails from guys at Warner Bros. saying, 'I don't do meetings at five P.M. on Fridays,' " recalled

Neil Davis, one of AOL's top salesmen. "So I'd call for a Monday morning meeting on the West Coast, which meant people in New York would have to fly to L.A. on Sunday night. They'd refuse."

AOL'ers just didn't understand how the media business operated, according to the people at Time Warner. You see, at Time Warner, journalists thought of themselves as artists; advertising may have been necessary, but it wasn't their problem. To AOL'ers, by contrast, artists (journalists, photographers, and actors) were "content providers," whose job it was to fill the empty spaces between advertisements. In the hope of securing a giant advertising deal with Victoria's Secret, AOL wanted HBO to air Victoria's Secret's fashion show. HBO was incensed: the fashion show wasn't creative programming; it was advertising in disguise! On demand, AOL expected Warner Bros. to have Mel Gibson record the famous voice-over that greets tens of millions of AOL subscribers every day ("You've got mail!"). When Warner Bros. pointed out that actors like Mel Gibson didn't actually work for the company, AOL accused Warner Bros. of being obstinate. Similarly, AOL demanded the right to use photographs from Time Inc.'s magazines on its Web site. Editors at Time Inc. then had to explain they didn't own those photographs; they effectively rented them, paying photographers for a onetime use of their work. Convinced that Time Inc. was trying to undermine AOL, a frustrated AOL'er finally blurted out: "We can't get anything done with you guys!"

Single-mindedly, ignoring the lack of compliance on the part of the Time Warner people, Pittman forged ahead. There were so many ways to save money and encourage cooperation!

■ ■ ■

IN LATE 2000, EVEN BEFORE THE AOL TIME WARNER DEAL HAD closed, Pittman had came up with another idea. Why not switch the whole company over to AOL's e-mail system? It made no sense for the company to be paying software licensing fees to outsiders when AOL could take care of everybody's e-mail all at once. "We can save $30 million with the flick of a switch," Pittman told Norm Pearlstine, Time Inc.'s editor in chief, and Paul Zazzera, Time Inc's chief information officer.

That sounded reasonable to Pearlstine, who was anyway looking to upgrade Time Inc.'s e-mail system. So a group of AOL techies was dispatched to New York from Dulles to extol the wonders of AOL e-mail. As part of the demonstration, by way of example, they showed Pearlstine how efficiently, how easily, AOL's e-mail and instant messaging could be used to invite employees to a company beer bash. "I remember sitting through this thing for an hour and thinking, These guys use e-mail to say there's a beer bash at five o'clock; I use e-mail to read three hundred articles a week, to deal with people who use both PCs and Macs, and for attachments that require high levels of security and are difficult to download," Pearlstine told me. "So I said, Oh my God! And I went back to Zazzera and told him, 'You know, they think e-mail is about beer bashes at five.' "

Still, Pearlstine agreed to adopt AOL e-mail. It would save the company $30 million, after all. What's more, AOL'ers raved about their system, especially about AOL's instant messaging. "It's a fabulous way to run your company," said Pittman's lieutenant Mayo Stuntz. "No paper. Instant access twenty-four hours a day, seven days a week. Look how fast you can get things done!" Levin was enamored of instant messaging; Steve Case practically lived on it. Yes, the new system had to be tweaked to suit the needs of Time Warner's various divisions, but to techies at AOL, tweaking was second nature.

Over the course of six months, starting in May 2001, Time Warner employees switched over to AOL's e-mail. Chaos ensued. Originally designed for consumers, AOL e-mail flopped as a corporate tool. It couldn't handle large attachments, it crashed, it randomly locked out users, it kept losing messages, it automatically erased e-mails after seven days. It was a farce. When sales executives at *En-*

tertainment Weekly tried e-mailing an important presentation to an advertising agency, AOL's e-mail system wouldn't accept the file, it was so big. Instead, an *Entertainment Weekly* staff member had to be dispatched to deliver the presentation by hand.

Pearlstine delivered the bad news to Mayo Stuntz, who was sympathetic, of course; but aside from telling AOL's techies to work on the problems, there wasn't much he could do. "We just have to stick with it," he told Pearlstine. "Bob has committed to the board that we'll save $30 million by using this e-mail system."

Months passed, the problems were never fixed, and Pearlstine's complaints got lost between New York and Dulles. AOL had more urgent issues to deal with, bigger fish to fry. Besides, in the view of AOL'ers, the folks at Time Warner were exaggerating; they were whiners. "There was no real understanding on the part of people at AOL of how our divisions were different from their own," Pearlstine explained. "From their point of view, to the degree we were different, we should adjust. You know, 'Twelve thousand people at AOL are using this e-mail, so what's wrong with you?' "

Meanwhile, on deep background, one or more Time Warner employees leaked word of the disastrous AOL e-mail experiment to the *New York Observer.* The article implied, accurately, that the e-mail fiasco, while apparently minor, reflected a growing chasm between the two sides of the combined company. "AOL's giving us dog food and making us eat it," whispered one employee to the *Observer,* hiding behind his or her anonymity. "It's a nightmare," said another. "Everybody's bitching and moaning."

Caught off guard, AOL executives were enraged by the *New York Observer* article. They'd been betrayed by members of their own family! When it came to the art of backstabbing, AOL'ers weren't amateurs; in this case, however, they couldn't understand why and how anyone in the company would leak information that could hurt the share price.

"The whole culture at AOL was share price, share price, share price. Why else were we in business?" asked a bewildered senior AOL executive, explaining to me how the skirmish over e-mail became a massive fault line. "They pretended they cared about share price, too. Our naiveté was in not understanding that there were other agendas."

Which agenda did he have in mind? According to AOL'ers, people at Time Warner were out to humiliate them and undermine AOL's leadership of the combined company. Surely, in their view, Norm Pearlstine himself, or his deputy, John Huey, must have been responsible for the story leaked to the *New York Observer.* "Let's be serious," Huey responded. "If we wanted to orchestrate a leak, we'd have done it a lot sooner and a lot better. There are 2,000 journalists here with shitty e-mail. How long did you think it would be a secret? It's amazing it was kept a secret for so long."

On March 20, 2002, less than a month after the article appeared in the *Observer,* and after fiddling with e-mail for nearly a year, AOL Time Warner gave up; now each division could choose its own e-mail system.

■ ■ ■

PITTMAN'S MAIN GOAL WAS TO CENTRALIZE ADVERTISING SALES. The company's sales force was urged to promote large, multidivisional deals, selling national advertisers a package of ads that would run across all of AOL Time Warner properties—its magazines, its cable TV channels, and its Internet service. Pittman observed the obvious: AOL shared only four advertisers with Time Inc. and Turner Broadcasting. Imagine how much advertising could be sold once the divisions pooled their resources—if all of Time and Turner's advertisers signed on for AOL and vice versa! "Cross-platform advertising and marketing initiatives will increasingly become a key driver of the company's future growth," he proclaimed in a press release.

To devise those cross-platform initiatives, a committee of AOL

Time Warner's top sales and marketing executives was set up. Beginning in early 2001, under Pittman's watch, the Advertising Council, as it was known, got together every two weeks to brainstorm and think "holistically" (Pittman's term) about advertising. "It's a matter of coming in, talking to customers, and saying, 'What big strategic issues are you wrestling with?' "—that's Pittman, outlining the Ad Council's job.

To show Time Warner's advertising executives how profitable cross-media deals could be, and to get the ball rolling, Pittman himself called on potential clients, using some of his best connections. Before long, the Ad Council had cobbled together so many potential deals that the list of names filled fifteen pages of single-spaced type. Every week, just about, AOL Time Warner issued another glowing press release touting the Ad Council's latest "strategic marketing alliance." Where was the advertising downturn people were going on about? It hadn't affected AOL Time Warner!

By the end of summer 2001, the Ad Council boasted of having twenty-two strategic marketing alliances worth $700 million. Most of these companies were doing business with AOL already or, in the case of Kinko's, they were partly owned by AOL. One advertiser, Cendant Corp., Century 21's parent company, was Pittman's former employer; in turn, Pittman was a director and shareholder of Cendant. Others, such as WorldCom, Foundry Networks, Compaq Computer, Nortel, and Cisco, were major AOL suppliers; buying advertisements was one of the costs of doing business, apparently. After AOL threatened to stop using WorldCom's telecommunications network, WorldCom wisely decided to buy $180 million worth of advertising on AOL. Philips Electronics agreed to spend $30 million over three years on AOL Time Warner ads—but only after being assured that AOL Time Warner would buy more of its cable TV set-top boxes. And so on, round and round in a circle.

Was the money generated by these deals advertising revenue? Or was some of it a rebate—a discount on a supplier's product that showed up as ad revenue? If AOL invested in a company that in turn bought advertising from AOL, wasn't that really a form of barter? To Pittman, such questions were irrelevant and tiresome. Money was money. If he was calling in personal favors to prop up ad revenue, that's how business worked, tit for tat. "If we're one of their big customers, we expect them to be one of our big customers," Pittman said unapologetically. To which Myer Berlow added: "If you can't do business with your partners, then what's wrong with you?"

The answer to Berlow's question would come later in the day. Known as "round-tripping" or "lazy Susans," barter agreements aren't illegal, as long as the goods and services you're swapping are being valued at their fair market price. Still, because they inflate revenue, lazy Susans can distort a company's numbers badly. Instead of admitting that the company's reciprocal, or round-trip, deals made no substantial difference to the bottom line, AOL used them to inflate its results. For example, AOL booked WorldCom's ad sales as revenue; at the same time, AOL recorded the purchase of services from World-Com as an expense. The bottom line hadn't changed; but the top line—AOL's revenues—had been jacked up. Investors who focused on the top line were impressed; the company was growing quickly, as expected.

Round-tripping was such an effortless way to boost revenue that AOL Time Warner adopted the practice internally, moving money from one division to the other. One of those deals involved Oxygen Media, a start-up media company with Web sites and a cable television channel for women. Since its launch in early 2000, Oxygen TV hadn't managed to get much distribution on cable systems; it hadn't made a dent in Time Warner Cable, which by and large had kept the nascent channel out of the New York City market. Limited to distribution in just thirteen million homes, Oxygen was ignored, or it was considered a flop. But in April 2001, out of nowhere, Oxygen got lucky: AOL, an early minority investor in the company, decided to invest another $30 million to $50 million in Oxygen. At the same time,

AOL arranged for Oxygen TV to be carried on Time Warner Cable systems.

Normally, cable channels pay a "carriage fee" to get on cable systems, and in the case of Oxygen TV, the carriage fee to Time Warner Cable might have been as high as $100 million. But Oxygen paid no carriage fee. Instead, the struggling TV channel promised to spend a massive $100 million in advertising on AOL Time Warner properties, but mostly on AOL online advertising. That promise was good news for the AOL unit, but not for the cable division. To remedy that situation, the AOL division proceeded to compensate Time Warner Cable for the loss of Oxygen's carriage fee by buying tens of millions of dollars in ads on Time Warner Cable. Manipulating Oxygen's carriage fee like that wasn't just round-tripping; it was also double booking. The same money was booked twice, once as ad revenue at the AOL division and then as ad revenue at Time Warner Cable.

■ ■ ■

BY THE SPRING OF 2001, THE COUNTRY WAS OFFICIALLY IN A RE-cession. Stuck with excess inventory that no one wanted and no one needed, companies were doing everything possible to get their sales and stock prices moving again. Between January and April 2001 alone, the Federal Reserve Bank cut interest rates four times. Still stocks kept plunging. America was undergoing what *The Wall Street Journal* would later call "the most wrenching bear market in stocks since the Great Depression."

The advertising market was weak. Sales of television commercials were down sharply from the previous year. The magazine industry, which generally lags behind television by about six months, braced itself. Online advertising was already slumping badly. In early April 2001, Yahoo! announced its first ever decline in revenues, a drop of 22 percent from the previous year. In the opinion of analysts, those numbers would fall even further, as much as 30 percent for the full year. Reacting to their predictions, shares of Yahoo! hit an all-time low that month: at $11.38, they were down a staggering 70 percent since January. In the somber post-Internet economy, it seemed unimaginable that in the heady days of early 2000, Yahoo! had traded for $239 a share.

By a miracle, on April 18, AOL Time Warner had wonderful news to report: In its first quarter as a merged company, advertising revenue had increased by 10 percent, in line with projections. Most of the Time Warner divisions had done badly. At the AOL unit, however, advertising and e-commerce revenue was up 37 percent to $721 million, from $538 million a year earlier. It was astounding. "This puts us on track to meet the financial goals we've set for the calendar year," Levin told reporters proudly. Wall Street couldn't have agreed more. "This sets the tone for a big year for the company," one analyst told *The Wall Street Journal*. "It shows their resilience in the face of a difficult advertising market."

Impressed by the quarterly results, investors bid up AOL Time Warner's stock price by 12 percent to $49 that day alone. Less than five weeks later, on May 21, AOL's stock had climbed another 19 percent to $58.51. Since the beginning of 2001, AOL was up an incredible 85 percent. Like a Hovercraft, the company was riding "above normal market dynamics," just as Levin had promised.

Meanwhile, helping the company's stock to climb higher and higher, Steve Case was rapturously promoting the "big strategy" behind AOL Time Warner: "The basic bet is that convergence is going to happen, and it's not just about the TV," he told a reporter in June 2001. "It's about knitting together the PC, the TV, the telephone, and the stereo to allow people to be entertained in better ways, to be educated in better ways, to communicate in better ways, to change people's lives."

As chairman of AOL Time Warner, Case had become the company's elder statesman, making visionary speeches about the digital age and predicting the coming of the great convergence. Busy tending to his charitable foundation and his family, he was increasingly out of touch with his key executives in 2001. Nonetheless, just about anyone inside the company could have told him the facts: In 2001, there *was* no big strategy at AOL Time Warner—unless cutting costs to save $1 billion is a strategy. Whether Case recognized it, his job wasn't "to allow people" to be educated in better ways; it was to make sure that AOL Time Warner could meet the numbers he'd promised to Wall Street.

By June, the company was running out of tricks. Every division of AOL Time Warner was struggling, and yet outsiders had no idea what was going on. As the largest division and the supposed driver of AOL Time Warner, the AOL unit just had to meet its targets.

In the late spring of 2001, Myer Berlow confronted Barry Schuler, head of the AOL division. He couldn't meet AOL's advertising numbers for the year, period.

"You've got to find a way to do it," Schuler pleaded.

"Barry," Berlow replied, "we've got first quarter and we've got second quarter, but after that, you've got to find a way to get this taken care of because we're not going to make third quarter."

Nervous, other division heads confronted their bosses. In meeting after meeting with Jerry Levin, Bob Pittman, and Mike Kelly, for example, Time Inc.'s Don Logan argued that the targets should be revised. He couldn't make the numbers promised to Wall Street, he told them. But the targets weren't revised; instead, Logan, Berlow, and others were ordered to work harder, faster. Costs were cut further, more people were fired, and employees who remained were pushed to work longer hours. "Bob Pittman's never missed a number in his life," they were told. "And he's not going to miss this one."

Meanwhile, demonstrating that the targets he'd set were realistic and within range, Levin had been charging ahead with AOL Time Warner's stock buyback program. Between February and June, AOL Time Warner spent an incredible $1.3 billion of the company's money buying back its own stock on the open market. That was good news for investors: AOL Time Warner's stock had to be undervalued!

Or maybe the stock wasn't undervalued. Because while the $1.3 billion buyback was going on, AOL Time Warner's top executives were unloading their personal holdings, selling hundreds of millions of dollars' worth of shares. Between February and May 2001, Steve Case made $100 million by dumping two million AOL Time Warner shares. He may have distanced himself from the day-to-day operations at AOL Time Warner, but he hadn't lost his sense of timing. Pittman got rid of nearly all his AOL Time Warner stock in the spring of 2001, cashing in 1.5 million shares worth a total of $73 million. As for Dick Parsons, in April and May, he made a quick $35 million by selling 700,000 shares. At least a dozen other executives and directors sold shares that spring as well; among them were Mike Kelly ($19 million), David Colburn ($9 million), Mayo Stuntz ($22.8 million), Kenny Lerer ($10.5 million), George Vradenburg ($28 million) Ken Novack ($33.5 million), Miles Gilbourne ($19.7 million), Jim Barksdale ($10 million), and Ted Turner ($152 million). And there may well have been others who sold, too: there's no way to know for sure because the Securities and Exchange Commission does not require insiders at the division level to report their sales of stock.

How should those stock sales be interpreted? What did they signify? Were they, as some people would later allege, "a bail-out by them to pocket hundreds of millions before the truth about the failure of the merger and problems with AOL Time Warner became public and the stock collapsed," to quote the wording of a class-action lawsuit filed in April 2003? Or were the top officers of AOL Time Warner setting aside a little money for a rainy day—a hundred million here and there—as "part of their long-term personal financial planning," in the words of a loyal company spokesman?

Years ago, insiders rarely sold stock. To do so was to declare openly that you lacked faith in the future of your own company. It was contrary to empire building. Curiously enough, or characteristically, the only AOL Time Warner executive who did not sell shares in 2001 was Jerry Levin. "As a matter of principle, I didn't sell any stock while I was CEO," Levin would later inform me, taking the moral high road.

Here's some historical context. Henry Luce never sold shares in Time Inc. When he died in 1967, he left 1,012,575 shares to his estate, almost 15 percent of Time Inc.'s outstanding stock. "Harry," his wife once asked, "don't you think it's a mistake to have all your eggs in one basket?" "It's all right," he answered, "as long as it's my basket."

Sam Walton, who founded Wal-Mart in 1945, took his company public in 1970 and died in 1992; in those twenty-two years, he never sold a single share of stock. At his death, Walton's stake in Wal-Mart was worth $25 billion. Then there's Warren Buffett, who, since buying Berkshire Hathaway for $11 million in 1965, has never sold a share in his company. Referring to his partner, Charles Munger, Buffett proudly declared in 1996 that "Charlie's family has 90 percent or more of its net worth in Berkshire shares; my wife, Suzie, and I have more than 99 percent."

By the late 1990s, however, men like Luce, Walton, and even Buffett had become anachronisms, and insider selling had become the norm. Somehow we'd become convinced by the founders and CEOs of Internet and telecom companies that selling huge blocks of shares in their own companies was perfectly natural. Just because people were rushing to cash out and cash in didn't mean they lacked faith in their company. They were seizing the day. Besides, who built companies for the long term anymore? The whole point of running a company was to make money on its stock. Didn't insiders deserve a piece of the action, too? "Why would I not sell?" one CEO told *Fortune* defensively. "I was a shareholder like any other shareholder."

The stock market is not a zero-sum game. As soon as an AOL Time Warner executive got out in the spring of 2001, some investor out there, convinced that the shares were undervalued, jumped in. Then the company's stock sank like a stone.

■ ■ ■

PITTMAN KEPT POUNDING THE TABLE. OF THE ONE HUNDRED biggest advertisers at Time Inc., Turner Broadcasting, and AOL, only four were shared by all three divisions, he told his executives, in the event they'd forgotten. In other words, ninety-six advertisers had to be sold on the benefits of cross-divisional advertising. Impatient with the lack of progress at Time Warner, AOL'ers would swagger into meetings, roll their eyes, look at their wristwatches, and say original things like "You people really need to start moving at Internet speed."

The reason Time Warner and AOL shared so few advertisers was obvious to the salesmen at Time Warner: AOL was a boiler-room operation, a bucket shop that attracted the dregs of advertising. Why share your best clients—high-class, major advertisers you've spent years wooing—with the upstarts at AOL? Why share revenue when you could keep it to yourself? Besides, it was important to distance yourself from what Time Warner's sales force regarded as AOL's quick and dirty sales tactics.

For instance, everyone at Time Warner had heard the story about the steak knife. In January 2001, just after the AOL Time Warner merger closed, a few of the company's salesmen had taken the CEO of Hasbro, Alan Hassenfeld, to a Manhattan steak house for lunch. AOL's Neil Davis came along, as did Stephen Heyer, Turner Broadcasting's president and chief operating officer.

For years, Hasbro had been a distant number two to Mattel in the toy business. But Mattel was doing badly; in 2000, with its growth in neutral and its stock falling through the floor, the company had abruptly fired its CEO, the flamboyant Jill Barad. Struggling to regain its footing, Mattel was in chaos. This was a perfect opportunity for Hasbro to assert itself as America's preeminent toy manufacturer, in the view of AOL's Neil Davis.

Over lunch, speaking on behalf of his colleagues, Davis made his pitch to Hassenfeld. Hasbro could overthrow Mattel by teaming up with AOL Time Warner. "Your competitor is a wounded animal," Davis announced. "You can either allow him to recover, which he will do with time, or you can do what we do to our competitors. . . ." Whereupon Davis grabbed his steak knife, raised it above his head, and slammed the knife straight down, cutting the tablecloth and impaling the table. While his Time Warner cohorts sat there wide-eyed, in disbelief, David looked up at Hassenfeld and continued: "You can jam a knife in his heart."

Delighted with his stab at amateur theater, Davis returned to the office in high spirits. The lunch had gone very well, he told Heyer. A deal with Hasbro was imminent; Davis was sure of that.

The next morning, first thing, Myer Berlow dragged Davis into his office. "Pittman just called me," Berlow said. "Did you really take a steak knife and jam it into the table and tell Hassenfeld that's what we do to our competitors? Did you?"

Davis was unrepentant. "Absolutely," he replied. "It was a great meeting."

Back at the office, Heyer repeated the story. Davis had made all of them look like gangsters. He'd plunged his knife into the table! He was a barbarian! This was *not* how salesmen behaved at Time Warner. Heyer was embarrassed to be sitting at lunch with him. Pittman was furious. He called Berlow, saying: "How many times do I have to tell you guys to stop acting like cowboys?" The Hasbro deal never happened.

Throughout 2001, Time Warner and AOL clashed over almost every sale. "They all talk about integrated positions, but none of them do it," an executive at a major advertising agency said at the time. "I go to Turner Broadcasting and say, 'Okay, I want to do a cross-platform deal,' but they really don't get AOL and the magazines in

line. It's chaos. There's no strategic link, no coordination." Gene De-
Witt, former chairman and CEO of Optimedia USA, the big media-
buying agency, concurred: "The individual operations at AOL Time
Warner have no interest in working with each other, and no one in
management has the power to make them work with each other.
From day one, it was just wheels spinning."

An early dispute centered on American Airlines. American was
one of Time Warner's biggest advertisers; it was also its corporate
airline. In exchange for discounts on flights, Time Warner employees
always flew American. American had also been a major AOL advertiser, but in 2001 its contract with AOL expired and American didn't
want to renew it. With the economy so uncertain, the airline wanted
to avoid long-term financial commitments.

In response, using its trademark tactics of intimidation, AOL
threatened to replace American as its corporate airline. United Airlines was willing to sign a cross-divisional advertising deal. Time
Warner's executives balked when they heard that news. Time Inc. in
particular had a tight relationship with American Airlines going back
seventeen years. During golf games, fishing trips, dinners, and baseball games, Time Inc.'s top salesmen had bonded with the airline's executives. They'd worked closely together in good times and bad. They
were personal friends. They knew one another's spouses. They helped
one other's children land summer jobs. And all of a sudden, AOL was
about to dump American. That wasn't how business was conducted at
Time Inc., not at all. "One of the things that I personally and profes-
sionally hold dear is relationships: being there for your partners and
expecting them to be there for you, too"—that's Jack Haire, president
of Time Inc.'s Fortune Group, explaining his philosophy and, by ex-
tension, Time Inc.'s. "It's a two-way street, but it starts at home."

For months, Haire lobbied strongly against the United deal. He
begged Pittman to reconsider. American Airlines, a "preferred
client," deserved to be treated with special care, Haire argued. But
AOL's hardhearted salesmen weren't moved. Haire was being irra-

tional and sentimental. If American Airlines didn't want to pay up, they should be dumped. Business was a one-way street. Fuming, Haire pointed out that the United deal was worth only $5 million. Why alienate a longtime advertiser for peanuts? The battle over American Airlines became so heated, so impossible for both sides to discuss rationally, that in the end the fight had to be broken up by executives at the highest levels. United Airlines won.

According to Time Inc.'ers, United's $5 million advertising contract wouldn't even compensate for the discounts they lost on air travel with American. Maybe so. But to AOL'ers, the upside of the United deal was this: It meant they could issue another press release touting the stunning achievements of the Advertising Council. To Wall Street, the United deal would imply that AOL Time Warner's cross-media plans were on target. Pittman was making great progress!

■ ■ ■

PITTMAN WAS AN AMERICAN HERO. HIS APPEARANCE ON THE cover of *Business Week* in early 2001 had confirmed that. Exuding an easy confidence, his gaze cocksure, his arms folded just so, he was photographed wearing an open-collared shirt and a soft tweed jacket. Inside, splashed across seven pages, the article detailed Pittman's rise from rural Mississippi to the pinnacle of corporate America. Jerry Levin was hardly mentioned; eventually he'd be replaced by Pittman as CEO, the article predicted. After all, Pittman was the driving force behind AOL Time Warner. Wall Street and the media fawned on him. "The conventional wisdom in the media industry is that Mr. Pittman, 47, is set to become chief executive if and when Mr. Levin, who is 62, retires," wrote *the New York Times* in June 2001. "There is no reason to believe that Mr. Pittman would not get the job." *Fortune* named Pittman one of its "hottest business stories and people of 2001." *New York* magazine gossiped about his parties. Pittman's new wife, a stunning graphic designer named Veronique Choa, appeared in the May 2001 issue of *Harper's Bazaar.* Photographed by Patrick Demarchelier, she posed topless, breast-feeding their baby, Lucy, in a new age version of Madonna and child.

If you didn't know better, you'd think Pittman had everything under control. But it was now the summer of 2001, and as Pittman must have known, AOL Time Warner was in deep trouble. Despite the promise he'd made to Barry Schuler, Berlow hadn't made his second-quarter numbers after all. For the three months between April 1 and June 30, AOL's advertising and e-commerce revenue came in at $706 million, down sharply from the first quarter and nearly 10 percent lower than Wall Street's consensus estimate of $774 million. What's more, stories of accounting improprieties at AOL were slowly leaking out. In June, AOL Time Warner discreetly suspended two of David Colburn's salesmen, Eric Keller and Kent Wakeford. Details were hazy, but clearly something was wrong at the AOL division, where the number of new subscribers was slowing dramatically.

By July, even Mike Kelly, AOL Time Warner's CFO, was leaning on Levin and Pittman to lower the company's guidance to Wall Street—the projected numbers. AOL wasn't the only division having problems. Advertising sales had collapsed at the company's cable networks. Business was dismal at the magazine division. At Warner Music, sales were way way down. Everything was falling apart.

When AOL Time Warner released its second-quarter results on July 18, Wall Street was in shock. Who could have known? Overall revenues were just $9.2 billion, more than half a billion dollars less than analysts had projected. In a conference call to investors, Kelly cautiously tried to lower expectations for the second half of 2001: "We are assuming only a slight upturn in advertising," he said. (A "slight upturn" is not a downturn.) The $40 billion in revenue they'd promised for the full year was moving out of focus. "We're looking at the $40 billion being on the top of our range," Kelly added.

Kelly didn't admit to investors what everyone inside the company knew—that $40 billion wasn't in range, full stop. He sidestepped other discouraging news, assuring people that in the second half of the year, the company would make up the latest quarter's shortfall. As for Levin, he was still up in the clouds or on a mountaintop: "This has been a powerful quarter," he told more than one reporter in July 2001. "It's proof positive that the merger is working." Bob Pittman, the former disc jockey, played the song people wanted to hear, the request number: "The story of this quarter is that our synergies are hitting, and they're hitting big," he said with a straight face.

A few investors figured out that someone wasn't telling the truth. On July 18, the day that AOL Time Warner released its second-quarter numbers, the company's stock dropped by 10 percent. Convinced that the inflated numbers could still be met, Pittman wouldn't admit defeat. (Not that he had much to lose: by July 18, he'd sold nearly all his AOL Time Warner stock.) "Saying 'No' or saying 'I can't do it' was not in Pittman's parlance," explained George Vrandenburg, an AOL senior vice president. "[He'd say] 'Go take that hill!' And when his men said, 'It's unrealistic, sir,' he'd say, 'The hell it is! You go take that hill!' He wouldn't publicly admit there was a problem until he had a solution."

"Bob's style of management was that you have to keep pushing, because if you do not push very hard—it's just human nature—people slack off," added another AOL'er. "You don't throw in the towel on numbers until you know it's impossible to do it. And even once it's become impossible to make the numbers, you keep pushing and trying to find ways for success, and that's what drives great people and drives great companies."

AOL'ers who had worked with Pittman since 1996 trusted his instincts. They'd seen his management style work miracles. But by the summer of 2001, many of AOL's most senior executives doubted Pittman. More and more, for example, Schuler and Pittman were at odds. Exasperated by Schuler's leadership of the AOL division,

Pittman insisted angrily that Schuler wasn't devoting enough time and energy to ad sales. By then, however, Schuler had lost faith. In his opinion, Pittman was no longer in touch with reality.

Much later, after it was all over and the finger pointing had begun, Pittman would only say: "The promises were not my job. I was the operations guy. My job was once someone made the promise to make it happen."

■ ■ ■

PITTMAN'S VAUNTED CROSS-MEDIA DEALS WERE GOING NO-where. He'd exhausted most of his personal contacts. Any money that could be squeezed from his suppliers had been squeezed. Of the country's thirty biggest advertisers, AOL Time Warner's Ad Council had managed to sign on one. By the late summer of 2001, a few reporters and analysts were asking pointed questions about AOL's accounting. DO AOL'S ADS ADD UP? was the title of a short but prescient July 2001 article in *Fortune.* Among other slippery account-ing practices, the article noted, AOL was booking advertising revenue from barter deals in which no cash actually changed hands. Robert Olstein of the Olstein Financial Alert fund called it "phantom rev-enue."

By August, AOL Time Warner's stock price was below $40, some 30 percent off its high of three months earlier. That month, under extreme pressure, and refusing to call it a day, Pittman dreamed up yet another intracompany committee to implement cross-divisional ad deals. He called it the Global Marketing Solutions Group, and named as its leader his best salesman, the ingenious Myer Berlow, whose orders were straightforward: Take that hill, drag in an elephant, capture the big deal. "For me this is a dream come true," Berlow enthused at the time. "The promise of the merger always was to get the brands working together to sell more."

So the valiant Berlow captured a giant elephant: a $90 million deal with Burger King. It would be the ultimate in cross-divisional strategic alliances. Every issue of *Sports Illustrated* would include a "Whopper Sports Moment of the Month" (named for Burger King's Big Whopper sandwich); free Warner Music CDs would be given away with every Burger King purchase; Burger King customers could access a "BK Backstage" Web site on AOL featuring free music downloads and live chats with celebrities. There was more: Fun factoids about Warner Music performers would be printed on Burger King tray liners; and as a reward for exemplary performance on the job, Burger King employees would be given walk-on roles in Warner Bros. sitcoms—*Friends,* for example.

Of course, there was a stumbling block. Even before Berlow had approached Burger King, other members of the Global Marketing Solutions Group, salesmen from Time Inc. and Turner Broadcasting, had put together their own cross-media deal, with Wendy's. Worth some $30 million, the deal was ready to go as soon as it got a final sign-off from Berlow. Burger King was adamant: even though its $90 million deal wasn't ready to go, it had to be announced first. That was just fine with Berlow, for whom the Wendy's deal was a trifle, a child's portion; it hardly qualified as a "holistic" strategic alliance. "It didn't predicate itself on the transformation of a business," sniffed Berlow. "There was nothing big there. There was no involvement of the movie studio; there was no involvement of music; there was no taking advantage of what the total business was."

Even if the Wendy's deal wasn't "holistic," the Time Inc. and Turner salesmen felt obligated, as a matter of principle, to announce the Wendy's deal first, they told Berlow. It was about being there for your partners; it was a two-way street and all that. After all, Wendy's was under the impression that of all the hamburger chains, it was the only one signing a cross-media deal with AOL Time Warner; imagine what would happen when Wendy's read about the Burger King deal!

In October 2001, a meeting was called at 75 Rock to discuss the hamburger business. With Berlow and his fellow AOL'ers on one side of the table and Time Warner's sales force on the other, the discussion disintegrated into a brawl. "You're saying we have to give up the Burger King deal because Wendy's is going to be mad at us? That's absurd," Berlow argued. "There was no exclusivity to the Wendy's deal! There's no overlap between the two deals legally or morally!" When Turner's Larry Goodman, head of CNN's ad sales, suggested Wendy's was under the distinct impression that its deal was exclusive, Berlow exploded. Holding up the unsigned Wendy's contract, shaking it back and forth, he bellowed: "If they got that impression, they didn't get it from me or from this document or from any document that you've sent around internally."

"It's not in writing, Myer," ventured a nervous voice at the other end of the table, "but that was the spirit of the deal."

At that point in the meeting, Berlow lost it. "Don't tell me it was the spirit of the deal," he shouted, "because the whole reason we have these meetings, the whole reason we discuss these things, the whole reason we have all these internal documents, is so we know what was said. I do not have any evidence that Wendy's was given an exclusive. If one of you made that promise, tell me now." When the room fell silent, Berlow continued his rant: "Besides, the Wendy's deal hasn't been signed. We do not announce press releases without a signed deal."

That's when things got out of hand. Someone accused Berlow of purposely stalling on the Wendy's deal, refusing to sign off on it so that the Burger King deal would be done first. "Bullshit!" said Berlow. He was standing up now, gesturing wildly, threatening to walk out of the meeting. "We don't have a signature on that deal because their agency is bullshitting around. I haven't seen the goddamn papers."

It hardly matters now, the company's battle over Burger King and Wendy's. The point is, though, that it confirmed stereotypes. Implying that Berlow lacked scruples, that for enough money he'd stab his own mother in the back, Jack Haire (president of Time Inc.'s Fortune Group and friend to American Airlines) laid it on the table. "If it comes down to a question of a $100 million deal with Burger King or lying to somebody, I'll take my chances and lose the $100 million," Haire stated.

Thinking back on that day in 2001, Berlow remembered it as a defining moment. "They accused us of being whores, while they supposedly stood for purity," Berlow recalled with disgust. "The fact is they wanted to kill that deal for any reason they could find. And I sat and sat and sat and tried to understand what would possibly be the reason why you would say no to $90 million. Fundamentally, they didn't want one big company. Anything that drives toward centralization is the worst thing in the world for them."

Repeat those words to people at Time Warner, and they'll tell you Berlow was overwrought. The AOL Time Warner merger was a debacle because AOL's top executives were incompetent. End of story. "Those guys were fucking idiots about business—just fucking idiots," raged one Time Warner executive. Added Haire: "Myer was more of a guy to run a scrappy sales organization, not a sophisticated series of sales relationships. He was in way, way, way over his head."

"Get real," Berlow answered when I told him what the other side was saying. "I sold $2.5 billion worth of ads. They, at most, are responsible for $100 million; essentially they run small businesses." Going on and on about the insufferable pretensions of Time Warner executives and their high horses, and becoming more and more animated with every word, Berlow said: "They don't care about generating ad sales—all they want to do is win political battles. That place is full of people who don't have real jobs, who walk around in their suspenders and call themselves 'executive director' of this and of that and don't do anything. . . . To them, it's all about status; it's not about money. Anyone who believes it's about money is really looked down on. Well, what the fuck else matters when you're in business?"

The eloquent Berlow wasn't finished: "At Time Inc. they talk about having some sort of higher calling. What higher calling? I'll tell you, *People* magazine doesn't represent a higher calling. It's not what the Founding Fathers had in mind when they wrote the First Amendment. Is *Time* magazine uplifting? Is that a higher calling?"

TEN

Jerry Levin wasn't in New York when the World Trade Center came down. He didn't hear the hysterical screams of police sirens and ambulance sirens and fire sirens just after 9:15 A.M. on September 11, 2001. He didn't rush to his office window on the twenty-ninth floor of AOL Time Warner's headquarters to see flames and clouds of dark brown smoke engulfing the Twin Towers before they collapsed. Levin witnessed the horror on a television screen in Sweden, on the other side of the planet.

Sitting on the edge of his bed in the Grand Hotel in Stockholm, Levin watched as gaping holes opened in one tower, then in the other. Over and over, the scenes were replayed on CNN: the holes in the buildings like wounds, the planes disappearing into the towers, the charred bodies, the cacophony of sirens, the heroism, the ashes, the grief. The acrid smoke that Levin could not smell kept rising from the ruined towers. People were hurling themselves into space.

Jerry Levin collapsed on September 11, 2001. No one close to him had died in the terrorist attacks, none of his employees had been hurt, and yet he was weeping uncontrollably. At night in his hotel room, he'd wake up covered in sweat. As he would later explain, it was a belated "emotional response mechanism" to the 1997 murder of his son Jonathan. "It all came back to me—my son's death," Levin said. "I was a basket case. I was very emotional. I was naked and raw. It brought back a lot of memories."

When he returned to New York a week later, Levin visited ground zero. Wearing a hard hat and a face mask, he was escorted by an assistant police commissioner. Purposefully, Levin made his way through the wreckage. Bulldozers were digging, massive dump trucks were rolling in to remove the metal and scorched earth. Down on their hands and knees, firemen and other emergency workers were searching inch by square inch for any human remains. In the shadow of the twisted metal skeletons, Levin stood silently. "I thought I was with someone in mourning," said Kenny Lerer, who accompanied Levin that day. "I've never seen anyone fall apart, come apart at the seams like that. He was shell-shocked. It was horrifying."

Other people I've talked to used images of war and its aftermath to describe Levin's psychological state. In the view of Dick Parsons, Levin was suffering from posttraumatic shock syndrome. "After September 11, you could see a change come over him," Parsons said. "I've likened it to a Vietnam flashback: it's almost like it ripped open a scar that had scabbed over."

For an entire week, Levin did nothing but mourn with his employees. Traveling to every division of AOL Time Warner, he walked down every hallway of every building, shook people's hands, listened to them, and wept. "It was like going from wake to wake to wake. It was like he was everyone's father," recalled Lerer, who, along with Parsons, accompanied Levin on this exhausting cross-company journey of psychological displacement. "He didn't want to deal with anything else—business didn't matter."

Levin gave firm instructions to his division heads at Time Inc., CNN, and NY1 (the local all-news channel): Spend whatever you need to cover the war on terrorism. AOL Time Warner, he asserted, had a "fundamental moral responsibility to maintain and expand the process of creative freedom, journalistic independence, and democratic dialogue." Between September 11 and September 21, Levin sent out five long company wide e-mails intended to comfort his employees and give them something to cling to. "Nearly half a century ago, in the face of the enormous loss of innocent blood, Albert Camus asserted that those responsible would not triumph. 'Our faith,' he wrote, 'is that throughout the world, beside the impulse toward coercion and death that is darkening history, there is a growing impulse toward persuasion and life.' " Levin continued: "As individuals and as a Company, you've helped reaffirm that 'the impulse toward coercion and death' will ultimately be defeated, that our country and our communities will stand together, and that the work of building a better, freer, more just world will go on."

At the age of sixty-two, in September 2001, two months after AOL Time Warner's disastrous second-quarter results had come out, Levin had put on the armor of righteousness. Identifying himself with his shaky and shaken company, he told his employees that AOL Time Warner was not a detached, inhuman, unfeeling, impersonal corporate entity. On the contrary, AOL Time Warner comprised a community of souls dedicated to the principles of freedom and democracy and life and persuasion and so on: "The very things that the extremists seek to destroy—diversity of opinion, artistic expression, cultural and religious pluralism, civic dialogue, journalistic independence, creative freedom, the open flow of ideas, information, and images—are AOL Time Warner's reasons for being." Time Inc. had a higher calling after all: it was just what the Founding Fathers had in mind when they wrote the First Amendment.

Finally, perhaps to prove that his empathy and concern were genuine, Levin referred obliquely to his son's death: "The healing process will be long, but let me say here that you will not be alone. AOL Time Warner is a family—especially in times like these. . . . I know from painful, personal experience how critical this support is." When your child has died tragically, that's the sort of letter people write you.

■ ■ ■

IF SEPTEMBER 11 STIRRED UP LEVIN'S LATENT GRIEF FOR HIS SON, it also fueled his resentment against Steve Case. Using his moral authority to get the upper hand, Levin started by implying that Case lacked the compassion needed to lead AOL Time Warner through its time of emotional trauma. "People were hurting; they'd lost loved ones, they'd seen the horrors of what had happened," Levin recalled. "After 9/11, we needed to repair; we were a ministry. But Steve just wanted to get back to business. I said, 'I don't give a shit about business.' "

And Case didn't give a shit about ministries. When Levin demanded that Case cancel an AOL Time Warner board meeting scheduled soon after 9/11, Case refused. Seething, and partly unhinged, Levin argued that pushing the company to meet its financial projections was now irrelevant—the more urgent task at hand was ministering to employees and the community. Case, detached and unemotional as usual, countered that the best way to respond to the attacks was to get back to "business as usual."

As tensions between the two men increased, it dawned on Case, after the fact, that his first error in merging AOL with Time Warner had been to hand over the title of CEO to Levin and then, as chairman, to withdraw to the sidelines. It had seemed like a good idea at the time. Back then, Case had been attracted to the role of elder statesman. But now, sensing he was losing his hold on Levin (or sensing that Levin was losing his hold on himself), Case insisted that Levin keep him informed.

"He kept sending me e-mails, sometimes twenty-eight e-mails a day," said Levin, still frustrated at the memory of those e-mails flooding in. "He had an opinion on everything. He kept pressing me and pressing me." Levin would have none of it. For the past decade, guided by an internal compass, he'd run his company independently, with moral certainty, and he wasn't about to change.

Back and forth they went, Levin and Case, in a flurry of vitriolic e-mails. With condescension, Levin accused Case of failing to understand a media organization's responsibilities to the public. Furthermore, Levin implied, Case could not possibly know or feel the pain of losing a loved one. "The thing that bothered me was his lack of compassion with respect to 9/11," Levin explained. "Steve is an automaton. While he spoke of values, and he believed in those values, he has no spirituality."

As Levin was focusing on the work of mourning, one thing was clear to Case: His vision of AOL Time Warner's future was being distorted. Case didn't pretend to be a psychiatrist, but in his view, Levin was spiraling out of control. Levin himself admitted he was "a wreck," and though he attributed his condition to September 11, his breakdown had been triggered by more than that. On September 24, 2001, the company finally admitted publicly what insiders had known for some time: AOL Time Warner would miss its stated goals for the year, badly. Instead of growing by 30 percent, the company's cash flow would increase "in the 20 percent range." As for revenues, they would be up by 5 to 7 percent rather than by 10 percent. AOL Time Warner's stock, which in May had traded as high as $58.51, was hovering weakly around $30.

The world was in turmoil, and in response Levin was running a public ministry. There was no need to apologize to Wall Street for failing to deliver the numbers he'd promised. Evading the matter of shortfalls, and suggesting that any discussion of financials was disrespectful to the mourners and the mourned, Levin issued a curt written response to Wall Street: "No financial impact can compare to the terrible suffering and loss of life inflicted by the vicious attacks of September 11. The AOL Time Warner family is fully committed to continuing to do everything in our power to assist those who have been affected." It would have been crass to suggest that shareholders too had been affected.

Case, meanwhile, wanted to draw people's attention away from

September 11. Focusing on the big picture, he insisted that the company's financial results were a blip and a freak: "The bottom line is—despite this tragedy and the resulting economic effects—our unique mix of assets give[s] us confidence that we can generate strong earnings growth next year and into the future."

Case and Levin were no longer soul mates, celebrating over wine and chocolate mousse. As their squabbling grew more intense and more infantile, Levin made public pronouncements that were sure to infuriate Case and provoke him. For example, on November 9, Levin let investors know that he and his company existed on a high moral plane, whereas Wall Street worshipped Mammon. Echoing Henry Luce, Levin reminded his audience that AOL Time Warner "operates as a public trust as well as for our shareholders." When one analyst at the meeting dared to ask how the company's response to September 11 had managed to squeeze the profit margins, Levin raged: "I will provide whatever resources necessary to CNN, NY1, to all the magazines—will do whatever it takes. And I'm not interested in hearing what happens to margins with respect to those expenses."

Wait a minute. Just a few months earlier, in July 2001, Levin had promised to do whatever was necessary to meet AOL Time Warner's financial projections, assuring Wall Street: "We're running the company through the financial function." He'd boasted to a reporter, stating: "I'm a hawk on margins." Now, as if the company's finances were below his dignity, Levin let his audience know that the analyst's question about margins was not only an insult; it was "almost sacrilegious." Then, in what may have been a veiled threat to Case, Levin added: "I'm the CEO and this is what I'm going to do. I don't care what anyone says." As if to prove he meant every word he said, Levin proceeded to send out a grandiose, two-thousand-word company-wide e-mail outlining AOL Time Warner's strategy and its guiding principles. He did not ask for Case's input.

Levin's moral grandstanding didn't impress Case. But it did

have a mesmerizing effect on others, especially those who, having been spared mercifully on September 11, had vowed to lead more spiritual lives. Instead of writing about the very real problems at AOL Time Warner, the media praised Levin greatly. In late October, an 8,800-word article in *The New Yorker* portrayed Levin as a bold, capable leader at the very top of his game; Barry Diller, then CEO of USA Networks, was quoted: "[Jerry Levin] is, without any question or qualifications, the single most powerful person in media and communications." Levin himself noted that he had never been more satisfied: "For me, personally, this is the best it's ever been."

A few weeks later, in November, Levin was the subject of a sympathetic cover story in the *New York Observer.* It referred to AOL Time Warner's CEO as "a philosopher prince of the American media establishment" and concluded he had triumphed over all those rubes from Dulles, Virginia. *Fortune,* in a special issue devoted to "the New Future" and published on November 13, hailed Levin as "one of the smartest people we know." For the cover of *Fortune,* Levin was photographed with six other very smart people we know, including Bill Clinton and former secretary of state Madeleine Albright.

Inside AOL Time Warner, many senior executives were nervous, unsure how Levin's new found sense of purpose should be understood. A senior vice president who'd heard Levin's November 9 speech to investors explained his ambivalence this way: "I remember thinking that he was honorable—but also a little nuts." Insiders who'd watched Levin's devious corporate moves over the years wondered whether he wasn't using the events of September 11 as a red herring to draw attention away from his colossal mistake of having sold Time Warner to AOL in the first place. "[Levin] was in a panic— it was the first time I'd ever seen him like that," recalled another senior executive who worked closely with Levin. "He knew he'd failed on some cosmic level."

Case was neither nervous nor ambivalent: he was incensed. As was Ted Turner, whose hostility toward Levin had been gathering steam ever since he'd sold his company to Time Warner in 1997. Aside from watching the value of his shares deflate like a balloon the day after a birthday party, Turner had been given almost nothing to do since the AOL Time Warner merger. He was bored and he was bitter. Even his nominal job as vice chairman of the company was slipping away: the media were rife with speculation that Levin intended to dump Turner altogether once his contract expired at the end of 2001.

Combined with the collapse in AOL Time Warner's share price, Levin's increasingly irrational behavior was the opportunity Turner had been waiting for: it was the perfect excuse to launch an open attack on Levin. At first, when he started his campaign, Turner grumbled about Levin to a few friends. Then he took his cause public. To anyone who'd listen, Turner complained loudly that thanks to Levin, his fortune had been cut in half. At a cable industry conference in November 2001, he announced that his greatest regret was selling out to Time Warner. Instead, he said, he should have bought Time Warner "so I could have fired Jerry Levin before he fired me."

That same month, at an otherwise ordinary meeting of AOL Time Warner's board of directors, Turner turned on Levin. Banging his fist on the long conference table, yelling for all he was worth (which was less each day), he accused Levin of incompetence and negligence. Levin, Turner alleged, had destroyed the company— personally. And now he had the audacity to tell investors that he didn't care about profit margins! Raging, Turner loudly reminded the fifteen other directors of one hard fact: In just four months, AOL Time Warner's stock price had been halved.

Turner's outburst was followed by silence. Not one of the assembled AOL Time Warner directors defended Levin, not even Levin himself. Seemingly unruffled, his long face expressionless, his narrow shoulders bent, Levin didn't respond at all. Instead, as though nothing unusual had just occurred, he introduced the next item on the agenda. Levin was used to criticism. He had distanced himself from the world and its false gods. In his opinion, he was no longer obligated to Wall Street, or his directors, or his shareholders. Depressed, he took solace in eating fatty foods; that fall, while AOL Time Warner's stock price kept deflating, Levin ballooned to 174 pounds, about 20 pounds more than he weighed at the announcement of the AOL Time Warner deal.

Destiny was in charge, and the inevitable was about to happen. One perceptive insider who watched every scene of the play remarked: "Like all great Greek tragedies, you knew the plot before it played out—you knew who'd be sacrificed at the altar."

■ ■ ■

IN THE SUMMER OF 2001, AT&T'S CABLE SYSTEMS, KNOWN AS AT&T Broadband, had come up for sale. Levin dreamed about getting his hands on it. With fourteen million subscribers, AT&T Broadband was the biggest cable network in the country. If Levin were to combine it with AOL Time Warner's cable division, he'd wind up with a cable network three times the size of Comcast Corp., his nearest competitor. He'd then control one-third of the entire U.S. cable business, with an awesome twenty-seven million cable subscribers.

With the exception of having put HBO on satellite in 1975, nothing made Levin prouder than his longtime commitment to cable. In the mid-1990s, he'd gambled his whole career on it. Back then, he'd referred to cable as "the fundamental architecture of a dynamic new medium." Of course, the medium he'd had in mind hadn't been the Internet; it had been interactive television. Still, he'd always viewed cable as an essential conduit for the interactive future. Now, in Levin's view, cable was crucial to fulfilling the promise and prophecy of the AOL Time Warner merger. As Bill Gates had foreseen in 1997, the future of the Internet was not in twisted-copper phone lines; it lay in coaxial cable, otherwise known as broadband.

By the fall of 2001, without consulting Case, Levin started working on a deal to buy AT&T Broadband. When Case discovered what was up, he hit the roof, or blew a fuse, or both. It's not that Case disagreed in principle with the deal. Yes, cable was critical to the digital future, but in his opinion AOL Time Warner couldn't afford to buy AT&T Broadband, not then. If money was to be spent, Case argued, it should go toward upgrading AOL, not buying more cable systems. Demanding an explanation from Levin, who'd gone behind his back, Case was ignored at first. Then, imperiously, Levin informed Case that his involvement in the AT&T Broadband deal wasn't necessary until plans were further along. So far the internal discussions were only "tactical," as Levin put it, and therefore Case's input wasn't needed or wanted. On the contrary, replied Case, any potential acquisition was a "strategic" decision, and the deal was very much under his jurisdiction. It would have been comical, their battle of words, had so much not been at stake.

Levin was unmoved by Case and his arguments. Convinced that AOL Time Warner should buy AT&T's cable unit, he intended to pursue his single-minded vision despite the opinion of others. "I'm not like Steve Ross or Ted Turner or Steve Case—I'm not monomaniacal," Levin insisted. "But when I believe in something, I believe in it fully." When Miles Gilburne, Case's longtime strategist, questioned Levin's rationale for wanting to buy AT&T Broadband, Levin exploded, calling Gilburne a "fucking idiot." Being challenged by ignoramuses was far more than Levin could bear. "I understand cable: it's *my* business. I'm the guy who saw the possibilities of cable from the start—and for them to ask *me* why we should do the deal with AT&T. . . ." It was insulting.

Outraged by Levin's lack of respect for him and his people, Case threatened Levin outright: If he didn't drop the idea of buying AT&T Broadband, Case would take the fight to the board. For the first time in his career, Levin was facing an opponent as tenacious as himself. And this time Levin could not be sure the board would vote with him; for one thing, fully half of the new board had come from AOL.

What's more, in Levin's experience, when it came to the subject of cable, the AOL board members were clueless. "The AOL members of the board didn't understand cable; they were idiots," he told me. "To question whether we should be the biggest cable company! To hear these idiots try to understand issues that I have worked on for twenty—no, thirty years!"

Case had had enough. AOL Time Warner was *his* company, his creation. And with all his posturing, Levin was destroying it piece by piece. Shortly after Thanksgiving 2001, Case presented Levin with an ultimatum: Resign now or I'll convince the board to fire you. When Levin hesitated or stalled, Case started phoning every AOL Time Warner director, one after another, to make his impassioned argument. For the most part, the directors heard Case out and sympathized with him; very few were great supporters of Levin. At the same time, some directors were starting to lose confidence in Case: surely the problems in the AOL division were not Levin's fault. And though they didn't immediately voice their concerns to Case, it seemed to at least some directors that Case's cry for a palace coup was excessive— that ganging up on Levin was unseemly and inappropriate in a company as prominent as AOL Time Warner. Aware of Levin's fragile state of mind, a few directors even pitied him.

■ ■ ■

THE BOARD NEVER DID TAKE A VOTE ON WHETHER TO FIRE Levin. Instead, Levin decided not to risk it; he wouldn't give Case the satisfaction of seeing him fired. In all events, Levin was by this time exhausted, emotionally and physically. The "narcotic," as he'd once called his job, wasn't working anymore. With no one but the media left to manipulate, he found himself in a situation he couldn't get out of.

On Wednesday, December 5, 2001, at eight in the morning, Levin made a startling announcement to his board: He intended to take early retirement. So hastily was the unscheduled board meeting arranged that more than half of the sixteen directors participated by speakerphone. Even Dick Parsons was caught off guard by the suddenness of his Levin's decision. "He surprised us all," said Parsons.

At 1:46 that afternoon, Levin sent one final e-mail to all ninety thousand AOL Time Warner employees. Hinting that he had experienced a personal transformative vision, an epiphany of sorts urging him to change his life, he wrote vaguely about wanting to devote himself to "moral and social issues." The text and tone suggested he was being guided by something higher, more noble, than corporate profits. Levin signed off by quoting the Bible: "One of my favorite biblical passages is from chapter 2 of the Book of Ecclesiastes: 'To everything there is a season, and a time to every purpose under heaven.' "

That evening, speaking on CNN's *Lou Dobbs Moneyline,* Levin talked about his reasons for leaving—though, characteristically, he revealed very little. He was hunched over; he looked weary of it all. "I need to find out—people should understand—I'm not just a CEO corporate person. I am a real human being. I have strong feelings about things." Sounding from time to time as if he were talking to Oprah Winfrey and not to Lou Dobbs, Levin made a public confession: "You wouldn't know this—I'm not a suit anymore. There's a creative side. I want people to understand there's a real human being here. I am not and shouldn't be identified [as] the CEO of the world's largest media and entertainment company. I want to reclaim [my] individuality and do something that is socially significant but also creative." Levin—a man with the "nerves and toughness of a cat burglar," in the words of Dick Parsons—seemed to be on the verge of tears: "There is a real human being locked inside here, and, you know, I want the poetry back in my life."

Jerry Levin had spent thirty years working his way up: first at Time Inc, then at Time Warner, and finally at AOL Time Warner. Now, abruptly, his career was over.

ELEVEN

Officially, Jerry Levin was retiring on May 16, 2002. By early 2002, however, he'd already been forgotten at AOL Time Warner; he was a stranger. The company's 2001 annual report, issued in the spring of 2002, didn't mention him. "He's like the walking dead," one insider remarked. "When he walks into a meeting now, nobody pays attention to him—they literally don't acknowledge him."

Levin had always managed to keep his executives under control, on a tight leash. If there'd been little dissent during his tenure as CEO, it was because he didn't tolerate dissent. By the spring of 2002, however, a corporate civil war had broken out at 75 Rockefeller Plaza, with each partner at AOL Time Warner loudly accusing the other of sins of omission and commission. "The beginning of the real horror show was when Jerry left," concurred an AOL Time Warner division head. "All this tension and angst—Levin had kept it from boiling over; he'd kept it at 210 degrees with the lid on." With Levin gone, or invisible, the place was going to explode.

■ ■ ■

Bob Pittman would not succeed Levin after all. Instead, to the surprise of many onlookers, Dick Parsons, age fifty-three, was named CEO-in-waiting of AOL Time Warner. The decision to promote Parsons was explained to me this way: "He's the one who can keep all the guys on the playground playing nice." Times had changed, and visionaries like Steve Case had lost their currency at AOL Time Warner, as had Pittman with his gang of salesmen. What the company needed was someone thoughtful, someone who could understand the company's bitter, demoralized employees. Parsons was the right man. No one had a bad word to say about him. He was a born diplomat, people said, and a "teddy bear"; he was self-effacing and good-natured; he kept everything in perspective.

Recognizing the power of understatement, Parsons tended to portray himself as a gentle giant who, by a twist of fate, just happened to hold an important job. He once boasted that one of his children had given him a T-shirt that read, "I may not be bright, but I can lift heavy things." At the University of Hawaii, he dedicated himself, in his words, "to exercising my unalienable right to life, liberty, and the pursuit of coeds." "Richard," he claimed a teacher once told him, "you are to academic underachievement what Muhammad Ali is to boxing."

The truth about Parsons had to be far more complex. Charm and diplomacy are good things, but they don't explain how Richard Dean Parsons became one of only three African Americans to run a Fortune 500 company. In part, Parsons's modesty was strategic: he didn't seem to be a threat, and therefore people let down their guard. Meanwhile, slowly and steadily, Parsons moved forward, like the tortoise who beat the hare (aka Pittman on his Harley-Davidson). "Surviving is winning," Parsons noted soon after being named CEO of AOL Time Warner. "There's a certain amount of luck involved in anything in life, but I never had a doubt about how this would all work out."

Parsons's childhood was ordinary, as childhoods go. Born in Brooklyn's Bedford-Stuyvesant neighborhood on April 4, 1948, he was the second of five children. His father, Lorenzo, worked as an electrical airline technician for Sperry Rand (now Unisys Corp.) on Long Island; his mother, Isabelle, stayed at home raising the children.

When Dick Parsons was six, his family, like many aspiring working-
and middle-class African Americans, moved from Brooklyn to south-
east Queens, where they bought a tidy two-story house in South
Ozone Park, not far from the John F. Kennedy International Airport.
In 1964, Parsons graduated from John Adams High School with an
average record. "I got by, if just barely," he recalled.

Parsons left the University of Hawaii in 1968, six credits short of
graduation. Aimless, he had no idea what he wanted from life. His
girlfriend figured it out. Laura Ann Bush, a bright, determined, hard-
working student at the University of Hawaii, convinced her boyfriend
and future husband to apply to law school. "They were an odd couple,"
recalled Parson's fraternity brother and drinking buddy Scott Johnson, noting that while Parsons was a tall (six-foot-four-inch) black
New Yorker, Laura Bush was a short (five-foot-three-inch) white girl
from Oklahoma. "Here's this guy who's at the bar sixty-seven days in a
row and, as you can imagine, did very poorly in school. And then he
meets Laura, and Laura is this very efficient person, an excellent student with perfect habits, and they just hit it off. . . . He had no shortage
of brains; she just kind of helped him focus."

Parsons did well enough on his LSATs to be admitted to the
University of Albany Law School despite lacking an undergraduate
degree. He stopped spending evenings in bars. Law school, he later
noted, was "mind-changing and life-altering." In 1971, he graduated
from Albany Law School at the top of his class and took top honors in
the New York State Bar exam. "The logic of the law enthralled me,"
he said. "Its unyielding insistence on clear thinking, on building a case
piece by piece until the force of the argument had an irresistible mo-
mentum, captured my imagination."

In 1971, Parsons joined the administration of Nelson Rockefeller, then governor of New York, as a legal adviser. When Rockefeller was named vice president under Gerald Ford in 1974, Parsons
served as a senior White House aide. Later, returning to the law, he
became a partner at Patterson, Belknap, Webb & Tyler in New York.

In 1988, having abandoned both politics and law, he joining Dime
Savings Bank; named CEO in 1990 he was credited with saving the
company from insolvency during the savings and loan crisis. In 1991,
he joined the board of Time Warner. Four years later, in 1996, Jerry
Levin hired Dick Parsons as the company's president.

Levin had never wanted a second-in-command. He was chairman, CEO, and president of Time Warner; and since the position
of chief operating officer was vacant, Levin was effectively the company's COO. It had taken him years to consolidate all that power; why
would he willingly have diluted it? Because Time Warner's board of
directors, worried that Levin was overwhelmed by too much responsibility, insisted he hire someone to help out, and Dick Parsons was
the obvious choice. In the first place, Levin liked Parsons. More, he
acknowledged that Parsons had skills that he himself lacked. "Dick
had what I'll call judgment and wisdom beyond his years," Levin
said, thinking back to his decision to hire Parsons. "Secondly, Dick
had political skills. He had a nice touch. The way he thought about
problems was to accommodate different points of view."

There was something else: Parsons was no threat to Levin. A
lawyer, a politician, a banker—Parsons knew very little about the
entertainment and media business. Thus Levin had a plausible excuse
for delegating few responsibilities to Parsons, who was given no
specific portfolio when he started. Eventually, however, he made
himself indispensable at Time Warner. Using his skills as a mediator
and a politician, he took the edge off Levin's aloof management style.
"He struggled during much of the first year getting his footing,"
Levin conceded. "But then he became the ideal company man to me.
He handled problems that I couldn't or didn't want to handle,
whether with the board or with people externally, especially in Washington. I had very little patience for Washington."

Parsons's political skills were helpful in other ways. Throughout
the late 1990s, by never undermining or opposing Levin openly, Parsons survived the company purges. Smoothing ruffled feathers and

being agreeable; those were two of his great talents. He was black, he was Republican, he was six feet four, and he wore a thick beard; you might have expected him to take center stage at the company, but he never did. In 1999, Parsons served as one of Levin's few advisers on the AOL deal and helped negotiate its lax terms. In 2000, when regulators held up the merger for months, he was dispatched to Washington, where, skillfully, tactfully, he resolved the problems.

Whether Parsons actually believed in the AOL deal is anyone's guess—part of his genius was making both sides think he was their ally every step of the way. More than anything, that particular balancing act may explain how Parsons became CEO of AOL Time Warner in 2002. For despite his active involvement in crafting the merger, no one held him responsible for its catastrophic fallout. So he'd weathered that storm, but could Parsons really steer a huge company like AOL Time Warner through a hurricane? Few people thought so. "Caretaker" was the word used by one insider to describe Parsons's role as CEO.

■ ■ ■

FOR TWO YEARS, AOL TIME WARNER HAD BEEN MISLEADING reporters and shareholders; the company had glossed over its disappointing financial results and had withheld news that might destabilize the stock price. Things would be different now that Parsons was in charge. On January 7, 2002, in his first public statement since being named CEO-in-waiting of AOL Time Warner, Parsons told Wall Street: "We will try not to overpromise, and we will deliver." To herald the start of a new and temperate era at AOL Time Warner, he added: "My focus as CEO will be on building the long-term value. Short-term results are a means to an end, not an end in themselves. I think we've gotten that formulation a little bit out of whack in American business."

That same day, Parsons admitted that AOL Time Warner

would report only 5 percent growth for the year just ended. Revenues would come in at $38 billion, not $40 billion as promised. As for increasing the company's cash flow by 30 percent, there wasn't a chance in hell: the actual figure would be 18 percent. The prognosis was worse. Once upon a time, smiling, Levin and Case had promised shareholders that cash flow at AOL Time Warner would grow by 25 percent in 2002. Now, Parsons predicted, cash flow would grow just 8 to 12 percent. A few months later, in April, he would revise that figure again, to somewhere between 5 and 9 percent.

In just two years, AOL, the company's "crown jewel" (Levin's phrase), had become a millstone. Even Mary Meeker, a cheerleader for AOL Time Warner, had to acknowledge the obvious: AOL had reached what is politely and euphemistically referred to as "maturation." Growth in subscribers was slowing down, and for the first time, revenue from online advertising sales was actually falling. Worse, even after AOL increased its monthly fee by 9 percent in July 2001, the average amount actually paid by AOL subscribers was dropping. That's because the only way AOL could keep adding new subscribers was to lure them with promises of more and more months of free service. Gloating, MSN, Microsoft's Internet service provider, claimed that half its new subscribers were coming over from AOL. Meanwhile AOL's plans to use high-speed Internet connections to offer its subscribers Time Warner content had stalled; only a tiny number of subscribers had upgraded to AOL's uninviting and overpriced broadband service.

There was more discouraging news. In the first quarter of 2002, AOL Time Warner would write off a massive $54 billion of so-called goodwill. One of the largest write-offs in corporate history, it revealed just how sharply the value of the company had declined in the two years since AOL and Time Warner had announced their impending merger. Something else: According to the terms of a complicated agreement made with Bertelsmann AG in early 2000, AOL Time Warner was obligated to spend $6.75 billion in *cash* to buy the 49.5

percent of AOL Europe it didn't own already. It was bad enough that AOL Time Warner was being forced to spend nearly $7 billion it didn't have; the real fiasco, the absurdity of it all, was that the company was borrowing $7 billion to buy *half* of an asset analysts figured was barely worth $2 billion. In 2001, AOL Europe had lost $600 million on sales of just $800 million. Who in his or her right mind would value AOL Europe at $14 billion?

AOL Time Warner was in trouble. That's an understatement. The financial results weren't anywhere close to the numbers once promised to shareholders. The company was hobbled by a collapsing stock price, an overwhelming $28 billion of debt, a shaky credit rating, and a loss of confidence on the part of Wall Street. Its shareholders were angry and bitter; its employees had lost faith in the glorious future they'd been promised; and some of AOL Time Warner's big partners in joint ventures and subsidiaries were looking to get out. In short, the company was lost in the woods, and none of AOL Time Warner's top executives knew which way to turn. In April 2002, speaking to a group of MBA students, Parsons said offhandedly, "I'm desperately in need of a strategy." He was making light of things, but to anyone who knew the facts, he meant it. The company's top people—Steve Case, Dick Parsons, and Bob Pittman—couldn't agree on anything, except that something had to be done, fast.

Steve Case clung to his original strategy. As though nothing had changed since 1999, he was still using terms like "convergence" and "interactivity" to promote his business model: "The strategic logic of the merger is just as true today as it was two years ago—in some respects, more true," he insisted in the spring of 2002. Case's solution to the problems at AOL Time Warner was technology and more technology. The company had to invest heavily in upgrading the AOL service to meet the demands of the digital future, period. In his vision of the wonders to be, all creative content—music, movies, cartoons, TV shows, books, and magazines—would be converted from analog to digital; with broadband connections, cell phones, and wireless handheld devices, people would be accessing AOL Time Warner's proprietary content in all sorts of unforeseen ways. "This wave is going to crest—you don't know how high it'll be, or when it'll come, but it's inevitable," is how Ted Leonsis, vice chairman of the AOL division, explained Case's long-range view of things. You either ride the wave of the digital revolution or it drowns you.

At one time Case had been the resident oracle of AOL, revered by all his employees and their families. In the two years since he announced that America Online was buying Time Warner, however, Case had made few new friends or allies. He was aloof, distant, almost extraterrestrial. Some people were appalled by his raw, confrontational style. He liked playing devil's advocate.

"Darwinian management" was the phrase used by one AOL executive to describe Case's approach to decision making. From the viewpoint of several AOL executives, members of the Case fan club, his approach was an intellectual exercise, invented to help him work through a complex idea and, at the same time, test his managers' independence. It was a high-level mind game. "If you say 'Yes' all the time to him, he'll stop working with you," explained another AOL'er. "If you are a peer, you have to tell him that he's wrong—if you think he's wrong—and you have to tell him exactly what you think." There was a steep downside to Case's mind game: "If you didn't know him, you'd be insulted."

In fact, Time Warner executives *had* been insulted by Case, and they resented his arrogance and thick skin. During a strategy meeting in early 2002, for example, Case told Warner Bros. executives bluntly: "You guys will be out of business. The Internet's going to steal all your copyrighted material. What are you going to do?" Sensitive by nature, those guys took umbrage; they were being second-guessed, aggressively, by someone who in their opinion knew nothing about their business. "He thinks he's challenging people to do their best, to think creatively. But it doesn't motivate people—it pisses them off," explained an executive who attended the meeting.

What also pissed them off was Case's refusal to admit defeat. He was never wrong. People on the Time Warner side of the fence described him as "stubborn" and "tone-deaf." Anyone who disagreed with him hadn't seen the light, or wasn't logical, or hadn't weighed the facts, or was myopic.

If tenacity had worked for Case in the past, it was now working against him. It's not that anyone doubted his vision of the digital future; as visions go, it had become commonplace. But with Levin's departure, almost no one on the Time Warner side of the company expected the digital future to arrive as quickly or universally as Case had prophesied. As for his starry-eyed followers in Dulles, their devotion to Case reminded some people of the hysteria surrounding the cult leader Jim Jones: "Despite all of AOL's problems, Steve Case still drinks his Kool-Aid," complained one Time Warner executive. "This guy is so wedded to this situation that was maybe viable two or three years ago, but has been punctured by everyone in the world by now."

Bob Pittman's solution to the company's crisis was basic, immediate, and practical. AOL Time Warner had to market itself more aggressively, Pittman argued; it had to sell many, many more ads, especially on AOL; it also needed new tag lines, better spin, and more salesmen. Pittman had used that strategy to build AOL in the first place, and he intended to use it again, now that Parsons had sent him to Dulles to resuscitate the AOL division. Given enough time, Pittman was convinced he could turn around AOL.

But time was running out for Pittman. By the spring of 2002, the general view inside the company was that Pittman, more than anyone else, was responsible for scuttling AOL Time Warner. He'd punched a hole in the company behind its back, and that's why it was sinking. With contempt, the Time Warner people regarded him as nothing more than a glib salesman. "The division guys at Time Warner look at AOL and literally say, 'Fuck you. Get your business in order before you tell me what to do,' " reported a former Time Warner executive.

What about the new CEO, Dick Parsons: how did he see the future of AOL Time Warner? In early 2002, he had trouble articulating a far-reaching plan for the company. Asked to describe the big idea, the model justifying the merger of AOL and Time Warner, he paused, nodding his head thoughtfully. First he outlined his own view: "Putting AOL together with the preexisting suite of Time Warner businesses is just, you know, kind of the end result of vertical integration."

That said, he proceeded to outline Steve Case's view: "We need to marry up with all of that kind of content that exists in the Time Warner space and then we need to create a unified platform and we need to sort of drive convergence."

Using the same abstract, clotted rhetoric, Parsons explained how his vision dovetailed with Case's: "It's not like convergence is anything more than the ultimate expression of vertical integration; it's just that instead, now we have this big stack and we smoosh it all into one thing."

Parsons concluded: "The merger is about these larger notions of creating a truly vertically integrated company that is built offensively and defensively powerful in terms of protecting itself not only today in terms of the way the business is prosecuted and the way content is delivered, but going forward in the converging world." Sensing my bewilderment, perhaps, he added kindly: "Is that too long an answer?"

Who knows? What was clear was that the world's most powerful media and entertainment company had no strategy. Even if you managed to follow Parsons's circular logic, a question remained: Could Parsons, Case, and Pittman agree on how to integrate vertically and marry content and drive convergence and smoosh the stack into one thing? With each passing month and each downward tick in AOL Time Warner's stock price, the possibility of their success became more remote.

ON THURSDAY, MAY 16, 2002, THE ANNUAL SHAREHOLDERS' meeting of AOL Time Warner was held at the historic Apollo Theater in Harlem. The ceiling of the theater was chipped, the paint was peeling, the crimson velvet wall covering was stained. As some people observed, poetically, the shabby theater mirrored AOL Time Warner: both were desperately in need of renovation. Up on the stage, under the spotlights, Parsons and Steve Case spoke at length but said little.

One of the few memorable episodes of the two-and-a-half-hour meeting came when an angry, articulate shareholder approached the microphone. "Mr. Parsons," he said, "I hear you up here talking about your vision. You know what? I heard that vision last year. Now I want to see the job done." As the audience applauded, the shareholder added: "These are hard-earned dollars we entrusted to you, and you have decimated them. You have completely decimated them."

Toward the end of the meeting, Jerry Levin gave his final address as CEO. Introduced by Parsons as "a mentor, a teacher, a friend," Levin walked slowly onto the stage of the Apollo Theater looking haggard and distracted. Before a hushed audience of 1,500 people, solemnly, he thanked his board members and his executives, the company's shareholders, its 90,000 employees, and his "sturdy Irish wife" for their "faith, hope, and, above all, patience." He didn't apologize, he didn't explain. "I know the frustration you feel now is real," he said simply. "Have faith in this company. . . ."

"It has been a stunning ride," Levin concluded. "I now close my business career and fade away." He was echoing a speech given by General Douglas MacArthur in 1951 after he was fired by President Harry S. Truman. "Like the old soldier in that ballad," MacArthur said back then, "I now close my military career and just fade away, an old soldier who tried to do his duty as God gave him the sight to see that duty." The words to that ballad go something like this: "Old soldiers never die, never die, never die. Old soldiers never die, they just fade away." At AOL Time Warner, Jerry Levin had been fading away since December 2001.

After the shareholders' meeting was adjourned, a reporter for *The New York Times* approached Ted Turner and asked, "Can you give us your thoughts on the legacy Jerry Levin is leaving behind?" "I have no comment," Turner said as he rushed out of the Apollo Theater. All of a sudden, he stopped in his tracks. Turning to face the reporter, Turner blurted out: "We're going to miss him. Ha, ha, ha."

■ ■ ■

FOUR WEEKS LATER THE GAME WAS UP, THOUGH NO ONE KNEW IT right away. On June 14, 2002, a reporter for *The Washington Post,* Alec Klein, drove out to AOL's offices in Dulles to deliver a twenty-one-page single-spaced letter to John Buckley, head of the AOL division's corporate communications department. According to the text of Klein's letter, AOL had been playing a giant shell game. For the past two years, Klein alleged, the company had been inflating revenues, distorting earnings, and misleading investors; it had also concealed serious problems in its advertising division. Drawing on dozens of confidential company documents and on interviews with former and current employees, the letter claimed that AOL had converted fees from legal settlements and deal terminations, disguising them as ad sales. As well, it had booked barter deals and stock options as advertising revenue. On good evidence, Klein added a few colorful details: AOL executives had snorted cocaine from the hood of a car and, on group outings, had visited strip clubs. His report was so comprehensive that it delved into the matter of David Colburn's hair weaves, which had apparently been imported from South America.

From hand to unsteady hand, Klein's letter circulated among AOL Time Warner's top executives. The accusations were incredible, those people reassured one another. Besides, who was this Alec Klein person that anyone should take him seriously? I mean, who would believe his report? He was a thirty-five-year-old kid who'd been covering AOL Time Warner since joining *The Washington Post* in the summer of 2000. From the perspective of AOL Time Warner's corporate communications department, Klein was a minor league reporter. Overwhelmed by his beat, he'd be easy to brush off. No problem.

The AOL Time Warner beat was grueling—AOL was one of the biggest business stories in America, and the competition to break news on the company was fierce. Unlike the *Wall Street Journal,* which had half a dozen reporters to cover every angle and square inch of AOL Time Warner, *The Washington Post* had few resources. Not only was Klein the only *Post* reporter following AOL Time Warner full-time, but until he started on that beat he'd known almost nothing about the company and its business. He was, by his own admission, "clueless," or he had been. Klein got the hang of things quickly. He developed his own sources, befriended former AOL employees and partners, and began to question the official company line. To be a good reporter, you need a touch of paranoia. Maybe you call it cynicism.

Klein hadn't recognized it back then, but his big break had come in the summer of 2001, when an anonymous source phoned *The Washington Post* with a tip: A senior AOL salesman by the name of Eric Keller had been suspended. Why did that matter? Klein asked himself. He'd never heard of Keller. And what big company doesn't suspend an employee from time to time? Cryptically, the source hinted that the Keller story was urgent; beneath it lurked dark and dirty facts about AOL.

Calling around, Klein learned this much: Keller, a senior vice president in David Colburn's business affairs division (with its "BA Specials"), had been placed on something called "administrative leave" pending an internal investigation into a partnership between AOL and PurchasePro.com, a shaky Las Vegas–based company with serious accounting problems. The details of the investigation were vague and sketchy. AOL wasn't talking, and Klein didn't get very far. On June 19, 2001, he published a 380-word article about Keller that was soon forgotten.

Two months later, on August 14, Jeffrey Skilling quit as CEO of

Enron Corp. By December 2001, Enron was in bankruptcy, and all of
a sudden corporate fraud was the hottest story in America. The mania
for stocks in the late 1990s had not been a glorious expression of
democracy after all, the media concluded; it had been an expression of
greed—a parade of the deadly sins. Stock options had not empowered
employees; they had encouraged executives to boost their company's
stock price, often by distorting earnings. Enron, Tyco, WorldCom:
every day new, unbelievable stories about those and other huge companies were coming to light. So Alec Klein starting thinking about
Eric Keller again.

Month after month, from the fall of 2001 to the late spring
of 2002, Klein gathered information about AOL's business affairs
department. Worried that AOL would trace his calls, he spent
hours each week on a pay phone in the lobby of a Washington hotel.
He interviewed AOL's advertising partners, debriefed former employees, and learned about Colburn's "BA Specials" in all their horror.
Unraveling AOL's convoluted deal with PurchasePro.com (the deal
Eric Keller had negotiated), Klein discovered the following. In
essence, AOL had bought stock warrants in PurchasePro for $9.5 mil-
lion in late 2000; then AOL marked up the value of those warrants to
$30 million and booked the difference as advertising revenue. The
money gained from the PurchasePro deal didn't make a significant
difference to the bottom line, and the accounting for the deal may
have been legal, strictly speaking. But to Klein it had become clear
that AOL's ledgers weren't what they appeared to be. They'd had
years of cosmetic surgery. By June 2002, having built a strong and
solid case against AOL, Klein wrote the twenty-one-page letter that
he delivered to Dulles.

To understand AOL Time Warner's reaction to Klein's letter,
you should know something about the company's approach to the
media. Before the merger with AOL, Time Warner had been fairly
relaxed with journalists. True, Jerry Levin had avoided reporters,
convinced they were out to get him (he was not always wrong). In-

terviewed for a *Business Week* cover story, for example, Levin had stormed out of the room—twice. To compensate for his boss, Ed Adler, Time Warner's longtime head of public relations, would discreetly give reporters the information they asked for. Adler was an optimist. Surely people who wrote negative stories about the company could be convinced to change their point of view, he thought. Besides, what was the point of clamping down on reporters or on executives and employees who spoke to reporters? As Adler knew, in the media and entertainment world, information inevitably made its way out through one channel or another. He tended to ignore leaks within the company.

AOL's approach to public relations was another story. Having started his career organizing political campaigns, Kenny Lerer ran the PR machine at AOL as if he were fighting a vicious congressional race, as did his colleague, John Buckley, who had been director of communications for Bob Dole's 1996 presidential campaign. In Lerer's mind, reporters had to be tightly controlled, their information rationed. First AOL's PR machine would come up with the official corporate spin on some issue; then the spin was repeated over and over again by spokespersons. A few executives were allowed to speak directly to the press, but they knew to stay on message, to parrot the company line. Their performance was carefully tracked, and leaks to the press weren't tolerated. Journalists who criticized AOL were cut off, ignored, or accused of incompetence and ignorance. Reporters on the AOL beat told a story about Lerer: Determined to track the source of internal leaks, Lerer obsessively traced every phone call and e-mail from reporters to anyone inside the company. The story was surely apocryphal, but it reflected the media's fear and loathing of AOL's corporate communications department.

AOL Time Warner's response to Klein's letter was immediate and blunt and arrogant. As you might expect, the company denied all of Klein's allegations. It also used every tactic of intimidation legally available to people with deep pockets. Right away, faster than you can say "Enron," an outside lawyer, Thomas Yannucci of the firm Kirk-land & Ellis, was hired to represent AOL.

In media circles, Yannucci was notorious—one of the country's "most dangerous" media plaintiff lawyers, according to the trade publication *Editor & Publisher.* In 1993, representing General Motors in a case against *Dateline NBC,* Yannucci forced the TV news-magazine to fall on its knees and confess that it had embellished a tel-evised crash scene by rigging GM trucks with hidden explosives. In 1995, acting for the tobacco firm Brown & Williamson, Yannucci had prevented CBS from airing an interview on *60 Minutes* with Jeffrey Wigand, a whistle-blower in the tobacco industry. And in 1998, after catching an investigative reporter hacking into the voice mail system of Chiquita Brands International, Yannucci extracted a front-page apology from the *Cincinnati Enquirer* and a reported $18 million in damages. Now Yannucci's job was to make sure *The Washington Post* didn't run Alec Klein's story about AOL.

For six weeks, AOL and *The Washington Post* negotiated. The stakes were high, and communications were intense and nasty. AOL, threatening a major defamation suit, told the *Post* to back off. For one thing, AOL claimed, Klein had misunderstood and misinterpreted the confidential documents in his possession. His sources were dis-gruntled, resentful former employees, and his information lacked context. "The accounting for all of these transactions is appropriate and in accordance with generally accepted accounting principles," Yannucci stated in a letter to *The Washington Post* dated June 21. As further evidence of AOL's innocence and unblemished bottom line, Yannucci produced a written statement from AOL Time Warner's auditors at Ernst & Young, who swore that AOL's accounting was ac-curate and verifiable.

At ten A.M. on June 27, after a long series of letters, e-mails, and phone calls, the two sides met at the *Post*'s offices. More than a dozen people were seated around the table in the fifth-floor conference room. Five top editors were present, including the *Post*'s executive editor, Leonard Downie Jr.; the managing editor, Steve Coll; and the business editor, Jill Dutt. Among the representatives from AOL were Yannucci, John Buckley, and AOL's general counsel, Paul Cappuccio. Line by line, the two sides reviewed every one of Klein's many allegations. Some of the facts in Klein's letter may well have been correct, AOL conceded; however, the assumptions he had derived from those facts didn't hold water. And yes, the company's accounting did tend to be somewhat aggressive—sometimes it "pushed the envelope"—but, AOL insisted, its accounting was neither illegal nor improper. Strict internal controls were in place to ensure that every financial transaction was legal.

After the meeting, in a letter written to the *Post* dated July 17, Yannucci said: "We believe such armchair speculation about AOL's accounting and financial disclosures by less than fully-informed 'experts' . . . is not only grossly unfair and unwarranted in light of the exhaustive facts we have presented to you, but is also reckless." It's not hard to decipher the subtext of Yannucci's letter: Klein was an unprincipled hack; by publishing his amateur and imaginary ramblings, the *Post* would almost certainly be committing libel, and there'd be hell to pay.

This time Yannucci's strong-arm tactics didn't work. *The Washington Post* refused to back down. On July 18 and 19, almost five weeks after Klein's letter had been delivered to AOL's offices, a long, two-part series titled "The Deal Makers: How AOL Hit the Numbers" hit the front page of the newspaper. And that was that. In a nutshell, Klein's article reported the following: In late 2000, before the merger of AOL and Time Warner had been made public, the online advertising market was just about to collapse. Desperate, and determined to see the AOL Time Warner merger go through, senior executives at America Online had concealed advertising shortfalls and had bullied their salespeople into inflating revenues. Some of Klein's most shocking revelations were on-the-record quotes from former AOL salesmen who attested to widespread trickery within the ranks of David

Colburn's army of thugs. "For nine months I tried to get these guys out of denial," said one salesman who'd left AOL four months earlier. "I tried to take the perfume off the pig."

■ ■ ■

PART ONE OF *THE WASHINGTON POST* ARTICLE RAN ON JULY 18. That was the day Bob Pittman quit his job at AOL. Surely it was a co-incidence, the timing, but one way or another the two events were linked. For months, the resentment against Pittman had been grow-ing inside AOL Time Warner. In the opinion of many insiders, the questionable accounting at AOL could be traced directly to Pittman. At the end of the day, his only choice was to resign.

One week later, on July 24, Dick Parsons revealed that the Securities and Exchange Commission had begun an investigation into the company's accounting practices. The following day, AOL Time Warner's shares hit an all-time low: at $8.70, the stock had dropped 85 percent in just over a year. Since the heyday of early 2000, when Steve Case and Jerry Levin had hugged and high-fived and announced their big deal, more than $200 billion of shareholder value had been wiped out. Then a criminal investigation was launched by the U.S. Justice Department. Shortly after that, around dinnertime on Friday, August 9, David Colburn received a phone call from Dick Parsons telling him his career at AOL Time Warner was over. The locks on Colburn's office door were changed, and his files were hauled away as evidence. AOL TIME WARNER BIGS ON THE SPOT, screamed the *New York Post;* "Fraud Charges Could Mean Time Behind Bars."

By August 14, 2002, chief executives had to certify the accuracy of their company's accounting, according to SEC regulations. That day, Parsons admitted publicly that at least $49 million had been "in-appropriately recognized as advertising and commerce revenues" between late 2000 and early 2002. It was only the beginning. By October, the $49 million Parsons had alluded to had turned into $190 million of "inappropriately recognized" revenue. A few months later, we learned that an additional $400 million of so-called revenue at AOL Time Warner may not have been revenue after all.

AOL Time Warner was in turmoil. One after another, eager lawyers were starting class-action suits, accusing the company and its executives of fraud. The newspaper headlines were scandalous. (So much for the moral legacy of Henry Luce.) Several people inside and outside the company argued that the merger should be undone, that AOL should be spun off. Was the AOL division about to be dumped? Would the company survive at all? How long would it be before the acronym AOL disappeared from the name AOL Time Warner?

One way or another, the reign of America Online was over. A year and a half after the cowboys from Dulles had conquered Time Warner, old media was back on top. Revelations about AOL's dubious accounting had caused the stock price to collapse. At the same time, Dick Parsons finally had the moral imperative he needed to enforce his power as CEO. With Pittman gone, Parsons named Don Logan and Jeff Bewkes, two of the harshest critics of the AOL deal, co–chief operating officers of AOL Time Warner. Case wasn't happy with his choice, but Case was no longer in charge.

Everything happened so fast. By the late summer of 2002, almost every senior AOL executive had been fired, forced out, or marginalized. Barry Schuler, head of the AOL division, lost his job in April. Mike Kelly was no longer the chief financial officer of AOL Time Warner; he'd been sent back to Dulles as chief operating officer for the AOL division. Myer Berlow was gone; months earlier, with AOL's advertising revenue in free fall and his vaunted Global Marketing Solutions Group in tatters, Berlow had managed to slip away. AOL's George Vradenburg had quit his post as AOL Time Warner's executive vice president for global and strategic policy. Mayo Stuntz,

Pittman's deputy, disappeared soon after his boss left. Even Kenny Lerer had pulled up stakes, leaving Time Warner's Ed Adler solely responsible for corporate communications.

Case was still chairman of AOL Time Warner, of course, but his power was ebbing. Having gained the upper hand and acres of moral ground, Parsons demoted him. None of the company's executives would be reporting directly to Case. He was becoming a passive "non-executive" chairman, the role Levin had envisioned for him in early 2000. As for Case's dream of "convergence," Parsons was having none of it. Each division of AOL Time Warner would operate as it had in the past, with total autonomy. The AOL "culture" of communal ideology was dead. To let everyone know that Case had been deported to executive no-man's-land, the company issued a statement on Parsons's behalf: "As C.E.O., Dick ultimately is responsible for managing the company, but he welcomes and seriously considers Steve's advice and counsel."

■ ■ ■

TED TURNER WAS IN PARIS WHEN HE GOT WORD OF *THE WASHington Post* exposé. He was raging. Since the announcement of the AOL Time Warner deal, Turner had seen the value of his shares in the company drop from $10 billion to $2 billion. His marriage to Jane Fonda had fallen apart. He'd lost his job. Short of cash, his charitable foundation had been scaled way back. For all that, Turner was still the single largest individual shareholder in AOL Time Warner, and he wasn't about to let anyone forget that fact. What's more, one of Turner's most trusted friends and allies was money manager Gordon Crawford of Capital Research & Management, a company that owned around 8 percent of AOL Time Warner.

For three decades, Crawford had been one of the country's most admired and imitated media and entertainment investors, owning massive positions in such companies as Viacom, the News Corporation, USA Interactive, and AOL Time Warner. According to both Turner and Crawford, the man responsible for the mess at AOL was Steve Case. Using their considerable influence, Turner and Crawford began lobbying other major shareholders and directors to demand Case's resignation. In August 2002, shortly after AOL Time Warner admitted, reluctantly, that its revenue had been inflated, Crawford met Case in New York, informing him he should resign. The next day, Case phoned Crawford to ask what he could do to patch up their relationship. "Not very much," was the matter-of-fact reply.

Case insisted he had done nothing wrong. To the extent he acknowledged that the AOL Time Warner deal had been a fiasco, Case portrayed himself as a victim of other people's incompetence. "He had this vision. They did this grand deal. Then the guys running it screwed it up." That's Crawford, describing the excuses Case had given him.

Crawford and Turner weren't the only ones who wanted Case out of there. On the Time Warner side, some people were convinced that getting rid of Case would solve the company's problems and reverse the fall. To them, he epitomized everything that had gone wrong with the company in the past two years. Above all, what grated on Time Warner executives and investors was the collective belief that Case had fleeced them, and yet here he was, day after day, hanging around headquarters, rubbing salt in their wounds, a constant reminder that they had been taken. With an uncanny sense of timing, Case had used AOL's artificially inflated stock to buy their company. For AOL shareholders, the Time Warner deal was a masterstroke; without it, they'd have been left holding shares worth a fraction of AOL Time Warner's shares. The people who lost out on the deal, and lost out big, were Time Warner shareholders and employees. Their retirement accounts had been destroyed; their stock options were worthless. Meanwhile, in 2001 alone, Case had sold $100 million of

AOL Time Warner stock. In total, in the decade since AOL had gone public, Case had exercised and sold about $700 million worth of AOL stock options.

Feeding on leaks from hysterical insiders, the media speculated that Case's departure was imminent. How much longer could he hold out? How thick was his skin? By September 2002, shortly before a scheduled AOL Time Warner board meeting, reports in *The New York Times* and the *New York Post* suggested the company's directors might vote to fire him. At AOL's Dulles headquarters, where attacks on Case were taken personally by his devoted employees, flyers started appearing in hallways and elevators, stuck up with tape. They read, "We support Steve." On one of the flyers the word *strongly* had been added by hand, as in "We *strongly* support Steve."

The speculations about Case were so intense that on September 19, once AOL Time Warner's board meeting had ended without a formal change in his status, a company spokesperson took the unusual step of telling reporters, "Steve Case is the company's chairman and he will remain so. . . . Steve Case's role at the company was not on the [board's] agenda and not discussed."

That announcement did nothing to stop the intrigue and hostility at AOL Time Warner. It was November 2002 now, and Gordy Crawford had promised to use his large position in AOL Time Warner shares to vote against Case at the next annual shareholders' meeting. Turner, presumably, would do the same. "There's no shareholder in the company of any substance that wants him around," Crawford insisted. "There's nobody at the Time Warner companies that wants him around. I don't believe Dick Parsons wants him around. I don't think the majority of the board wants him around. So his only constituency is the AOL board members. . . . That's all that stands between him and the door."

███

ON SUNDAY, JANUARY 12, 2003, STEVE CASE RESIGNED AS CHAIRman of AOL Time Warner. "As you might expect, this decision was personally very difficult for me," his statement read. "However, after careful consideration, I believe stepping down is in the best interest of the company."

Case had decided to sacrifice himself for the sake of the digital future. "I believed in America Online when we built it," he concluded. "I believed in AOL Time Warner when we created it; and I continue to believe in the great potential of this company and its people."

The next morning, on January 13, Case appeared on CNN's *American Morning* with Paula Zahn. "In a personal sense," Zahn asked him, "how badly do you feel about the almost $200 billion worth of shareholder value that has been wiped out? I mean, what do you say to the folks out there that were counting on their 401(k)s to fund their retirement?"

Case didn't feel bad or badly "in a personal sense." His face blank and pitiless as the sun, he answered her: "I recognize a lot of people have bet on this company and are disappointed by the results. But it's never over till it's over."

That said, Case counted his chips and walked away from the table.

EPILOGUE

The final chapter of *Fools Rush In* takes us to January 2003, the month Steve Case resigned as chairman of AOL Time Warner. Where are they now, the main characters in this morality play? What are they up to? Starting with the name of a company that no longer exists, and proceeding in alphabetical order, the catalog below is up-to-date as of November 2003.

AOL Time Warner

Glued together on January 11, 2001, the company known as AOL Time Warner lasted two years, nine months, and five days before it fell apart. On Thursday, October 16, 2003, the company was renamed Time Warner, and its "AOL" stock symbol was replaced on the New York Stock Exchange with Time Warner's old and respected symbol, "TWX."

Stock symbols are easy enough to change. Reversing the damage caused by the merger of AOL and Time Warner has not been so easy. In late 2003, Time Warner's stock hovered around $16, down 70 percent from January 2001, when the AOL Time Warner deal closed. Remember, in January 2000, the combined market capitalization of America Online and Time Warner was $250 billion. As this book goes to press almost four years later, the combined companies are worth $70 billion. To quote Rupert Murdoch, head of News Corp.: "They gave away their company for a mess of porridge, and they've got to live with that forever."

Myer Berlow

When he left the company in March 2002, Berlow became a "consultant" to AOL Time Warner. Since then, as he cheerfully admits, the company has not consulted him. Unemployed after decades as a high-powered salesman, Berlow has found a new vocation: he's a wood turner who spends eight hours a day at a lathe, making wooden bowls and other vessels in his workshop in Williamsburg, Brooklyn. Already he has taken two three-day courses from David Ellsworth, an American wood-turning master who lives in Quakertown, Pennsylvania. The last time I spoke to Berlow (in October 2003), he was on his way to the Glenstal Abbey in Limerick, Ireland, to study with Ciaran Forbes, a Benedictine monk and renowned wood turner. Berlow completes four wooden objects every day. As you can imagine, they keep piling up, hundreds of them. Wood turning is Berlow's form of therapy. "It's the process that I really enjoy," he said. "The pieces are just pieces."

Named as a defendant in two AOL Time Warner lawsuits, Berlow has been advised by his attorney to cut off all communication with his former partner and closest friend, David Colburn (see later). Berlow is fifty-three, he lives in Manhattan, and he does Pilates for recreation when he's not at his lathe. He still smokes a pack of Camel cigarettes every day. What will he do next? "Something interesting and fun," he replied casually.

Jeffrey Bewkes and Don Logan

If any two people epitomize the collapse of AOL, they're Jeff Bewkes and Don Logan. Fiercely opposed to the AOL deal all along, and viewed by AOL'ers as stiff-necked and unaccommodating, Bewkes and Logan are now the two most powerful executives at Time Warner, after Dick Parsons. "The old-media forces within AOL Time Warner Inc. [have] completed the reconquest of the world's largest media company," observed *The Wall Street Journal* in July 2002, the month Logan and Bewkes were named to their new posts.

Logan, fifty-nine, who once ran Time Inc., oversees the cable, magazine, and book publishing divisions; he's also in charge of AOL. Bewkes, fifty-one, the former head of HBO, is in charge of the company's music and films divisions, CNN, HBO, and the Turner Networks. He made $6 million in salary and bonus in 2002, as did Logan.

Determined to prove that the AOL Time Warner deal failed because of incompetent AOL'ers, people inside Time Warner make sure you know what a collegial and productive environment their company has become since the wheat was separated from the chaff. No one has an unkind word to say about either Bewkes or Logan. As Ann Moore, the new head of Time Inc., remarked when the two men were promoted: "I feel like the merger is starting today."

Christopher Bogart

Before the merger was announced in early 2000, Bogart was one of the few Time Warner executives to have worked closely with Jerry Levin on putting together the AOL deal. Once the deal was finalized, however, Bogart lost his job as general counsel, and AOL's Paul Cappuccio was named general counsel of the new combined company. Frustrated, Bogart decided to leave the company. He then changed his mind and in January 2001 accepted a senior management position at Time Warner's cable division.

It promised to be an exciting new job. With the growing importance of high-speed Internet access, cable was a key component of the AOL Time Warner merger. Bogart would help integrate Time

Warner's cable division with AOL and oversee new developments. He had wanted to move from law into business, and this seemed to be the perfect vehicle.

Then everything came to a halt. The cable division and AOL couldn't agree on anything. Bob Pittman and Joe Collins, head of the cable division, battled constantly; and regulators kept interfering with every proposal to merge Road Runner, Time Warner cable's high-speed Internet service, with AOL's high-speed Internet service. By the summer of 2001, Bogart's boss, Joe Collins, was no longer in charge of the cable division. Pittman intended to replace Collins (see later) with one of his own people, and that meant the cable division would be wonderfully changed, Bogart imagined.

You know what happened next: nothing much. Before long, Pittman had left the company. Working in the cable division was like working for a utility company: unexciting. In late 2002, Bogart started planning a spin-off of the cable division (an initial public offering of the company's cable assets would help pay down AOL Time Warner's growing debt). By the spring of 2003, the IPO was called off, and Bogart was moved back to AOL Time Warner headquarters, where he was given the official title of president and CEO of Time Warner Entertainment Ventures. His responsibilities included giving strategic advice to Dick Parsons, but in fact Bogart didn't have much to do. By the end of 2003 he'd pretty well left AOL Time Warner.

As one of the nation's most promising young corporate lawyers, Bogart was only thirty-three years old when he was named general counsel of Time Warner. Now, at age thirty-seven, he's not sure what to do with the rest of his life. He's weighing his options. Meanwhile he travels, he reads books, and he finally has time to spend with his three children, ages two, three, and five. "I kind of like my life right now," he told me. He lives in Bronxville, New York.

Timothy Boggs

In early 2001, having lost his job as Time Warner's senior vice president for global public policy (the job went to AOL's George Vradenburg), Boggs left the company. He had been with the firm for twenty years, first at Warner Communications, then at Time Warner.

Boggs is on his way to becoming an Episcopal priest. For the past year, while undergoing his "discernment period," he has worked with his parish in Washington, D.C. (Mount St. Albans) and with the bishop of Washington, the Right Reverend John Bryson Chane. At the same time, he's become a full-time graduate student at Georgetown University, studying philosophy, history, theology, and ethics. He plans to enter divinity school in the summer or fall of 2004. Now fifty-three, Boggs will be fifty-six when he's ordained.

In his free time, Boggs is a high-altitude mountain climber. Since leaving AOL Time Warner, he has reached the summits of Mount McKinley and Mont Blanc. He lives in Washington, near the Dupont Circle, and still holds a handful of Time Warner options. "I still think the AOL deal was a tragic mistake," he said recently. "But that's neither here nor there—it's become an opportunity for me to experience the rest of my life."

Daniel Borislow

Borislow left Tel-Save Holdings in late 1998. He then moved to Palm Beach and took up horse racing. His new career isn't all that different from his previous one, he told me: "They're both brutally competitive, and that's the reason I like both of them."

Borislow keeps forty horses in his Maryland stables, including Talk Is Money, a 2001 Kentucky Derby entrant. Retired from racing, Talk Is Money is at stud and earns $5,000 per mating session. Borislow's top colt, Toccet, won the 2002 Champagne Stakes and the 2002 Hollywood Futurity. In 2002, led by Toccet, Borislow's horses won thirty of their ninety-nine races, collecting $1.15 million in winnings. Unfortunately, 2003 was a less successful year: Toccet sat out much of the season because of bone remodeling. Still, Borislow foresees a great future for him as a stud. If Toccet has a successful comeback, as Borislow anticipates, he could earn as many as one hundred stud fees a year, at a rate of $30,000 to $50,000 per mating session.

Tel-Save Holdings, Borislow's old company, has been renamed Talk America. It still offers local and long-distance phone service. Though its revenues have barely increased since Borislow left in 1998, the company is now profitable; in 2002 it earned $45.4 million on revenues of $318 million. Once valued by the stock market at $2 billion, Talk America is now worth about $350 million.

Asked about his role in the history of America Online, Borislow replied with typical bravado: "I pretty much developed their business model. I saved their company. It's as simple as that."

Richard Bressler

He was Jerry Levin's loyal protégé; he helped to negotiate the AOL deal; he was chief financial officer between 1995 and 1999; he joined the company in 1988, a lifetime ago in corporate America. Despite all that, Rich Bressler was pushed out of AOL Time Warner.

After the AOL deal closed, Bressler was put in charge of making investments on behalf of the new combined company. In the chain of command he reported to Steve Case, who apparently found Bressler insufferable. By March 2001, only two months after the AOL deal closed, Bressler was out of there, thanks to Case. Having landed nicely on his feet, Bressler is now the chief financial officer of Viacom.

Why didn't Levin defend Bressler back then? "Because it was too late," Levin claimed. "Rich already had the offer from Viacom, and I knew that would be better than anything we could offer him." People inside the company dispute that account of history. Levin could have defended him back then, they insist; Bressler got himself a new job after his fate was more or less sealed. Not uncharacteristically, when Case went in for the kill, Levin looked the other way. One way or another, Bressler will be remembered as the first high-level victim of the AOL Time Warner merger. In retrospect, of course, he was lucky: he got out before disaster struck.

Since joining Viacom, Bressler, age forty-five, has kept a low profile. Like so many other people involved in this ongoing saga, he dabbles in revisionist history. According to friends and former colleagues, Bressler now says he never really supported the AOL deal. He was just a loyal and faithful servant, he says, following orders from above.

Paul Cappuccio

People at Time Warner now refer to Cappuccio as "one of us." That's an extraordinary compliment, given that Cappuccio is the most senior AOL'er left at the battered company. The former top lawyer for AOL, Cappuccio beat out Chris Bogart in January 2001 to become general counsel for the new combined company. He still holds that title at Time Warner, where most of his time is spent handling the SEC and Justice Department investigations. Cappuccio also played a significant role in settling AOL's antitrust suit against Microsoft in May 2003. Finally Microsoft agreed to pay a remarkable $750 million to AOL Time Warner, a sum large enough to make a dent in Time Warner's overwhelming debt and take some weight off Dick Parsons's shoulders.

A 1986 graduate of Harvard Law School, Cappuccio, forty-two, is rumored to be a prodigy, a true resident genius. Having served as U.S. Supreme Court clerk for Justices Antonin Scalia and Anthony Kennedy, he joined Kirkland & Ellis before coming to AOL in 1999. That late date may have something to do with how well he's managed to fit in at Time Warner: Cappuccio is one of a handful of senior AOL executives who arrived at the company too late to cash in and make a fortune.

Stephen Case

In January 2003, shortly after promising to take a more active role in the operations of AOL Time Warner, Steve Case resigned as chairman of the company, though officially he didn't step down until May. Case remains on Time Warner's board, despite pressure from large investors (Gordon Crawford, for example) to resign. At the company's annual shareholders meeting in May 2003, he was reelected to the board with 78 percent of the votes in his favor. Most other directors received more than 90 percent of the vote; only one director, former AOL'er Miles Gilburne, got fewer votes than Case did.

For all that, Case is one of the richest people in America. On the 2003 Forbes 400 list of richest Americans, he ranks 393rd, with a net worth estimated at $610 million. In 1999, his peak year, Case was worth $1.5 billion. With 12.5 million Time Warner shares, and another 19 million in exercisable options, he remains one of the company's biggest shareholders.

In late 2003, Case opened an office on Washington, D.C.'s K Street. From there he oversees his investments, which thus far have largely been restricted to Hawaii, his native state. "My macro investment thesis continues to be that Hawaii land has been pummeled over the past decade and is at an all-time low," Case wrote in a 1999 e-mail to his investment adviser. "Most of the landowners are old families who are land rich but cash poor and thus unable to make investments to maximize value."

In 1999 Case spent $40 million for a 41.2 percent stake in Maui Land & Pineapple, a company that grows and markets fresh and canned pineapples. Cash rich, he recently invested another $2.5 million in the company, bringing his stake to 43.5 percent. He also owns Grove Farm Company, one of the largest sugar plantations on Kauai, the most northern of Hawaii's main islands. Aside from its sugar plantation, Grove Farm owns twenty-two thousand acres of land with magnificent sand beaches known as Mahaulepu. The company plans to build a resort there. Case bought Grove Farms for $26 million (plus $65 million of debt) in late 2000 and installed his father as chairman.

As for philanthropy: The Stephen Case Foundation had assets of $83 million in 2001 (the latest year for which numbers are available). That year the foundation gave away $18.4 million in grants to such organizations as PowerUp ($7.3 million), a now defunct organization that helped bring computers and Internet access to poor communities; RocketTown ($2.3 million), a Christian youth services ministry; the Special Olympics ($1 million); and Hawaii Habitat for Humanity ($1 million).

Since stepping down as chairman of AOL Time Warner, Case has kept to himself, underground. He's given one interview, to *Business Week,* comprising a rambling series of questions and answers about the role of technology in our economy. Case didn't mention AOL Time Warner, not once.

Case is only forty-five. What will he do next? One of his friends thinks that Case's next venture will be a major nonprofit organization, something like Bill and Melinda Gates's foundation, though on a far smaller scale. Other soothsayers predict that Case will buy back AOL one day. (In the fall of 2002, when he was still chairman of AOL Time Warner, he did muse about reclaiming his old company.) In the meantime, though, he is defending himself against approximately 50 shareholder lawsuits. His lawyers have filed a motion on his behalf: after the merger with Time Warner, Case wasn't directly responsible for the AOL division, they argue. Therefore he's not responsible for any improper accounting practices that have come to light (and may still come to light).

Case, his wife, Jean, and their two children live in the Reserve, a 258-acre gated community of stately neo-Colonial mansions in

McLean, Virginia. "The Reserve is a journey into the ultimate living experience," the sales brochure promises in breathtaking prose. "It is the quality of life you have always dreamed of, filled with luxury and a convenience rarely found. The Reserve is for those of you who know where you are going, and desire the greatest luxury of all time."

David Colburn

David Colburn has had nothing to do with AOL Time Warner or with Time Warner since being forced out of the company in August 2002. His business career has collapsed. He's been named a defendant in various lawsuits against the company and its executives. And some people in the media have accused him of bringing down AOL almost single-handedly. *Business Week* named him one of its "Worst Managers" of 2002, along with other well-known mis-managers: Martha Stewart; Salomon Smith Barney's Jack Grubman; WorldCom's Bernie Ebbers; Jerry Levin; and Bob Pittman. Bruised but somehow resigned to his fate, Colburn has devoted the past year and a half to self-examination. He has reset his priorities. Avoiding former colleagues and the media (not once has he been quoted on the record), he has more or less gone into hiding with his wife and their three young children at their home in Potomac, Maryland.

A Modern Orthodox Jew, Colburn has always been drawn to a life of the spirit. As reported by Alec Klein of *The Washington Post,* in 1999 Colburn made a firm promise to three rabbis: if they would pray for AOL's stock to rise, he would donate $1 million to a Jewish cause. AOL's stock rose. Since leaving AOL Time Warner, Colburn has become utterly devout; much of his time and money are dedicated to philanthropic causes. In 2002, the latest year for which figures are available, his foundation gave away $3.5 million, more than double the amount it gave away in 2001. He has donated large sums of money to Operation Embrace, a group that helps Israeli victims of terrorists attacks. He's given $600,000 to the Jewish Federation of Greater

Washington. And he's given $400,000 to Chai Lifeline, an organization that helps children with life-threatening diseases. At the Charles E. Smith Jewish Day School in Rockville, Maryland, Colburn has funded a new gymnasium named after Daniel Pearl, the *Wall Street Journal* reporter who in 2002 was tortured and killed by terrorists in Pakistan. At the same time, Colburn is working with the Community Wealth Venture to help nonprofit organizations generate revenue through business ventures and corporate partnerships (as opposed to fund-raising alone). Quietly, he is also involved with a real estate development project in Virginia and has been doing some consulting work, giving strategic advice to a handful of private companies.

In the spring of 2001, Colburn exercised and sold $9 million worth of AOL Time Warner stock options. He is forty-five years old, plays tennis and basketball, and is represented legally by a former prosecutor for the Justice Department, Roger Spaeder, who specializes in white-collar crime.

Joseph Collins

Other division heads who opposed the AOL deal (namely Don Logan and Jeff Bewkes) wound up on top of the heap. Joe Collins, the long-time head of Time Warner's cable division, wasn't so lucky. From day one he and Bob Pittman were at each other's throats.

In the summer of 2001, only six months after the AOL deal closed, Collins lost his powerful job and impressive title. To console him, or compensate him, Levin made Collins head of something called AOL Time Warner Interactive Video, which oversees such advanced cable technologies as video on demand. "Pittman probably would have fired Joe," explained a former cable division executive. "Instead, Levin created a new venture for him."

For months Pittman looked for someone to replace Collins, who is now fifty-nine, but few people wanted the job. Jeff Bewkes turned down Pittman's offer flat. The able Tom Rutledge, an executive vice president in the cable division, left the company to run Cablevision's cable division. By then, most people with antennae sensed impending doom; besides, who wanted to work for Pittman? Ultimately, Collins's deputy, Glenn Britt, a lifelong Time Inc.'er, accepted the job.

Robert Daly and Terry Semel

Left over from the Steve Ross era, Bob Daly and Terry Semel stepped down in December 1999 as chairmen and co-CEOs of Warner Bros. film and music divisions. For nearly twenty years, working together, the two men ran the Warner Bros. studio. After Michael Fuchs was fired in 1995, the music group was added to their portfolio. Semel first arrived at Warner Bros. in 1965 (he was twenty-two then). Daly arrived in 1980. As Hollywood's longest-serving studio heads, Daly and Semel built the film and music divisions into a $11 billion behemoth.

By the late 1990s, the two men seemed to be anachronistic—a reminder of an age when all-powerful studio heads ruled Hollywood and reported to no one. After Time Warner bought Turner Broadcasting, Ted Turner complained loudly: Daly and Semel were too powerful, and their salaries were inflated. As the music business continued to lose market share, the men were criticized for spreading themselves too thin. The movie studio started to slip. By 1999, panicking about his company's lack of an Internet strategy, even Levin had grown disenchanted with his two long-serving studio chiefs. To him Semel and Daly represented everything that was wrong with Time Warner, technically speaking: why, they barely used e-mail!

Casually, meeting Semel at a wedding they both attended in 1999, Levin told him the sad fact: Semel's and Daly's contracts wouldn't be renewed at the end of the year. "Those days are over," Levin said, referring to Semel's and Daly's outsize compensation packets. In May 1999 Hollywood was shocked when Semel and Daly announced their intention to retire at the end of the year.

A few months later, in October 1999, Daly was named managing partner, chairman, and chief operating officer of the Los Angeles Dodgers. Born in Brooklyn (where the Dodgers were originally based), Daly presented himself as a lifelong Dodgers fan who dreamed of returning the team to glory. That never happened. In October 2003, the Dodgers were sold to Frank McCourt, a Boston real estate developer, and Daly announced his retirement. Under Daly the Dodgers had a 349–299 record; despite one of the biggest payrolls in Major League Baseball, the team never made the playoffs.

As for Terry Semel, since leaving Time Warner he has emerged as one of the most powerful and successful executives in the Internet world. Named chairman and CEO of Yahoo! in May 2001, Semel, who is sixty, has done a remarkable job of turning around the company. Wall Street was skeptical at first: it seemed unlikely that a long-time Hollywood player, a man who couldn't find his way around Silicon Valley, would know how to salvage Yahoo!. Since Semel's arrival at Yahoo!, however, the company's revenue and profits have reached record highs, and the stock has more than doubled.

Charles Dolan

After Time Inc. took over his ailing HBO in 1973, Chuck Dolan founded Cablevision Systems, which today has a market cap of about $6 billion. With three million cable subscribers in the New York metropolitan area, Cablevision is the seventh largest cable operator in the country. It also owns Madison Square Garden; the New York Knicks basketball and New York Rangers hockey teams; a twenty-five-year lease on Radio City Music Hall; and a 54 percent stake in such cable television channels as American Movie Classics, the Independent Film Channel, and Women's Entertainment.

Some things never change. In the process of upgrading the company's cable system, Chuck Dolan and his son, president James "Jimmy" Dolan, spent so much of the company's money to upgrade its cable systems that Cablevision wound up bloated with debt and facing a cash crunch. It then had to sell off assets. Between May 1999 and August 2002, Cablevision's stock price fell from $183.75 to $4.85. Recently, the stock has come back somewhat, to around $20. In part that's because the company has pared back and slimmed down. There's this, too: Rumor has it that Time Warner is eager to get its hands on Chuck Dolan's cable assets. At seventy-seven, Dolan may be eager to cash out—this time at a profit.

Michael Fuchs

Jerry Levin fired him on Thursday, November 16, 1995. For more than a year Fuchs was in shock. He'd spent eighteen years at Time Inc. and then Time Warner. He was addicted, as he put it, to the "metronome, the urgency" of his huge job—and then, all of a sudden, at the age of forty-nine, he was out of work. "You walk into the building on a Thursday a master of the universe and you walk out that night a man without a country," Fuchs explained to me. "I didn't realize what it would be like to wake up the next day with nowhere to go. . . . It was incredibly disconcerting."

For a time, Fuchs imagined he'd be hired to run another big media and entertainment company. It was reported he was negotiating for the top job at Sony Pictures Entertainment. In fact, no one offered Fuchs a job. "People were afraid that I'd come in and change things and move the furniture around, and that was probably true," he said. "But people were always more afraid of me than they should have been. I was never that much of a killer—I was just outspoken and I wasn't afraid of anyone." Eventually, Fuchs packed his bags and moved on: "I spent about a year waiting for something to happen, waiting to run another media company, and then it dawned on me that I'd never really be able to run a big machine again. . . . After a year I decided I never wanted to be back in a corporation. I decided that life wasn't for me."

At least Fuchs was rich. He (or his lawyer) had negotiated a fantastic severance package: Time Warner gave him somewhere in the range of $50 million to $100 million in stock (depending on whom you believe). The company also agreed to pay five years' rent on his new spacious office at 9 West 57th Street (one of Manhattan's most iconic high-rises) and threw in another $500,000 for decorating. Having settled into his new office overlooking Central Park, Fuchs started spending his money. During the Internet boom, he plowed $20 million into something called MyTurn.com that went under before it took off. He was an early investor in Autobytel, which has survived; he remains chairman. He has backed a handful of theater productions in New York and London, including *Hairspray, Little Shop of Horrors, La Bohème,* and *The Vagina Monologues.* A few years ago Fuchs bought seventy acres of land in Hawaii, where he is planning a large development. In 2003 he bought half of a natural medicine company that sells an herbal migraine preventive called MigreLief. He has also backed Maer Roshan's new *Radar* magazine, whose tagline is, "Pop. Politics. Scandal. Style."

Now fifty-seven, and thinking of writing a book about his years at HBO, Fuchs is in the "very early stages" of trying to start a new cable channel. "I'd like to go against the current one more time," he said, comparing the impact he made with HBO to what he hopes to achieve with his new cable channel.

Fuchs can still get nostalgic thinking about his old company. "I get a few pangs," he conceded. "I still get up in the middle of the night and think of what could have been." Fuchs loves speaking to reporters about the good old days. Proudly, he arrived at the 2002 AOL Time Warner annual shareholders meeting like a decorated hero home from the wars. In September 2003 he hosted an HBO reunion party at his second home in Katonah, New York. About 150 people showed up: they included former Time Inc. CEO Dick Munro; Jerry Levin's estranged wife, Barbara Riley; former Time Warner CEO Nick Nicholas; and the former head of Time Warner's cable division, Joe Collins.

Fuchs lives in Manhattan. He travels regularly, plays tennis, collects Latin American and pre-Columbian art, serves as chairman of the Bryant Park Restoration Corporation, and has two children, ages eleven and four. He has never been married.

Peter Haje

Time Warner's longtime general counsel is now retired. Having been frozen out of the negotiations with AOL in 1999 while he was still general counsel, Haje, sixty-nine, left Time Warner just as the company's merger with AOL was being announced. Since then he has done some consulting work; he has also written a novel about corporate lawyers and the ethical pressures they face. Titled *Looking the Other Way,* it has not been picked up by a publisher so far.

Richard Hanlon

When the AOL Time Warner merger closed in January 2001, Hanlon was named senior vice president of investor relations, pushing aside Time Warner's longtime head of investor relations, Joan Nicolais Sumner. (Nicolais is now vice president of strategic planning for Viacom.) In March 2003, Hanlon quit, following the exodus of most of the other senior AOL'ers. "I'd always had fun doing what I did— never more so than at AOL," he told me. "But my new job had not been fun for two years."

Describing his activities since leaving the company, Hanlon, fifty-six, said simply: "I've just been getting my life in order. I have no burning desire to do anything 'next.' I'm not anxious to get back into investor relations." If Hanlon decides to do anything, it will likely be helping small private companies raise money, perhaps in the role of a venture capitalist. For now he's content being a board member of Michaels Stores, a $3 billion (market cap) chain of arts and crafts stores based in Dallas, Texas. He has also helped start, and is an investor in, two hedge funds: Maverick Capital ($8 billion in assets) and Emancipation Capital, which invests in software.

Along with many other AOL'ers (Steve Case, George Vradenburg, Ted Leonsis, and Jack Davies), Hanlon serves on the board of Venture Philanthropy Partners. Rather than just funding various programs, VPP tries to take an entrepreneurial and business approach to philanthropy by making sure it gets a good "return" on its investments. Hanlon is also on the board of the Washington Ballet. He and his wife, a retired registered nurse, live in Great Falls, Virginia. Hanlon still holds stock in Time Warner.

Andrew Heiskell

Chairman and CEO of Time Inc. from 1960 to 1980, and the last of Henry Luce's handpicked successors, Heiskell died in July 2003 at his home in Darien, Connecticut. He was eighty-seven.

Having retired from Time Inc. after forty-three years with the company, Heiskell became renowned for his philanthropy and his remarkable contributions to civic improvements. In 1981 he was named chairman of the New York Public Library. Together with Brooke Astor, he raised hundreds of millions of dollars to restore the library's landmark Fifth Avenue building, improve the library system citywide, and clean up historic Bryant Park, the dilapidated park behind the main library. As chairman of the Enterprise Foundation's New York advisory board, he helped raise $600 million to build low-cost housing in some of the poorest, most dangerous parts of New York City.

Over the years, Heiskell expressed his sadness at what had become of Time Inc. In his memoirs, Heiskell wrote with resignation: "I left my company in good shape—financially, spiritually, ethically. Times change." According to one of his friends and former colleagues, he deeply regretted ever having referred to Jerry Levin as Time Inc.'s "resident genius."

Michael Kelly

It's a tough call: which AOL'er did the people at Time Warner hate most, Bob Pittman or Mike Kelly? Jerry Levin regarded Kelly as a brilliant chief financial officer; that's why he became CFO of AOL Time Warner in January 2001. Ten months later, in November 2001, Kelly was demoted and sent back to the AOL division as chief operating officer. Wayne Pace, the longtime chief financial officer of the Turner Broadcasting System, replaced him as CFO.

Why was Kelly demoted? He was too bombastic and impulsive, some people said. For example, he once told Merrill Lynch analyst Jessica Reif Cohen to "fuck off." As well, Kelly was responsible for negotiating the disastrous deal with Bertelsmann in which AOL Time Warner was forced to spend $6.75 billion to buy half of AOL Europe. Kelly's defenders will tell you a whole different story. Despite appearances, they insist, Kelly was not demoted; he was sent back to the AOL unit because the division needed his help, desperately. When Barry Schuler, head of the AOL division, lost the confidence of his bosses, Kelly effectively took charge.

One way or another, Kelly, forty-seven, has become a minor player at Time Warner. In mid-2003, when Jonathan Miller was named head of the AOL division, Kelly was moved over to the side; he now oversees AOL International.

A defendant in all the lawsuits against AOL Time Warner, Kelly exercised and sold $19 million worth of company shares in the spring of 2001.

Kenneth Lerer

Shortly before his old friend Bob Pittman left AOL Time Warner in July 2002, Lerer gave up his position as head of the company's corporate communications and investor relations departments. For the remainder of 2002, under the official title of executive vice president, office of the Chief Executive Officer, he served as an adviser to Dick Parsons. Lerer left the company in January 2003, having exercised and sold $10.5 million worth of AOL Time Warner stock options in the spring of 2001.

In September 2003, Lerer began teaching an undergraduate course at the University of Pennsylvania's Annenberg School for Communication: "The Modern American Corporation and the Media." He has also returned to politics; currently he's helping the Brady Campaign to Prevent Gun Violence hone its attack on the National Rifle Association. "I've gone back to my roots," he told me recently, clearly relieved to have traded corporate politics for the politics of gun control.

Lerer, fifty-one, lives with his wife, Katherine Sailer, in Manhattan and is chairman of the board of the Joseph Papp Public Theater. He still owns stock in Time Warner and is a defendant in lawsuits against the company and its executives. His old corporate communications firm, Robinson, Lerer & Montgomery, was sold to Young & Rubicam Inc. in early 2000.

Gerald Levin

Jerry Levin has distanced himself from his past yet again. From time to time he does think about his old company, but in a detached sort of way. He rarely communicates with former colleagues or associates. "I'm not in the Hollywood community, I'm not in the media community. That's not where I'm looking for my sustenance," he told me in October 2003. Levin has a new life. He also has a new vocation: the healing arts. Together with his fiancée, Laurie Perlman, a psychologist, Levin is helping to create a holistic mental health institute in Los Angeles, California. Called Moonview Sanctuary, and conceived of by Perlman and her partners before she met Levin, it is described on its

Web site as "a sanctuary of calm and order in a world of chaos, pressure, and fear." As well: "Moonview provides a sanctuary for individuals who are challenged by emotional, physical, social, or spiritual upheavals."

Moonview Sanctuary is expected to open in early 2004. Already Levin and Perlman have signed on a distinguished staff of professional healers: psychiatrists, psychologists, acupuncturists, chiropractors, hypnotherapists, aromatherapists, and animal and equine therapists. The couple also plans to launch an imprint dedicated to books that "affect the human condition," to quote Levin. He compares the new imprint to an independent film house or to HBO; instead of publishing mass-market self-help books, he and Perlman intend to publish "meaningful" books with "integrity." Their own book (as yet unfinished), an early example of the genre, is called *Soul Communion*. An ode to the couple's "belief system," it addresses, among other things, their understanding of "couple-ship, life, death and God."

Since early 2003, Levin and Perlman have been living in her apartment in Marina del Rey, California. He's lost thirty pounds now that he's left AOL Time Warner, and he works out at the Sports Club/L.A. almost every day. One week a month he's back in New York dealing with unfinished business. In the process of divorcing his wife, Barbara Riley, Levin is liquidating most of his assets. Although he once earned as much as $11 million a year in salary and bonus, and held plenty of options in AOL Time Warner, he's cash poor. The value of his stock options has either collapsed or evaporated: in 2003, two blocks of Levin's ten-year options expired, worthless. Over the years, he and his wife (Barbara Riley) had taken out huge loans, mostly to buy and decorate their four houses. "I used to joke about one of our earlier houses; how I'd come home from a business trip and she'd have things completely changed around," Levin once remarked on the subject of his wife's tendency to decorate and redecorate. "It's like the Greek philosopher—I mean, I never walked into the same room twice."

In order to pay down their debts, rumored to be as high as $20 million, Levin needs cash. In late 2002 and early 2003, he was forced to sell most of his AOL Time Warner stock at low prices. He sold his stake in a vineyard in California's Santa Ynez Valley for $4 million. His New York apartment, a triplex in River House, is on the market for $6.5 million (down from $7 million). His luxury condominium in Santa Fe is on the market for $3.2 million. Rumor has it that his other homes (in Dorset, Vermont, and in Key West, Florida)—both featured in *Architectural Digest*—will soon be put up for sale. What's keeping Levin afloat is his annual pension of $362,000 (half of which will presumably go to his wife) plus the $1 million a year he'll receive from Time Warner until 2005.

Levin isn't troubled by his financial problems. In fact, he's never been happier, he assured me. "I'd make a much better CEO now," he said. "I'm more centered. I'm balancing all parts of my internal being. I'm more in touch with the feminine side of myself."

What does sadden Levin from time to time is this: that during his long tenure as CEO of Time Warner, he was misunderstood and misinterpreted. "I tried to stand for values and humanity, but the perception was very different. That's who I really am, and it's who I am now, but I couldn't succeed in getting that infused in the company." Does he regret selling Time Warner to AOL? "I don't have any regrets," he said matter-of-factly. "I'm not defensive about it, either. It is what it is."

Don Logan

See Jeffrey Bewkes, earlier.

Henry R. Luce, Portrait

When Steve Case stepped down as chairman of AOL Time Warner in January 2001, the portrait of Harry Luce was taken down from the wall of Case's office. Moved from 75 Rockefeller Center back to the

Time-Life Building, the portrait was reframed; in late 2003 it was hung in a new conference center on the second floor.

Henry Luce III

The eldest son of Harry Luce, Hank Luce retired as an employee of Time Inc. in 1981 and as a member of the Time Warner board in 1996. In 2002, after forty-five years as chairman of the Henry Luce Foundation, Luce was replaced by his cousin Margaret Boles Fitzgerald. He remains a member of the foundation's board and is chairman emeritus.

The Luce Foundation, which was funded with Harry Luce's Time Inc. shares, gave away $19.5 million in 2002 (the latest available figures). Since 1936, when the foundation was created, it has given away $550 million to fund higher education, studies in religion and theology, cultural and intellectual exchanges between Asia and the United States, exhibitions and scholarships in American art, environmental research, and scholarships for women in the sciences. Of the foundation's $687 million in assets, only about 6 percent remains in Time Warner stock.

Now seventy-eight years old, Luce is dispassionate about what has become of the company his father created. At the time of the AOL deal, no one from Time Warner thought of phoning him with the news, though he did later speak to Dick Parsons about it. He hasn't seen Jerry Levin in years. "I've not been in touch," he told me. "I've not tried to be in touch." Asked if he feels any personal connection to Time Warner, he answered: "Hardly at all." He lives in Manhattan with his wife, the travel writer Leila Hadley.

Richard Munro

After retiring as CEO of Time Inc. (and, briefly, as co-CEO of Time Warner) in 1990, Munro remained on the board of Time Warner until 1996. For a few years, until he turned seventy in 2001, he also served on the boards of Exxon (and ExxonMobil), Kellogg, and Genentech. In the 1990s, he was chairman of the Points of Lights Foundation (which encourages volunteers to donate their time and energy to social causes) and of the Juvenile Diabetes Research Foundation (both his children are diabetic). He currently serves as a trustee for Save the Children, which works to improve the health and education of children around the world.

Upon his retirement from Time Warner, Munro was given a retirement package worth $7 million over ten years. At the time, he assumed $7 million was lavish, a huge amount of money. "I was embarrassed to take it," he recalled. "Back in the Time Inc. days most of us didn't even know how much money we made. We never had contracts. We just never thought about it. You didn't come to Time Inc. to get rich." In an era when former CEOs like Jack Welch (of General Electric) are awarded pensions valued at $8.4 million *a year,* Munro's $7 million isn't much, relatively speaking. He's not poor, of course; he still holds about eight hundred thousand Time Warner shares, worth $12 million before taxes. But in the decade since leaving Time Warner, Munro has held on to almost all his stock, which is to say he made a bad financial decision.

Now seventy-three, Munro is scaling back, trying to preserve whatever capital he has. He has sold his apartment in New Canaan, Connecticut, and is trying to sell his house in Weston, Vermont. "It's water under the dam now," he told me on the subject of his financial shortsightedness. "A lot of people, myself included, grew up feeling that you didn't sell your stock until you really needed the money."

By nature, Munro is gracious and even tempered; however, he can't help sounding resentful when Jerry Levin's name comes up. Looking back, he suspects he was duped by Levin. And he has other regrets. Why didn't he stand up to Levin on that fateful day back in 1992, when Levin staged the coup against Nick Nicholas? Given a opening, Munro will rage against Levin's rewriting of corporate history. According to Munro, the contributions he and others made to Time Inc.'s video group, especially to HBO, have not been properly acknowledged; Levin has taken all the credit. Above all, Munro is troubled by what he considers to be a personal attack: the reason he agreed to buy Warner Communications rather than accepting Paramount's hostile bid, some people will tell you, is that he wanted to save his job. "I will go to my grave bothered that our integrity was questioned," he stated. "We may have been stupid, but our integrity was like the Rock of Gibraltar."

Like other former Time Inc.'ers, Munro tends to be nostalgic: "When you spend forty years with a company, it becomes a part of you. Hardly a day goes by when I don't think of it." In September 2003 he attended the HBO reunion party hosted by Michael Fuchs and Nick Nicholas. "It brought back so many fun memories of that era," he said. "God, it was fun!"

Nick Nicholas

Fired as co-CEO of Time Warner in 1992, Nicholas received $16 million in severance—a small amount by current standards. He sold all his Time Warner stock options around 1997, just as the stock began to recover. Since then he has owned no stock in the company.

For the past decade, Nicholas has been a private equity investor, making early stage investments in various Internet companies. His most successful investment to date has been Priceline.com, which he backed even before its launch in 1998. He served on Priceline.com's board from its founding until June 2003. Mostly, however, Nicholas spends his time and energy as chairman of the board of trustees for Environmental Defense, a nonprofit, nonpartisan advocacy group devoted to domestic and global environmental issues.

Since leaving Time Warner, Nicholas, sixty-four, has become the grandfather of eight. In September 2003 he co-hosted an HBO reunion party with Michael Fuchs. "It was like a high school reunion," he said nostalgically. "It was great—just great." Nicholas lives in Manhattan with his wife, a retired psychologist.

Richard Parsons

As CEO of Time Warner, Dick Parsons is charged with cleaning up what may be the messiest merger in the history of corporate America. It's a thankless job. And although Time Warner's stock nearly doubled in Parson's first year on the job, from a low of $8.70 in July 2002, lately it's been stuck in the region of $16.

Determined to stabilize Time Warner and give it credibility on Wall Street, Parsons has approached his job cautiously. He is pushing for steady growth and lower costs. He has improved morale and actually seems to be getting employees to work in tandem. To encourage cooperation, he meets Don Logan, Jeff Bewkes, and CFO Wayne Pace for breakfast every Monday morning. Determined to pare the company's debt from $29 billion to $20 billion by the end of 2004, Parsons has sold the company's CD and DVD manufacturing business, its Atlanta Hawks and Thrashers sports teams, and its stakes in the Comedy Central cable network and Hughes Electronics Corp. On November 24, 2003 he announced the sale of Time Warner's music division for $2.6 billion. And he has raised $750 million by settling AOL's antitrust lawsuit against Microsoft. By the end of 2004, Time Warner's debt should be back to about what it was before the AOL deal.

Some analysts believe Parson will, or should, dump the AOL unit—but given how badly the division is doing, it may not be worth much. But who knows? Maybe Steve Case will wind up buying back his old company.

Despite Parsons's strategies, Time Warner is in limbo until the SEC and Justice Department investigations of the company's accounting are over; no one knows when that will be. Already the investigations have dragged on for a year and a half. And so far neither the company nor any of its former or current executives have officially been charged with a crime. Time Warner has admitted to exaggerating revenues by $190 million over a two-month period beginning in the fall of 2000. The SEC contends that an additional $400 million of revenue has been overstated; Time Warner and its auditors disagree. Until that dispute is settled, Time Warner and Dick Parsons will have a hard time moving forward.

Then shareholder lawsuits have to be resolved. Time Warner is trying to have the suits dismissed. Its lawyers contend that the company never committed fraud: they say that the company disclosed its questionable accounting practices—round-trip deals and all—right from the beginning. The plaintiffs, naturally, disagree. Their lawyers are excited by the potential damages, which have been estimated at anywhere from $1 billion to $100 billion, depending on who's doing the math. The largest settlement of a securities fraud class-action lawsuit was $2.83 billion, paid by Cendant Corp. in 1999. As the plaintiffs' lawyers in this case are happy to point out, however, Time Warner is nearly seven times bigger than Cendant was in 1999.

For someone fighting a tough battle, Parsons is surprisingly calm and cheerful. He's not easily rattled. His job as CEO is just that: a job. In late 2002, Parsons was asked how he responds to employees who sulk about the loss in value of their retirement plans. "Get over it," he answered. "I say to them, 'You have to get over it because you can't go back and undo the past.' " That may be easy for Parsons to say: in 2001 he exercised and sold $35 million worth of stock options.

Robert Pittman

Jerry Levin and Steve Case negotiated the deal. Bob Pittman wrecked it. That's the party line over at Time Warner. He's puzzled by the animosity he's managed to stir up, and he's stung by personal attacks on his integrity. As far as Pittman is concerned, he was only doing his job, and his job was to produce sales. Even more, he went out of his way to treat people on the Time Warner side of the company gently; so what's the problem? Ironically, some senior AOL'ers argue that Pittman failed as co-COO of AOL Time Warner because he was too nice; he gave people so much rope, they managed to hang him.

After being pushed out of AOL Time Warner in July 2002, Pittman spent nearly a year in seclusion with his wife, Veronique, and their two children. They traveled to Asia, Mexico, and Europe; he reconnected with old friends and with family in Mississippi; and, uncharacteristically, he avoided the spotlight. Then, in mid-2003, he started his career over again.

Ignoring the shareholder lawsuits in which he remains a defendant, Pittman, now fifty, has started a private equity firm named the Pilot Group to invest in small media properties, mainly television and radio stations. Working from new four-thousand-square-foot offices at 625 Madison Avenue, between 58th and 59th streets, Pittman has raised about $500 million from former associates and partners. His new team includes his former lieutenant at AOL and AOL Time Warner, Mayo Stuntz, and Robert Sherman, former president of interactive marketing at AOL. According to his friends and family, Pittman is back to his old self. "In the last year, he has been happier than I have seen him since first grade," remarked his brother, Tom.

In 2000, after the AOL Time Warner deal had been announced but before it closed, Pittman exercised and sold $22 million of AOL stock options. After the deal closed in 2001, he unloaded another $73 million of AOL Time Warner stock. He still holds sixteen thousand Time Warner options, which, in accordance with his severance agreement, have an extended expiration date of 2007. Pittman is confident that Time Warner's stock will rebound. "As American business comes out of the economic slowdown," he wrote in a recent e-mail to me, "I think you'll finally see the full value of these assets and you'll see Dick's skill at getting them to all work together." He always was an optimist. As a friend of his noted: "When it rains, Bob says it's sunny."

Joseph Ripp

Poor Joe Ripp. For a fleeting moment, he was chief financial officer of the world's biggest media and entertainment company. That was in late 1999, when Jerry Levin named Rich Bressler, Time Warner's longtime CFO, to head the new Time Warner Digital Media. The AOL deal happened only a few months later, and soon Ripp was pushed aside to make way for Mike Kelly, AOL's CFO. Though he had been at Time Inc. and then Time Warner since 1985, Ripp hadn't been consulted on the AOL deal.

After the AOL merger, he was CFO of the AOL division. By September 2002, as AOL's accounting problems were made public, Ripp, fifty-two, was named vice chairman of the AOL division, even though his replacement as CFO was not hired until the following spring. Whether his new job is a promotion or a demotion is not clear.

Barry Schuler

For six months after he was pushed out of his job as head of the AOL division in April 2002, Schuler was adrift, literally. Living on his eighty-three-foot yacht, *Expedition,* Schuler, along with his second wife, Tracy, and two of his four children cruised around Central and South America. Far from Dulles, Virginia, and the pressures of his old job, Schuler managed to decompress.

After spending the summer of 2003 at his home in Fire Island, New York, Schuler and his family settled in his dream home in California's Napa Valley. There, on thirty-five acres of land, he tends to his Medior Vineyard, producing about fifty cases of Cabernet Sauvignon a year for friends and family members. The rest of the grapes are sold to other winemakers. The vineyard is named after the interactive TV company Schuler sold to America Online in 1995.

In the fall of 2002, Schuler put up the money to co-found Blue Oak School, a progressive elementary school in downtown Napa. He's also investing in new business ventures; one of them is a start-up involved in laser technology. His free time (there's plenty of it) is devoted to art. Using both watercolors and oils, Schuler creates still-lifes, portraits, and pastoral scenes. His studio in Napa is equipped with a kiln for the ceramics he makes. And he's become an expert in digital art.

Since leaving AOL, Schuler has lost fifty pounds.

Terry Semel

See Robert Daly, earlier.

Time Warner

The AOL Time Warner deal was a fiasco; we've established that. But what about the merger of Time and Warner in 1990—how has that deal stood the test of bad times? Here's the bottom line: Say a shareholder had bought $10,000 worth of Time Warner stock on January 10, 1990, when the Time Warner merger closed, and had held on to that stock. He or she would now own shares worth $15,750. That's a dismal rate of return. A shareholder who had parked his money in the staid S&P 500 index during that same period would have tripled his money.

Time Warner Center

Often compared to the Taj Mahal, the new $1.8 billion Time Warner Center (previously known as the AOL Time Warner Center) opened on November 15, 2003. Rising eighty stories above Manhattan's Columbus Circle, Time Warner's glittering, glistening, glimmering new headquarters (2.3 million square feet) is the most expensive single-building construction project in U.S. history. In light of the company's problems and balance sheet, it has been called a monumental folly, like the tower of Babel.

The Time Warner Center is ample. It includes 1.1 million square feet of office space; 191 luxury condominiums (one was bought by a British financier for $45 million); a 149-room five-star hotel (the Mandarin Oriental); a 574-space parking garage; an amphitheater; two fancy restaurants; a seven-tier retail "atrium"; a health club; and a street-level broadcast studio for CNN.

Ted Turner

In the end, Ted Turner finally gave up. He'd been marginalized at AOL Time Warner. No one at the company would listen to him. He wasn't even consulted about CNN's new management team. In late January 2003 he quit his job as AOL Time Warner's vice chairman, packed his things, and moved out of the office he'd occupied at CNN's Atlanta headquarters for sixteen years. His new office is two blocks away, at 133 Luckie Street.

For the past months, Turner, sixty-five, has devoted much of his time to bemoaning the collapse of his enormous fortune. For a few days after the AOL Time Warner deal was announced, Turner's stock in the company was worth about $10 billion. Since then, on paper, he's lost $8.5 billion. According to the 2003 Forbes 400 list of richest Americans, Turner's net worth is now $2.3 billion. He owns seventy million Time Warner shares; 1.9 million acres of land (the largest landholding in America); and $800 million in bonds and cash. Still, Turner is upset. "I'm the stupidest person in the world not to have sold earlier," he told *Fortune* on the subject of his Time Warner stock.

What's Turner's next move? "Right now I'm kind of like Rhett Butler walking out the door on his way to Charleston to look for a more noble life," he quipped. One of his new projects is a chain of restaurants specializing in bison burgers. The first Ted's Montana Grill opened in 2002; there are now fourteen of them—in Ohio, Georgia, Tennessee, and Colorado. "I can see a day when this company has five hundred restaurants and a billion-dollar market cap," he prophesied. His restaurants have a noble agenda. Described as "eco-friendly," they're intended to popularize bison meat. In turn, sales of bison meat will encourage bison ranching and save the species from extinction. Bison are one of Turner's obsessions. He owns about 10 percent of the world's bison population, a herd of thirty-seven thousand.

Back in 1997, Turner promised to give $1 billion over ten years to the United Nations. It was a grand and spontaneous gesture, the sort of gesture Turner loves. As he explained to *The New York Times:* "I like gallantry, and the UN was an idealistic thing." He still owes the UN $600 million, a debt he has sworn to honor. The rest of his philanthropy has been scaled back. In 2001, Turner pledged stock then worth $250 million to his Nuclear Threat Initiative, whose mission is preventing the spread of nuclear, biological, and chemical weapons. By the time he actually handed over the money, the value of those shares had dropped by more than half. The value of Turner's personal foundation has been likewise affected.

When it comes to the subject of the disastrous AOL Time Warner deal, Turner presents himself as an innocent country boy who got conned by big-city slickers. "I'm an old-media guy," he said not too long ago. "I had a general knowledge of what AOL did, but my emphasis was television, not the Internet."

George Vradenburg III

Named senior vice president for global public policy in January 2001 (when his Time Warner counterpart, Tim Boggs, was sidelined), AOL's Vradenburg suffered a heart attack less than six months later and quit his post. Then he was named a "strategic adviser." In November 2003 he left the company altogether, but not before exercising and selling $39.5 million of AOL Time Warner stock options.

A resident of Washington, D.C., Vradenburg, sixty, is busier than ever. He co-chairs the Potomac Conference, a group of political, business, and civic leaders who address regional issues like homeland security and Washington's bid for the 2012 Olympic Games. He's chairman of the board for the Phillips Collection, a modern art museum off Dupont Circle. He's co-publisher of *Tikkun,* a magazine devoted to Jewish affairs and the Middle East. He co-chairs the fund-raising campaign of the Inova Heart Institute in Fairfax, Virginia; and he is also a board member of the greater Washington Board of Trade. Those are only some of the organizations Vradenburg is involved with. His favorite project is the Bee Vradenburg Foundation, which he established in honor of his mother; for thirty-seven years, until her death in 2000, Bee Vradenburg had served as manager of the Colorado Springs Symphony Orchestra. The foundation supports the performing arts in Colorado Springs.

Vradenburg doesn't regret the AOL Time Warner merger. "The strategy was right," he assured me. "The deal terms clouded people's perception." A devoted follower of Steve Case, Vradenburg regrets that the messianism that once defined AOL was overshadowed by the Time Warner deal. "There once was a positive social energy that at least some of us at AOL were driven by," he insisted.

NOTES AND SOURCES

Most of the research for this book derives from the hundreds of hours of interviews I conducted between 2000 and 2003. At the same time, I am indebted to the work of many outstanding journalists and scholars who came before me. These notes attest to that.

Among the many books cited below, five should be singled out. On Henry Luce and the history of Time Inc.: James L. Baughman's *Henry R. Luce and the Rise of the American News Media* (Johns Hopkins University Press, 1987), and Curtis Prendergast's *The World of Time Inc.* (Atheneum, 1986). On the history of Time Inc. and the Time Warner deal: Richard M. Clurman's *To the End of Time* (Simon & Schuster, 1992). On Steve Ross and the Time Warner deal: Connie Bruck's *Master of the Game* (Simon & Schuster, 1994). On the history of America Online: Kara Swisher's *AOL.com* (Three Rivers Press, 1998).

My reporting was in many ways shaped by the work of other business journalists. A handful of those journalists deserve special mention: Ken Auletta and Connie Bruck of *The New Yorker;* Julia Angwin, Laura Landro, Martin Peers, and Eben Shapiro of *The Wall Street Journal;* Alec Klein of *The Washington Post;* David Carr, Geraldine Fabrikant, Saul Hansell, Laura Holson, David Kirkpatrick, Steve Lohr, Floyd Norris, and Seth Schiesel of *The New York Times;* Marc Gunther and Carol Loomis of *Fortune;* Johnnie Roberts and Allan Sloan of *Newsweek;* David Lieberman of *USA Today;* and Sallie Hofmeister of the *Los Angeles Times.* Thank you all.

PROLOGUE

xi "I have long believed that Henry Luce had it right": Gabriel Snyder, "AOL Time Warner Marches On!," *New York Observer,* April 16, 2001.

xii Levin's allusion to Heraclitus: Steven M. L. Aronson, "Vermont Life and Times," *Architectural Digest,* May 1999.

xiii $200 billion of shareholder value had vanished: In January 2000, when their deal was announced, the combined market capitalization of AOL and Time Warner was $250 billion. By the summer of 2002, AOL Time Warner's market cap was $40 billion.

xiii Insider stock sales: During a three-year period beginning in January 2000, when the AOL Time Warner deal was announced, insiders sold $936,849,013 of stock according to *Regents of California and The Amalgamated Bank as Trustee for The Longview Collective Investment Fund v. Richard D. Parsons, et al.,* Superior Court of the State of California, County of Los Angeles, April 11, 2003.

xv "It's been wonderful to discover that I can really have a life": Leslie Cauley, "After a Tense Exit, Levin Tells His Side," *The New York Times,* February 2, 2003.

Part I
CHAPTER 1

3 "I believe that I can be of greatest service in journalistic work": W. A. Swanberg, *Luce and His Empire* (Charles Scribner's Sons, 1972), pp. 34–35.

4 Luce and Hadden's prospectus for *Time:* James L. Baughman, *Henry R. Luce and the Rise of the American News Media* (Johns Hopkins University Press, 1987), p. 27. (This page number, as well others from Baughman, refers to the Johns Hopkins paperback edition of 2001.)

4 Luce and Hadden comparing *Time* to the *Literary Digest:* Alden Whitman, "Henry Luce, 68, Dies in Phoenix," *The New York Times,* February 29, 1967.

4 Money raised to launch *Time:* Curtis Prendergast with Geoffrey Colvin, *The World of Time Inc.: The Intimate History of a Changing Enterprise Volume Three: 1960–1980* (Atheneum, 1986), p. xiii.

4   Number of investors in *Time:* Alden Whitman, "Henry Luce, 68, Dies in Phoenix," *The New York Times,* February 29, 1967.

4   "It was of course not for people who really wanted to be informed": Swanberg, p. 57.

4   *Time* was pilloried by intellectuals: Henry Grunwald, *One Man's America: A Journalist's Search for the Heart of His Country* (Doubleday, 1997), pp. 126–27. (This page number, as well as others from Grunwald, refers to the Anchor Books paperback edition of 1998.)

5   "Where it will all end, knows God!": Wolcott Gibbs, "Profiles: Time . . . Fortune . . . Life . . . Luce," *The New Yorker,* November 28, 1936.

5   "fantastic faith in the industrial and commercial future of this country": John K. Jessup, ed., *The Ideas of Henry Luce* (Atheneum, 1969), p. 385.

5   no magazine in history passed the half-million mark so quickly: Baughman, p. 92.

5   For a detailed history of *Sports Illustrated,* see Michael MacCambridge, *The Franchise: A History of Sports Illustrated Magazine* (Hyperion Press, 1997).

6   On Theodore White, Time's correspondent in China, see Swanberg, p. 3; see also Grunwald, pp. 102–103.

6   "began to entertain the delusion common among press lords": Thomas S. Matthews, "Tall, Balding, Dead Henry R. Luce," *Esquire,* September 1967.

6   Luce's frequent use of the word *righteousness:* Alden Whitman, "Henry Luce, 68, Dies in Phoenix," *The New York Times,* February 29, 1967.

7   "I am a Protestant, a Republican and a free enterpriser": Dwight Martin, "Henry R. Luce: His Time and Life," *Newsweek,* March 13, 1967.

7   "helped shape the reading habits, political attitudes, and cultural tastes of millions": Alden Whitman, "Henry Luce, 68, Dies in Phoenix," *The New York Times,* February 29, 1967.

7   "overstyled understatement": Ada Louise Huxtable, "Some New Skyscrapers and How they Grew," *The New York Times,* November 6, 1960.

7   Time Inc.'s share of the advertising market in the 1960s: Prendergast, *The World of Time Inc.,* p. 5.

7   John F. Kennedy receiving early copies of *Time:* Ibid., p. 30.

8   "An ignoramus, vintage Princeton '54": John Gregory Dunne, "Your Time is My Time," *The New York Review of Books,* April 23, 1992.

9   One black writer felt so vulnerable: Grunwald, *One Man's America,*
    p. 327.

9   "He's short; let's face it, he's fat; and he's Jewish": Ibid., p. 348.

9   "Galley slaves": Richard M. Clurman, *To the End of Time: The Seduc-
    tion and Conquest of a Media Empire* (Simon & Schuster, 1992), p. 36.

9   "comes as close as anything in America to being a czar": Prendergast,
    The World of Time Inc., p. 24.

9   Luce's shares in Time Inc. at his death: Ibid., p. 206.

9   Luce's funeral: McCandlish Phillips, "2,000 Pay Tribute to Henry R.
    Luce," *The New York Times,* March 4, 1967.

10 Statement by Lyndon Johnson on the death of Luce: Public Papers of
    the Presidents, Lyndon B. Johnson, February 28, 1967; the American
    Presidency Project, University of California, Santa Barbara. Available
    at www.presidency.ucsb.edu

10 Agnew confronting Time Inc.'s editors: Grunwald, *One Man's America,*
    p. 441; also (in a slightly different version) Prendergast, *The World of
    Time Inc.,* pp. 350–351.

11 "Newsweek has a fresher feel to it": A. Kent MacDougall, "Time Inc.'s
    Trials: Big Publisher Pledges New Projects Despite A Series of Set-
    backs," *The Wall Street Journal,* April 15, 1969.

11 *Life*'s losses in 1970–1972: Prendergast, *The World of Time Inc.,* p. 276.

11 "It violates everything Luce stood for": Andrew Heiskell with Ralph
    Graves, *Outsider, Insider: An Unlikely Success Story* (Marian-Darien
    Press, 1998), p. 182.

11 "Everyone know they're anti-Semitic": Luce resented charges that he
    was anti-Semitic. His supporters insisted that he was not. Richard
    Clurman, himself a Jew and *Time*'s chief of correspondents between
    1960 and 1969, said: "Harry isn't anti-Semitic. It's just that he hasn't
    known many Jews . . . He often asks me about this or that issue: 'What
    do you think of it as a Jew?' I always have to tell him that I don't think
    'as a Jew.' " (Grunwald, *One Man's America,* p. 348)

12 Time Inc.'s initial investment in Sterling: Prendergast, *The World of
    Time Inc.,* pp. 489–490.

13 "giving advice to people who were really doing something": Clurman,
    To the End of Time, p. 149.

13 "the ugly and the good side of human nature": David E. Lilienthal,
    Management: A Humanist Art (Columbia University Press, 1967), p. 17.

14 "business itself is the highest art form": Peter Kerr, "A Video Visionary Sees a Future in Print," *The New York Times,* September 16, 1984.

14 "very little difference between water, electricity and television": Clurman, *To the End of Time,* p. 149.

14 "he was the only one who understood it": Heiskell, *Outsider, Insider,* p. 132.

15 HBO was a hopeless proposition: Apart from Levin, another senior executive, James Shepley, Time Inc.'s president and chief operating officer under Andrew Heiskell, strongly supported HBO. Over the years, Shepley's crucial role in developing Time Inc.'s cable strategy, including HBO, has been greatly understated. "Jim Shepley was the believer, he was the godfather. He was not the guy who managed it to be successful, but he was the man with the vision," a colleague is quoted as saying in Prendergast, *The World of Time Inc.,* p. 492.

15 "I might have known enough never to start HBO at all": Heiskell, *Outsider, Insider,* p. 133.

16 "an electrifying kind of experience": Peter Kerr, "A Video Visionary Sees a Future in Print," *The New York Times,* September 16, 1984.

16 "Suddenly the whole meeting began to be HBO-oriented": Clurman, *To the End of Time,* p. 150.

16 "Resident genius": Connie Bruck, "The World of Business: Deal of the Year," *The New Yorker,* January 8, 1990.

16 "Snake-oil salesman": Prendergast, *The World of Time Inc.,* pp. 508–09.

16 "There is *no one* like Jerry Levin": Ibid, p. 509.

17 Samuel and Anna Levin's arrival in America: Samuel Levin household, 1910 U.S. Census, Philadelphia County, Pa. Ward 16, E.D. 252, S.D. 1, sheet 27A, dwelling 481, family 526.

17 Samuel Levin's estate: Samuel A. Levin estate file, Philadelphia Administration File No. 2187 of 1918, Philadelphia Register of Wills Office.

17 Pauline Shantzer's parents and date of arrival in America: Philadelphia County Marriage License No. 560408 of 1928, Philadelphia County Orphans' Court, Philadelphia, Pa. (Pauline's maiden name is spelled "Shantzer" on her marriage license; however, the 1930 U.S. Census and the 1925 Philadelphia City Directory lists her uncle's surname as "Schantzer." According to Samuel Levin, some branches of his mother's family spelled it one way and some the other.)

18   Marriage of David Levin and Pauline Shantzer: Philadelphia County Marriage License No. 560408 of 1928, Philadelphia County Orphans' Court, Philadelphia, Pa.

18   David Levin's age at time of marriage: David Levin's marriage license gives his date of birth as January 18, 1908. However, his birth record states his date of birth as January 18, 1909. The date on the marriage license may have been an error, or David Levin may have added a year to his age in order to appear older than his new wife.

18   The 720 Copley Road purchase and mortgage: Delaware County Deed Book 934:306 (1932), Delaware County Recorder of Deeds Office, Media, Pa.; also, Delaware County Mortgage Book 1086:409 (1932), Delaware County Recorder of Deeds Office, Media, Pa.

18   One of a handful of Jewish families in Upper Darby: Thomas J. DiFillippo, *The History and Development of Upper Darby Township,* 2d ed. (King of Prussia, Pa.: privately printed for Delaware County Historical Society, 1992), pp. 117 and 119.

19   "Synagogue in formation": In 1950, a synagogue, Temple Israel of Upper Darby, was built in Upper Darby.

20   Sale price of 720 Copley Road: Delaware County Deed Book 1590:208 (1951), Delaware County Recorder of Deeds Office, Media, Pa.

20   The 150 Trent Road purchase: Montgomery County Deed Book 2164:27, Montgomery County Recorder of Deeds Office, Norristown, Pa.

21   "When I met Jerry, he was sixteen going on forty-seven": Michael Oneal, "The Unlikely Mogul," *Business Week,* December 11, 1995.

22   "The symbol of Jesus . . . became so powerful to me": Clurman, *To the End of Time,* p. 148.

22   Quakerism "endowed me with a moral certainty": Connie Bruck, "The World of Business: Strategic Alliances," *The New Yorker,* July 6, 1992.

Chapter 2

25   "Publishing is more gentlemanly": Prendergast, *The World of Time Inc.,* p. 509.

26   "When I became chairman, I didn't know what a balance sheet was": Ibid., p. 555.

26   "I can't recall ever shaking his hand": Ibid.

26 "He is a man who has absolutely no interest in food or drink": Clurman, *To the End of Time,* p. 44.

27 "In those days all you had to do was add and subtract": Ibid., p. 69.

28 HBO's losses on Teletext and subscription television: Curtis Prendergast, *The World of Time Inc.,* p. 511.

28 HBO's losses on TriStar Pictures: Connie Bruck, *Master of the Game: Steve Ross and the Creation of Time Warner* (Simon & Schuster, 1994), p. 253. Bruck writes: "Time Inc. and HBO spent more than $1 billion for something that should have cost $500 million—a loss that was so embarrassing to Munro that it was hidden from Wall Street by amortizing the extra $500 million expense against the profit-and-loss statement over many years."

29 "Nicholas was not as tough as he looked and Levin a lot tougher": Grunwald, *One Man's America,* p. 550.

29 "The reason I didn't quit": Clurman, *To the End of Time,* p. 99.

29 "A failure. My big failure": Heiskell, *Outsider, Insider,* p. 201.

30 "The company is perceived": Bruck, *Master of the Game,* p. 256.

30 "This is not a company that worships deities": Clurman, *To the End of Time,* pp. 24–25.

31 "Time has what we call an immunologic system": Connie Bruck, "The World of Business: Deal of the Year," *The New Yorker,* January 8, 1990.

32 "I hate calculators; they're the equalizer": Ibid. In *Master of the Game,* p. 355, Bruck reports that Ross could "multiply a three-digit number by another three-digit number in his head."

33 "Mr. Warner dominated Warner Brothers": Vincent Canby, "Jack Warner, 75, Resigns Top Job," *The New York Times,* July 25, 1967.

33 "But wait until tomorrow: I'll be just another rich Jew": Nick Tosches, "Who Killed the Hit Machine?" *Vanity Fair,* November 2002.

34 "Time has such pizzazz": Bruck, *Master of the Game,* p. 281.

36 "Steve is such a warm, embracing human being": Connie Bruck, "The World of Business: Deal of the Year," *The New Yorker,* January 8, 1990.

36 $25,999 spent at the Villa Eden pro shop: Bruck, *Master of the Game,* p. 212.

36 "Steve is like a kid in a candy store": Tony Schwartz, "Steve Ross on the Spot," *New York* magazine, January 24, 1983.

37 Paramount initially offered to pay $175 a share for Time Inc. before increasing its offer to $200.

37   "Ross is a gentleman. Davis is a son of a bitch": Clurman, *To the End of Time,* p. 223.
38   "Tell him to go fuck himself": Ibid., p. 221.
39   "the greatest incursion in United States business history into the rights of shareholders": Robert A. G. Monks and Nell Minow, *Corporate Governance,* 2nd ed. (Blackwell Publishers, 2001). Available at www.ragm.com/library/books/corp_gov/cases/cs_twx.html
40   Time Warner's stock finally reached the equivalent of Paramount's $200-a-share offer in July 1997. Note that in 1992, Time Warner's stock was split four for one, making the $200-a-share offer equivalent to $50 after 1992.

CHAPTER 3

45   "I want Time Warner's success to be part of Steve Ross's legacy": Diane Mermigas, "Twelve to Watch in 1993: Gerald Levin," *Electronic Media,* January 25, 1993.
46   Levin's weak chin: Kim Masters and Stephen Fried, "The Precarious Throne," *Vanity Fair,* October 1995.
46   Levin following a track of giant footsteps: Robert Lenzner and Esther Wachs Book, "The Testing of Gerald Levin," *Forbes,* February 27, 1995.
46   The $90,000-an-hour interest on Time Warner's debt was calculated by entertainment analyst Harold Vogel. See Kim Masters and Stephen Fried, "The Precarious Throne," *Vanity Fair,* October 1995.
46   "the barons really have all the power": Spoken by John Malone in Michael Oneal, "The Unlikely Mogul," *Business Week,* December 11, 1995.
47   Steve Ross "wasn't a creator like Luce": Robert Lenzner and Esther Wachs Book, "The Testing of Gerald Levin," *Forbes,* February 27, 1995.
48   "Someday, 15 percent of New Yorkers will be paying their phone bills to Time Warner": Ibid.
48   On Malone and the five-hundred-channel universe, see Mark Robichaux, *Cable Cowboy: John Malone and the Rise of the Modern Cable Business* (John Wiley & Sons, 2002), pp. 122–23.
48   "I've staked my career on it": Laura Landro and Johnnie L. Roberts, "Dodging Gossip: Time Warner's Levin Tries to Rise Above the Takeover Talk," *The Wall Street Journal,* March 25, 1994.

50   "I was one card away from beating him": Catherine Hinman, "TV
     Clicker Takes a Wekiva Family into a New World," *Orlando Sentinel,*
     December 15, 1994.

50   The Internet is "an anarchistic electronic freeway": Philip Elmer-
     Dewitt, "First Nation in Cyberspace," *Time,* December 6, 1993.

51   "It's a little like holding the Indy 500 on a two-lane plank road": George
     Garneau, "A Calling in Cyberspace," *Editor & Publisher* magazine,
     May 13, 1995.

54   "Jerry went off to the mountaintop": Connie Bruck, "The World of
     Business: Jerry's Deal," *The New Yorker,* February 19, 1996.

55   "It is going to be something totally different, as it must be": Michael
     Oneal, "The Unlikely Mogul," *Business Week,* December 11, 1995.

55   "I'm used to being in charge": Anita Sharpe, "Not So Retiring: Used to
     Being Boss, Ted Turner Is Mulling His Time Warner Role," *The Wall
     Street Journal,* November 27, 1995.

56   "Show me your tits!": Ken Auletta, "The Lost Tycoon," *The New
     Yorker,* April 23 and 30, 2001.

56   Turner smashing a reporter's tape recorder: Peter Ross Range, "Ted
     Turner: *Playboy* Interview," *Playboy,* August 1983.

56   "I like the romance of the Confederacy": Peter Ross Range, "Ted
     Turner: *Playboy* Interview," *Playboy,* August 1978.

58   "I will take on myself the responsibility for anybody who is killed":
     Ken Auletta, "The Lost Tycoon," *The New Yorker,* April 23 and 30,
     2001.

59   "I learn more from CNN than I do from the CIA": William A. Henry
     III, *Time,* January 6, 1992.

59   "*I'm* being clitorized by Time Warner": Speech to the National Press
     Club, Washington, D.C., September 27, 1994.

60   "The biggest mistake I made was trusting Jerry too much": Patricia
     Sellers, "Gone With the Wind," *Fortune,* May 26, 2003.

63   "Jon is my mother's son": Andrea Peyser, "Sis: 'Jon Wouldn't Want Us
     Bitter,' " *New York Post,* November 11, 1998.

64   "a combination of Jesus, Buddha, and Gandhi": Metropolitan Devel-
     opment Association Annual Meeting, Onondaga County Convention
     Center, Syracuse, NY, December 13, 2001.

64   ENTER GOD, WITH $1 BILLION: "Enter God, with $1 Billion," *The
     Economist,* June 14, 1997.

65 Between October 1996 and October 1997, AOL's stock price (adjusted for all stock splits through 2003) went from $1.42 to $5.65.

66 "The world has never experienced as rapid/violent a commercial evolution": Mary Meeker, "U.S. and the Americas Investment Research," Morgan Stanley Dean Witter, September 26, 1997.

66 Levin described as "strong, decisive, and farsighted": Nelson D. Schwartz, "Suddenly, Jerry Levin's Stock Is Hot," *Fortune*, March 30, 1998.

Part II
CHAPTER 4

69 "The geeks don't like us": Joshua Cooper Ramo, "How AOL Lost the Battles but Won the War," *Time*, September 22, 1997.

72 "I believe in love, availability and direction": Andy Serwer, "The Word on Dan and Steve Case—From Mom," *Fortune*, November 22, 1999.

73 "I was always more conventional": Alan Deutschman, "How Sibling Rivalry Created AOL," *GQ*, August 1997.

74 Case's *Saturday Night Fever* party as a "multi-media extravaganza": "News Briefs: Case and Beckett Plan Disco Party," *Williams Record*, Williams College, April 11, 1978.

74 Case accused of "laissez-faire capitalism": Jeff Kovar, "Night Fever and the Sickness unto Death," *Williams Record*, Williams College, May 9, 1978.

74 He lost $350 on the *Saturday Night Fever* party: Steve Case letter to the editor, *Williams Record*, Williams College, May 12, 1978.

74 A "distraught" Case "sprawled out on a foam cushion between sets": Andy Clark, "Jukes Storm Towne but ACEC Loses $5,000," *Williams Record*, Williams College, October 27, 1978.

75 "It was just exhilarating": Kara Swisher, *AOL.com: How Steve Case Beat Bill Gates, Nailed the Netheads, and Made Millions in the War for the Web* (Three River Press, 1998), p. 27. (This page number, as well as others from Swisher, refers to the paperback edition of 1999.)

77 Quantum's main online service was named America Online in 1989. But the company wasn't officially named America Online until 1991, when the Quantum name was eliminated.

79 "The coming of a whole new civilization in the fullest sense of

the term": Alvin Toffler, *The Third Wave* (William Morrow, 1980), p. 349. (This page number refers to the Bantam paperback edition of 1981.)

79   "I had worked cleaning houses, cleaning toilets": Julia L. Wilkinson, *My Life at AOL* (1st Books Library, 2000), p. 5.

82   Case withdrew permission to use his personal photos: Swisher, *AOL.com,* p. 147.

82   Case quibbling over details with *The Washington Post:* Mark Leibovich, *The New Imperialists: How Five Restless Kids Grew Up to Virtually Rule Your World* (Prentice Hall Press, 2002), pp. 221–224.

85   "Breast-feeding" journalists: James B. Stewart, *Den of Thieves* (Simon & Schuster, 1991), p. 377. Lerer denied he said this: "I would never in a billion years talk like that; never ever. Someone made it up out of whole cloth," he told me.

86   "I've seen this movie before": Robert Pittman, AOL conference call with reporters, October 29, 1996.

87   "Bob always wanted to be rich and famous": Ron Powers, "The Cool, Dark Telegenius of Robert Pittman," *GQ,* March 1989.

CHAPTER 5

89   Churches in Brookhaven, Mississippi: see churchesofmississippi.com/lincoln.html#brookhaven

89   Brookhaven is perhaps best known by historians for Lamar Smith, a black civil rights activist who, in retaliation for encouraging blacks to vote in the Democratic primaries, was shot dead on the town's courthouse lawn one busy Saturday afternoon in 1955. In *Local People: The Struggle for Civil Rights in Mississippi* (University of Illinois Press, 1995), p. 54, John Dittmer reports that "although the sheriff saw a white man leaving the scene with 'blood all over him,' no one admitted to having witnessed the shooting."

90   "If you have an artificial eye, you're different": Ken Auletta, "Leviathan," *The New Yorker,* October 29, 2001.

90   "It changed my life": Ibid.

92   Pittman's WMAQ-AM as the greatest success stories in the history of radio turnarounds: www.museum.tv/archives/etv/P/htmlP/pittman robe/pittmanrobe.htm

93   "I figured out how to read people and get along": Steve Acker, "Robert W. Pittman: From MTV, Nick-at-Nite, Six Flags to Century 21," *Mississippi Business Journal,* August 7, 1995.

94   " 'cause that says a lot about a person": Michael Gross, "The Couple of the Minute," *New York* magazine, July 30, 1990.

94   Sandy Hill and Bob Pittman made "passionate" love: Jennet Conant, "Snow Blind Ambition," *Vanity Fair,* August 1996.

94   "Many coattails were wrinkled by Sandy Pittman": Joanne Kaufman, "Socialite Scales Highest Peaks: Six Down, One to Go," *The Wall Street Journal,* March 21, 1996.

94   "An ample supply of Dean & DeLuca's Near East blend": Jon Krakauer, *Into Thin Air: A Personal Account of the Mount Everest Tragedy* (Villard, 1997), p. 117. Sandy Hill Pittman is perhaps best known for having been one of the amateur climbers on the expedition detailed by Krakauer in which eight climbers died in a blizzard: her life was saved by a guide who carried her out of the blizzard and back to base camp.

94   "The socialite everyone loves to hate": Deborah Mitchell, "Pitons Are Served," Salon.com, June 11, 1997.

94   "The Martha Stewart of the outdoors" and THE COUPLE OF THE MINUTE: Michael Gross, "The Couple of the Minute," *New York* magazine, July 30, 1990.

95   "Steve Ross had probably one of the greatest impacts on my life": Catherine Yang with Ronald Grover and Ann Therese Palmer, "Show Time for AOL Time Warner," *Business Week,* January 15, 2001.

97   "I don't know what's gotten into him": Jennet Conant, "Snow Blind Ambition," *Vanity Fair,* August 1996.

99   In fiscal 2000, ended June 2000, its last full year before merging with Time Warner, America Online reported $1.986 million in "advertising, commerce and other" revenue.

101   "AOL does not have many other tricks": Amy Barrett, "AOL Downloads a New Growth Plan," *Business Week,* October 14, 1996.

103   Daniel Borislow on the verge of selling Tel-Save to a "very big company": Henry Goldblatt, "AOL's Long-Distance Telco," *Fortune,* May 25, 1998.

106   "When you see that 40 percent of all online traffic": Marc Gunther, "The Internet Is Mr. Case's Neighborhood," *Fortune,* March 30, 1998.

107 In March 1999, N2K became part of CDNow. In July 2000, on the brink
    of bankruptcy, CDNow was bought for $3 a share by Bertelsmann.

107 "Borislow has a criminal record": Alex Berenson, "Tel-Save's Tortured
    Tale: A Bull Market Fable," TheStreet.com, November 13, 1998. Bori-
    slow confirms he was convicted for weapons possession in New Jersey
    in 1992, adding that the gun in question was registered in Pennsylvania.
    He insists, however, that he never lied to *Fortune*. "I got expelled in the
    11th grade. I'm not much for structure," is what he told *Fortune* (May
    25, 1998). According to Berenson's article of November 1998, however,
    Borislow did graduate from Plymouth-Whitemarsh High School on
    June 11, 1980. When Berenson asked about the discrepancy, Borislow
    said he "couldn't remember" whether he'd graduated. More recently,
    when I spoke to him in October 2003, Borislow insisted he was indeed
    expelled. He explained that the records may show he graduated be-
    cause he completed requirements for his high-school diploma at a local
    community college.

109 "I can buy 20 percent of you or I can buy all of you": Swisher, *AOL.com,*
    p. xv.

109 Microsoft as "the enemy," "the beast," and "Hitler": Defendant's Ex-
    hibit #1345, *United States of America v. Microsoft Corporation,* U.S. Dis-
    trict Court for the District of Columbia, Civil Action No. 98-1232,
    October 28, 1998. In a draft of an October 1995 memo from Case to
    executives at Netscape, Case proposes that AOL and Netscape join
    forces against "the common enemy," namely Microsoft. He added: "My
    recollection is that Stalin teamed with Roosevelt and Churchill, and
    that was that Grand Alliance—that unified partnership—that beat
    Hitler."

109 Netscape "jilted at the altar" and as "a wounded duck": *United States
    of America v. Microsoft Corporation,* U.S. District Court for the District
    of Columbia, Civil Action No. 98-1232, October 28, 1998, volume 7,
    2:02 P.M. session.

111 "We really go through great pains": Gary Rivlin, "AOL's Rough Rid-
    ers," *Industry Standard,* October 30, 2000.

112 "For weeks it was, 'You're great, you're great, you're great' ": Ibid.

112 Autobytel lawsuit: *Auto-by-Tel Corp v. America Online Inc.,* Superior
    Court of the State of Delaware in and for New Castle County, Civil Ac-
    tion No. 97C-09-15 JEB, September 3, 1997.

114 "They think you'll be good for the stock": Paul Keegan, "Making AOL Rock," *Upside* magazine, November 1, 1998.

115 AOL's stock prices reflect all splits through 2003.

116 Number of millionaires at AOL: Beth Brophy, "You've Got Money," *Washingtonian,* October 1999.

118 On June 12, 1998, Woolworth Corporation was renamed Venator Group. In November 2001, the company changed its name again; it's now called Foot Locker Inc.

118 A note about "cash flow": Throughout this book, the term "cash flow" is used as shorthand to mean earnings before interest, taxes, depreciation, and amortization (EBITDA). However, it is worth remembering that EBITDA is nowhere near as valuable as real operating cash flow—at least not to investors. For AOL and AOL Time Warner, on the other hand, EBITDA was a way to dress up earnings by ignoring big expenses that were being amortized, or written off, over many years. Note that in the 1990s, Time Warner had used the less opaque EBITA (earnings before interest, taxes, amortization) as its measure of cash flow. Only after the AOL merger did the company switch to using EBITDA.

119 "I am loath to predict the future": Saul Hansell, "Now, AOL Everywhere," *The New York Times,* July 4, 1999.

119 AOL would generate more ad revenue than ABC or CBS: Marc Gunther, "AOL: The Future King of Advertising?" *Fortune,* October 11, 1999.

119 "When the history books are written": "America Online: An Incredible Success Story," CNBC, *Business Center,* February 23, 1999.

119 "AOL in the same vein as a Coca-Cola or a Gillette": Cory Johnson, "AOL Rides Its Credibility to Blue-Chip Status," TheStreet.com, April 5, 1999.

119 "AOL is *the* Internet blue chip": "America Online an Incredible Success Story," CNBC, *Business Center,* February 23, 1999.

Part III
CHAPTER 6

123 Case on the cover of *Business Week,* again: Ira Sager and Catherine Yang with Linda Himelstein and Neil Gross, "A New Cyber Order," *Business Week,* December 7, 1998.

123 "Steve Case was better than Harriet Tubman": "America Online's Next Frontier: If I Ran AOL . . . ," *The Wall Street Journal,* March 19, 1999.

124 For evidence that Case's fears of MSN were legitimate, see Walter S. Mossberg, "In the Battle of the 7s, MSN's Access Service Gains Ground on AOL," *The Wall Street Journal,* November 15, 2001; see also Julia Angwin and Rebecca Buckman, "Dialing In: In Internet Access, AOL Begins to Feel Microsoft's Breath," *The Wall Street Journal,* October 14, 2002.

124 NetZero went public on September 24, 1999. By the end of its first day of trading, it was worth $3 billion, almost as much as United Airlines. One year later, the stock had dropped 90 percent.

127 Salomon Smith Barney's rank in Internet IPO underwriting: Thomson Financial Services, 1999.

127 "I don't even know the names of anyone over there": Jonathan Rabinovitz, "Eduardo Mestre: Surprise Dealmaker for AOL Time Warner," *Industry Standard,* January 12, 2000.

129 In hindsight, Sumner Redstone of Viacom claimed that he too had been approached by AOL: "Jerry did the deal that we rejected," he later boasted to David Faber ("The Big Heist: How AOL Took Time Warner," CNBC, January 9, 2003). In fact, no one from AOL talked to Redstone about doing a deal.

132 "I could name 50 other people at Time Warner": Frank Rose, "Reminder to Steve Case: Confiscate the Long Knives," *Wired* magazine, September 2000.

133 "I've obviously been an idealist my whole life": Ken Auletta, "Leviathan," *The New Yorker,* October 29, 2000.

133 "Presbyterian muscularity": Gerald M. Levin, "Value for the Digital Age: The Legacy of Henry Luce," keynote address delivered at the Third Annual Aspen Institute Conference on Journalism and Society, August 7, 1999.

133 "I share this conviction": Ibid.

134 "a future I will do all my power to make happen": Ibid.

134 *Time* news tours of the 1960s: Prendergast, *The World of Time Inc.,* pp. 199 and 253.

135 Warner Bros.' co-CEOs Bob Daly and Terry Semel were the only division heads who did not attend the Time Warner News Tour. Only two weeks before the trip was to begin, they begged off (Daly apparently

announced that he didn't like "group trips") and in so doing greatly offended Levin.

140 "perceived as a merger of equals": Ken Auletta, "Leviathan," *The New Yorker,* October 29, 2000.

141 "poison pill": Named after the cyanide pills that secret agents are instructed to take if their capture is imminent, poison pills are designed to prevent corporate takeovers. Typically, poison pills allow shareholders of the targeted company to fend off a hostile bid by buying additional shares at a deep discount to fair market price.

145 Turner was more interested in NBC than AOL: Martin Peers and John Lippman, "Ted Turner Still Wants Time Warner to Buy a Major Television Network," *The Wall Street Journal,* November 26, 1999.

146 "I want one of everything": Speech at the California Cable Television Association's Western Show, December 15, 1999.

147 Between October 10, 1999, and December 10, 1999, AOL's stock (adjusted for all splits through 2003) climbed from $60.53 to $91.75.

147 On December 31, 1999, AOL's market capitalization was $176 billion. Berkshire Hathaway, $85 billion; McDonald's, $54 billion; J.C. Penney, $52 billion; PepsiCo, $51 billion.

147 $11,500 invested in AOL in 1992 would now be worth $8 million: "America Online's Board of Directors Declares Two-for-One Stock Split," *Business Wire,* October 28, 1999.

149 "There was only so far I could go": Steve Lohr and Laura M. Holson, "Price of Joining Old and New Was Core Issue at AOL Deal," *The New York Times,* January 16, 2000.

149 AOL as one of the most inflated stocks: Loren Fox, "The 20 Most Inflated Tech Stocks," *Upside* magazine, August 1, 1999.

149 For an outstanding history of stock manias, see Edward Chancellor, *Devil Take the Hindmost: A History of Financial Speculation* (Farrar, Straus & Giroux, 1999).

149 Barbra Streisand as stock picker: Jeanne Lee, "Barbra Streisand's Latest Role: Stock Picker," *Fortune,* June 21, 1999.

150 "There's such an overvaluation of tech stocks": Speech to the Society of American Business Writers and Editors, September 24, 1999.

150 "It's a matter of self-preservation": Joseph Nocera, "Do You Believe? How Yahoo! Became a Blue Chip," *Fortune,* June 7, 1999.

153 "Biggest Gainer of the '90s": E.S. Browning, "Goodbye Golden De-

cade. Now What Will the '00s Bring," *The Wall Street Journal,* December 13, 1999.

CHAPTER 7

174 One example of a deal undone by a company's board of directors occurred in November 2000 when Coca-Cola Co.'s board voted to reject a deal to buy Quaker Oats for $15.75 billion. So imminent was the announcement of the deal that publicity shots had already been taken of the two CEOs together.

174 "Don't you think we ought to vote more enthusiastically?": Johnnie L. Roberts. "Desperately Seeking a Deal," *Newsweek,* January 24, 2000.

178 "My first thought was, 'Oh, my God' ": David Faber, "The Big Heist: How AOL Took Time Warner," CBNC, January 8, 2003.

179 "The new media stock-market valuations are real": Steve Lohr, "Media Megadeal: The Strategy: Medium for Main Street," *The New York Times,* January 11, 2000.

180 "It's a brilliant deal for Steve Case": David Wallis, "Act 2.0," *Wired* magazine, May 2000.

181 "Pushing a boulder up an alp": Carol Loomis, "AOL + TWX = ???" *Fortune,* February 7, 2000.

181 "But we know it's big": Ibid.

181 Henry Blodget thought that AOL would now go after Wal-Mart: Marc Gunther, "These Guys Want It All," *Fortune,* February 7, 2000.

182 "A minnow in a pool with a very big fish in it": David Faber, "The Big Heist: How AOL Took Time Warner," CBNC, January 8, 2003.

182 "now it's go digital or die": Peter Huber, "AOL & Time Warner Inc.: The Death of Old Media," *The Wall Street Journal,* January 11, 2000.

182 "Everyone is trying to figure out where they go next": Susan Pulliam and Paul M. Sherer, "Anything Goes! After AOL Time Warner, Who's Next?," *The Wall Street Journal,* January 11, 2000.

183 "We're at the cusp of what we think will be a new era": Jim Lehrer, "MegaMerger Masters," *The NewsHour with Jim Lehrer,* PBS, January 12, 2000.

184 "The growth rate will be like an Internet company": Richard Siklos and Catherine Yang, "Welcome to the 21st Century," *Business Week,* January 24, 2000.

Part IV
CHAPTER 8

187 "A company that isn't old enough to buy beer": Martin Peers, Nick Wingfield, and Laura Landro, "Media Blitz: AOL, Time Warner Leap Borders to Plan a Mammoth Merger," *The Wall Street Journal,* January 11, 2000.

187 For a thorough debunking of the myth of market populism, see Thomas Frank, *One Market Under God: Extreme Capitalism, Market Populism, and the End of Economic Democracy* (Doubleday, 2000).

188 "returns will continue to average about 25 percent per year": James K. Glassman and Kevin A. Hassett, *Dow 36,000: The New Strategy for Profiting from the Coming Rise in the Stock Market* (Times Books, September 1999), p. 13.

188 "I think we can see Nasdaq 6000 in the next 12 to 18 months": Beth Piskora, "NASDAQ on Fast Track: Hits 5000," *New York Post,* March 10, 2000.

191 "we thought we could get digital by injection instead of by evolution": Frank Rose, "Reminder to Steve Case: Confiscate the Long Knives," *Wired* magazine, September 2000.

192 "Measuring Jerry Levin's office for curtains": "Who'll End Up Running AOL Time Warner? Bet on Bob Pittman," *Washingtonian,* February 2000.

192 "Ted went white": Ken Auletta, "The Lost Tycoon," *The New Yorker,* April 23 and 30, 2001.

192 "a title you give to somebody you can't figure out what else to do with": Ibid.

193 Ted Turner is "a transcendent figure": Jim Rutenberg and Alessandra Stanley, "At 63, Ted Turner May Yet Roar Again," *The New York Times,* December 16, 2001.

193 "Ted Turner has been a hero of mine": Speech at a press luncheon celebrating CNN's twentieth anniversary, June 1, 2000.

193 "I said, 'I'm your best friend?' ": Speech at the California Cable Television Association's Western Show, November 28, 2001.

197 "Black hole": Don Logan used this term at the American Magazine Conference, Boca Raton, Florida, November 1995. Asked how much money Time Inc. had spent in the past year to develop Pathfinder,

he replied: "It's given new meaning to me of the scientific term *black hole.*"

198 "Of all the cable operators, Time Warner is my worst customer": Marc Gunther, "Dumb & Dumber," *Fortune,* May 29, 2000.

201 For a thorough study of Wall Street's obsession with quarterly numbers in the 1990s, see Alex Berenson, *The Number: How the Drive for Quarterly Earnings Corrupted Wall Street and Corporate America* (Random House, 2003).

201 According to Thompson Financial/First Call, 278 companies on the S&P 500 index beat consensus estimates by one penny during at least one quarter of 1999. In many cases, those companies beat their estimates by one penny in more than one quarter—and some companies (including Costco Wholesale Corp., Cisco Systems, Express Scripts, First Data Corp., The Home Depot, Harley-Davidson, and Kohl's Corp.) beat their estimates by exactly one penny in all four quarters of 1999.

203 "The worst is yet to come": Mylene Mangalindan, "Yahoo! Drops 15% As Web Analyst Questions Revenue," *The Wall Street Journal,* November 11, 2000.

203 "the environment continues to worsen": CBS MarketWatch, August 28, 2000.

205 "Everybody has been hurt by the crashing dot-com advertising": CNN Moneyline News Hour, October 18, 2000.

206 "They are out of $": Alec Klein, "Unconventional Transactions Boosted Sales," *The Washington Post,* July 18, 2002.

207 24dogs.com ads on AOL: Ibid.

208 "Why can't you get this deal closed?": Ibid.

208 Reviews of *Little Nicky:* Charles Taylor, "Little Nicky," Salon.com, November 10, 2000; Steve Tilley, "Dumb and Dumber Little Nicky is Just Plain Offensive—and Unfunny," *Edmonton Sun,* November 10, 2000; John Murray (aka Mervius), "Little Nicky," *Fantastica Daily,* at fantasticadaily.com.

209 It has been suggested that either AOL or Time Warner could have pulled out of the deal by paying the breakup fees listed in the merger agreement ($5.4 billion for AOL; $3.9 billion for Time Warner). In fact, there was only one condition under which those breakup fees would be paid: If either side broke off the planned merger to do a deal with an-

other company. In other words, Time Warner couldn't simply pay $3.9 billion to prevent itself from being swallowed by AOL.

211 Levin's refusal to back out of the AOL deal would cost shareholders $200 billion: See note on p. 312 (xiii).

211 Christopher Bogart, Time Warner's general counsel, insisted that the lack of a collar on the AOL Time Warner deal had not been an oversight or even a concession to AOL. Instead, he told me, the deal did not include a collar because it was a "merger of equals": "You use a collar for the acquiree in a purchase-and-sale transaction, but this was not a purchase-and-sale transaction. Now, you can say in retrospect, 'Hey, they were sold a bill of goods: of course it was a purchase!' But it was structured and presented to both boards as a merger of equals, and the governance even today operates in a merger of equals setting. . . . At the end of the day, if the thing is not going to be an acquisition, you don't put a collar on it. You just don't. . . . It's kind of unfair now to come along and say, 'Hey, the Time Warner guys should have put a collar on the deal.' We were as gullible as but no more gullible than everybody who lost money on dot-com stocks."

CHAPTER 9

214 "Our company rides above normal market dynamics": Edmund Sanders, "Company Town: AOL Time Warner Restores Confidence with Strong First-Quarter Earnings," *Los Angeles Times,* April 19, 2001.

214 Case assures analysts that AOL Time Warner is on track to revenues of $100 billion: Peter Loftus, "AOL Time Warner CFO: 2001 Guidance Remains the Same," Dow Jones News Service, January 31, 2001.

214 "We believe our shares are undervalued": "AOL Time Warner Launches $5 Billion Share Repurchase Program," Business Wire, January 18, 2001.

215 "The company must hit the numbers expected of it": Catherine Yang with Ronald Grover and Ann Therese Palmer, "Show Time for AOL Time Warner," *Business Week,* January 15, 2001.

216 "He personifies Southern charm": Ibid.

216 "we're trying to get more out of them": Christopher Grimes and Richard Waters, "Pittman's Progress," *Financial Times,* March 19, 2001.

216 "Are you going to make your numbers?": Alec Klein, "New Firm to Follow 3 Leaders," *The Washington Post,* December 15, 2000.

218 Money saved by pizza cutbacks at *Sports Illustrated:* Gabriel Snyder, "AOL Time Warner Marches On!" *New York Observer,* April 16, 2001.

218 *Time*'s mock issue "In Memoriam": David D. Kirkpatrick and David Carr, "A Media Giant Needs a Script," *The New York Times,* July 7, 2002.

218 Pittman's mission as a "jihad": Seth Schiesel, "Planning the Digital Smorgasbord," *The New York Times,* June 11, 2001.

222 The *Entertainment Weekly* presentation had to be delivered by hand: Matthew Rose and Martin Peers, "AOL's Latest Internal Woe: 'You've Got Mail'—'Oops! No You Don't,' " *The Wall Street Journal,* March 22, 2002.

222 "AOL's giving us dog food": Sridhar Pappu, "Off the Record," *New York Observer,* February 25, 2002.

223 "a key driver of the company's future growth": "AOL Time Warner Creates Global Marketing Solutions Group to Drive Growth of Cross-Brand Advertising and Marketing Initiatives," Business Wire, August 17, 2001.

224 to think "holistically": Joe Fine, "Crunchtime," *Advertising Age,* May 7, 2001.

224 " 'What big strategic issues are you wrestling with?' ": Ibid.

225 "If we're one of their big customers": Martin Peers and Julia Angwin, "AOL's Grand Strategy for Ads Proves Hard to Boot Up," *The Wall Street Journal,* October 23, 2001.

225 "If you can't do business with your partners": Julia Angwin, "Amid Advertising Slowdown, AOL Parlays Partnerships into Revenue," *The Wall Street Journal,* April 16, 2001.

225 For details on the deal between AOL and WorldCom, see Laurie P. Cohen, Jared Sandberg, and Martin Peers, "Questionable AOL Revenue Has WorldCom Link," *The Wall Street Journal,* August 23, 2002; see also Julia Angwin and Rebecca Blumenstein, "AOL Dealmaker Was Renowned for Tough Style," *The Wall Street Journal,* August 23, 2002.

225 For details on the deal between AOL Time Warner and Oxygen, see Julia Angwin and Martin Peers, "Officials Probe AOL's Actions

with Partners," *The Wall Street Journal,* August 26, 2002; see also
Martin Peers and Laurie P. Cohen, "SEC Probes AOL-Oxygen Pact for
Double-Booking of Revenues," *The Wall Street Journal,* October 7,
2002; and Martin Peers and Julia Angwin, "Leading the News: AOL to
Restate Two Years of Results," *The Wall Street Journal,* October 24,
2002.

226 According to the National Bureau of Economic Research, the recession
began in March 2001.

226 "the most wrenching bear market": E. S. Browning and Ianthe Jeanne
Dugan, "Stocks Unwind: Aftermath of a Market Mania," *The Wall
Street Journal,* December 16, 2002.

226 First-quarter 2001 revenues were Yahoo!'s first year-over-year decline.
Measured quarter over quarter, however, it was the second time
Yahoo!'s numbers had fallen.

227 Yahoo!'s share price hit a split-adjusted all-time high of $238.50 on January 3, 2000.

227 "This puts us on track to meet the financial goals we've set": Peter Loftus, "AOL Time Warner CEO: Co. on Track To Meet Yr Targets,"
Dow Jones News Service, April 18, 2001.

227 "This sets the tone for a big year": Analyst Frederick W. Moran of Jefferies & Co., quoted in Julia Angwin and Martin Peers, "AOL Time
Warner Narrows Loss, Meets Targets," *The Wall Street Journal,* April
19, 2001.

227 "The basic bet is that convergence is going to happen": Seth Schiesel,
"Planning the Digital Smorgasbord," *The New York Times,* June 11,
2001.

229 When the amount paid to exercise underlying options is taken into account, the $73 million grossed by Bob Pittman comes to a net figure of
$66.1 million. Dick Parsons's gross was $35 million; his net was $27 million. Steve Case's net was about the same as his gross because the cost of
his underlying options was negligible. All other figures are also gross
numbers.

229 "A bail-out by them to pocket hundreds of millions": *The Regents of
California and the Amalgamated Bank as Trustee for the Longview Collective Investment Fund v. Richard D. Parsons, et al.,* Superior Court of the
State of California, County of Los Angeles, April 11, 2003.

229 "Part of their long-term personal financial planning": AOL Time

Warner spokesman Jim Whitney, quoted in Cassell Bryan-Low, "Do AOL Insider Sales Belie the Buyback?" *The Wall Street Journal,* May 30, 2001.

230 "Harry, don't you think it's a mistake to have all your eggs in one basket?": David Halberstam, *The Powers That Be* (University of Illinois Press, 2000), p. 53.

230 Walton's family (his wife, Helen, and their four children) is the richest in the world: the 2003 Forbes 400 list of richest Americans estimates their fortune at $102.5 billion, more than twice Bill Gates's net worth ($46 billion).

230 "Charlie's family has 90 percent or more": Warren E. Buffett, "An Owner's Manual," booklet published by Berkshire Hathaway, 1996. Available at berkshirehathaway.com/2001ar/ownersmanual.html

230 "Why would I not sell?": Mark Gemein, "You Bought. They Sold," *Fortune,* September 2, 2002.

233 "From day one, it was just wheels spinning": Matthew Rose, Julia Angwin, and Martin Peers, "Bad Connection: Failed Efforts to Coordinate Ads Signals Deeper Woes at AOL," *The Wall Street Journal,* July 18, 2002.

234 Pittman on the cover of *Business Week:* Catherine Yang with Ronald Grover and Anne Therese Palmer, "Show Time for AOL Time Warner," *Business Week,* January 15, 2001.

234 "The conventional wisdom in the media industry": Seth Schiesel, "Planning the Digital Smorgasbord," *The New York Times,* June 11, 2001.

234 Pittman as one of Fortune's "hottest business stories": "People to Watch 2001," *Fortune,* January 8, 2001.

234 *New York*'s gossip about Pittman's parties: Beth Landman Keil and Ian Spiegelman, "Intelligencer: So *That's* Where AOL Membership Fees Go," *New York* magazine, June 11, 2001.

236 "This has been a powerful quarter": Seth Schiesel, "AOL Time Warner Posts Mixed Results in Quarter," *The New York Times,* July 19, 2001; see also Alec Klein, "Ad Falloff Bites into AOL Revenue," *The Washington Post,* July 19, 2001.

236 "our synergies are hitting, and they're hitting big": Alec Klein, "Ad Falloff Bites into AOL Revenue," *The Washington Post,* July 19, 2001.

237 "The promises were not my job": Amy Harmon, "The Fading Fortunes of AOL's 'Bob Pitchman,' " *The New York Times,* July 19, 2002.

237 DO AOL'S ADS ADD UP?: Jeremy Kahn, "Do AOL's Ads Add Up?" *Fortune,* July 23, 2001.

237 "For me, this is a dream come true": Jared Sandberg, "New AOL Ad Unit Will Promote Marketing Across Multiple Media," *The Wall Street Journal,* August 20, 2001.

CHAPTER 10

247 "No financial impact can compare": "AOL Time Warner Comments on Its Business Outlook for 2001 and 2002," AOL Time Warner press release, September 24, 2001.

248 "The bottom line is—despite this tragedy": Ibid.

248 "I'm a hawk on margins": Ken Auletta, "Leviathan," *The New Yorker,* October 29, 2001.

248 "I'm the CEO and this is what I'm going to do": Speech at the JP Morgan H&Q Millennium.01 Global Telecom and Media Conference, New York City, November 8, 2001. As reported by Landon Thomas Jr., "Gerald Levin Grabs the Moment," *New York Observer,* December 3, 2001; see also Maxwell Murphy, "AOL's Levin Excited About Content, International Growth," Dow Jones News Service, November 9, 2001.

249 "this is the best it's ever been": Ken Auletta, "Leviathan," *The New Yorker,* October 29, 2001.

249 "A philosopher prince of the American media establishment": Landon Thomas Jr., "Gerald Levin Grabs the Moment," *New York Observer,* December 3, 2001.

250 "so I could have fired Jerry Levin before he fired me": Speech at the California Cable Television Association's Western Show, November 28, 2001.

251 "the fundamental architecture of a dynamic new medium": Speech at the 1995 convention of the Newspaper Association of America in New Orleans. As reported by George Garneau, "A Calling in Cyberspace," *Editor & Publisher* magazine, May 13, 1995.

254 "One of my favorite biblical passages": Actually, it's taken from chapter 3 of Ecclesiastes, that verse.

CHAPTER 11

256 "I may not be bright, but I can lift heavy things": Adam Cohen, "Can a Nice Guy Run This Thing?" *Time,* December 17, 2001.

256 "what Muhammad Ali is to boxing": Richard D. Parsons, Commencement Speech, Albany Law School, May 27, 2000. Full text in "Richard Parsons: World Renowned CEO and Proud Albany Law School Graduate," *Albany Law School Magazine,* Spring/Summer 2002.

256 "Surviving is winning": Anthony Bianco and Tom Lowry, "Can Dick Parsons Rescue AOL Time Warner?" *Business Week,* May 19, 2003.

257 "I got by, if just barely": Parsons, Commencement Speech, Albany Law School, May 27, 2000.

257 "Mind-changing and life-altering": Ibid.

261 "I'm desperately in need of a strategy": Address to finalists of the 2002 Business Case Competition, "Leadership in the New Millennium," sponsored by the Executive Leadership Council and Goldman Sachs, New York City, April 23, 2002. As reported by Seth Schiesel, "Harvard Team Ranks First in Telling AOL What To Do," *The New York Times,* April 23, 2002.

261 "The strategic logic of the merger is just as true today": Marc Gunther and Stephanie N. Mehta, "The Mess at AOL Time Warner: Can Steve Case Make Sense of This Beast?" *Fortune,* May 13, 2002.

266 "We're going to miss him. Ha, ha, ha": Geraldine Fabrikant with Seth Schiesel, "At AOL, Parting Without the Sweet Sorrow," *The New York Times,* May 17, 2002.

267 380-word article about Eric Keller: Alec Klein, "AOL Opens Probe, Puts 2 on Leave; Firm Eyes Relationship With Internet Partner," *The Washington Post,* June 19, 2001.

270 one of the country's "most dangerous" media plaintiff lawyers: James Moscou, "Demolition Man," *Editor & Publisher* magazine, November 27, 2000.

272 AOL TIME WARNER BIGS ON THE SPOT: Dan Cox, "AOL Time Warner Bigs on the Spot: Fraud Charges Could Mean Time Behind Bars," *New York Post,* August 1, 2002.

274 "he welcomes and seriously considers Steve's advice and counsel": David D. Kirkpatrick, "Man in the Middle of AOL Deal Is Becoming Odd Man Out," *The New York Times,* July 27, 2002.

276 That Case exercised and sold $700 million of stock options is confirmed by calculations done for me based on SEC filings compiled by Thompson Financial.

276 Reports suggesting Case would be fired: David D. Kirkpatrick, "Some Directors Said to Seek Ouster at AOL," *The New York Times,* September 17, 2002; see also Keith J. Kelly, Tim Arango, and Lauren Barack, "Case Closed: AOL TW Chief on Way Out," *New York Post,* September 17, 2002.

EPILOGUE

280 "They gave away their company for a mess of porridge": Anthony Bianco and Tom Lowry, "Can Dick Parsons Rescue AOL Time Warner?" *Business Week,* May 19, 2003.

281 "The old-media forces within AOL Time Warner Inc.": Martin Peers and Julia Angwin, "AOL Shakes Up Its Management as New Media Makes Way for Old," *The Wall Street Journal,* July 19, 2002.

281 "I feel like the merger is starting today": Ibid.

284 Talk America's results do not include a non-cash-deferred income tax benefit of $22.3 million or an extraordinary gain of $29.3 million for 2002. With those gains included, the company's net income was $97 million.

286 "My macro investment thesis": Case's e-mail to his investment adviser was cited by Julia Angwin, "AOL Boss Case Faces Potent Foe in Hawaii: Eyeless Cave Spider," *The Wall Street Journal,* December 26, 2002.

288 Rabbis praying for AOL stock: Alec Klein, *Stealing Time: Steve Case, Jerry Levin, and the Collapse of AOL Time Warner* (Simon & Schuster, 2003), pp. 151–152.

289 Colburn exercised and sold $9 million of AOL Time Warner stock, but after paying for the underlying options, his net income from the sale was $5 million.

298 "I never walked into the same room twice": Steven M. L. Aronson, "Vermont Life and Times," *Architectural Digest,* May 1999. Levin is alluding to Heraclitus.

304 "Get over it": Presentation at a Variety Media Conference, New York City, November 22, 2002.

305 "Happier than I have seen him since the first grade": David A. Vise, "Pittman Reemerges as a Media Investor," *The Washington Post,* October 3, 2003.

307 On January 10, 1990, Time Warner traded at $119.375 or, on a split-adjusted basis, $9.95. During that same period the S&P 500 index has gone from $347.31 to $1,041.23.

308 "I'm the stupidest person in the world": Patricia Sellers, "Gone With the Wind," *Fortune,* May 12, 2003.

308 "I can see a day when this company has five hundred restaurants": Geraldine Fabrikant and Stephanie Strom, "Bison Burgers, for Humanity's Sake," *The New York Times,* October 5, 2003.

309 "I like gallantry": Ibid.

309 "I'm an old-media guy": Patricia Sellers, "Gone With the Wind," *Fortune,* May 12, 2003.

ACKNOWLEDGMENTS

I OWE THANKS TO MANY PEOPLE WHO HELPED ME WRITE THIS book. Elisabeth Rappold spent countless hours at the New York Public Library locating old articles; she also tracked down valuable sources and legal filings, helped research Bob Pittman's and Dick Parsons's childhoods, transcribed many recorded interviews, and carefully fact-checked much of my manuscript. Michael Rampage uncovered a trove of information on the early history of Jerry Levin's family. He assembled documents from the U.S. Census Bureau, the Philadelphia Register of Wills Office, the Delaware and Montgomery County Recorder of Deeds Offices, and the Philadelphia County Orphans' Court, and other public archives. David Whelan plowed through dozens of 990 Forms filed with the Internal Revenue Service. As well, he interviewed business school professors on the subject of mergers and acquisitions, ran any number of Nexis searches, and diligently fact-checked the spelling of every one of the 250-plus names mentioned in this book. Laura Kang photocopied mounds of articles from *Vanity Fair*'s library and ran down leads on hard-to-find printed sources.

I am also indebted to: Randall Lane and Jennifer Reingold, who convinced me to write a proposal for this book; to my agent Elyse

Cheney; and to my editor at HarperCollins, Marion Maneker, and his unwavering enthusiasm, even temper, and superb judgment. My photo researcher, Shawn Vale, worked under a tight deadline to gather the photographs that illustrate this book. Sona Vogel copyedited my manuscript fastidiously. The very able Edwin Tan helped shepherd my book to print. Anthony Munk and Oliver Corlette supplied every analyst's report I needed, and then some. With great efficiency, Scott DeCarlo made sure that all my references to stock prices and market capitalizations were correct. Graydon Carter encouraged me to follow (and keep following) the AOL Time Warner story. Graciously, he put on hold my commitment to his magazine so I could write this book. Bruce Handy and Tim Smith gave early versions of my manuscript exacting reads. Their insights and suggestions went a long way toward improving the final product.

My deepest gratitude goes to my mother, Linda Munk, a great scholar who has the best mind of anyone I know. Kindly, she assured people that she was only "weeding my garden and fixing a few semicolons here and there." In fact, she edited every word, sometimes more than once. This book could not have been written without her.

There are two others without whom this book could not have been written. My father, Peter Munk, taught me everything I know about business, perseverance, and fearlessness. He has never doubted me. My husband, Pablo Galarza, helped me at every stage of this book: He was a sounding board, a firm support, and a superb adviser. He made it bearable.

INDEX